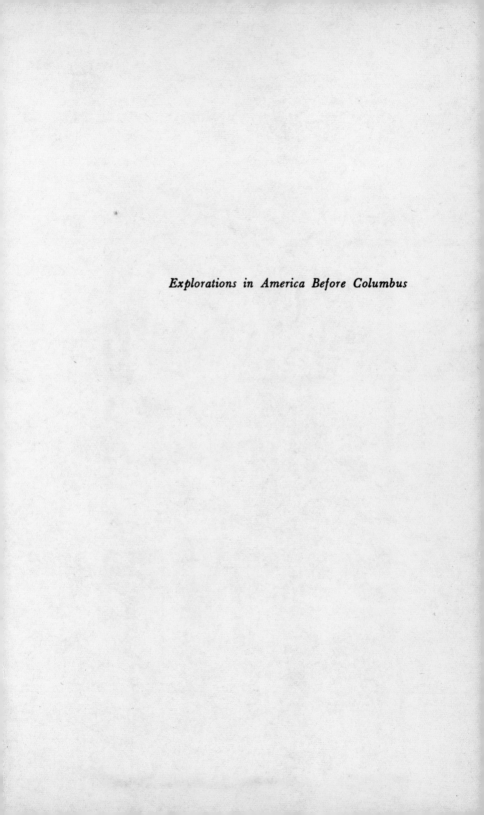

Explorations in America Before Columbus

The Kensington Monument in Alexandria, Minnesota.

Explorations
In America
Before Columbus

by Hjalmar R. Holand

TWAYNE PUBLISHERS, INC., NEW YORK

Second Edition, 1958
Third Printing, 1962

LITHOGRAPHED IN THE U.S.A.
BY NOBLE OFFSET PRINTERS, NEW YORK

Preface

*T*HERE IS no doubt that Norsemen—and perhaps others—did in fact reach America before Columbus, but scholars have come to very different conclusions concerning the location of these early discoveries and the extent of the exploration that followed them. These differences are largely due to the fact that scholars have tended to base their conclusions too much on surviving sailing directions for the Greenland to Vinland crossing while ignoring the detailed descriptions of topographical features that the Norsemen have left in their sagas and in other documents. The sailing directions, arrived at without benefit of modern navigational instruments and easily subject to clerical error by the copyists, are sometimes contradictory. The descriptions of topographical features by men familiar with many coastlines, on the other hand, can be more concretely dealt with and are subject to rather precise cross-checking. Whatever may be argued about sailing directions, when two or more explorers describe what is obviously the same progression of unique natural features, the evidence must indicate that they are sailing the same coastline.

A series of natural features may, however, be duplicated in other parts of the same shoreline. It is, therefore, necessary for the scholar to become minutely familiar with the American shoreline from Manhattan Island to Gaspé in order to avoid wrong identification. As far as I know, I am the only writer on Norse explorations of America to have made a detailed field study of this entire coastline.

A more important controversy than that concerning Norse penetration of the Atlantic coast, and a more notable part of the present volume, concerns Norse penetration of the inner continent by way of Hudson Bay and into central Minnesota. The center of this controversy is the Kensington inscription.

The Kensington Stone has had a strange history. It was found gripped in the roots of a tree growing near Kensington, Minnesota in 1898. At that time, a large part of the inscription baffled the scholars who first attempted to decipher it, and no complete translation was published until ten years later. In the meantime the inscription was condemned as a "clumsy fraud," and largely as a result of this first (and self-evidently incompetent) judgment, the later investigation of the stone has been attended by a kind of heat almost unprecedented in scholarly dispute.

Three sorts of scholars have investigated the stone in detail. The archeologists are unanimous in their verdict that nothing can be said for or against the authenticity of the stone on simply archeological grounds. The geologists who have examined the stone and who have submitted their detailed findings are unanimous in their judgment that the weathering of the inscription must have taken at least fifty to a hundred years, and overwhelmingly they read the weathering as evidence of much greater age. The dating here is important. Even the minimum estimate of fifty years would place the date of any possible forgery at a time when not a single Norwegian or Swede had settled in Minnesota. Any theory of a fraud requires a human agency, and there were no settlers in Douglas County where the stone was found until 1867. For several years before that time southern Minnesota was the scene of the terrible Sioux War in which 1500 pioneers were massacred. Finally there is the evidence of investigations undertaken by philologists, and here opinion divides sharply. The larger number of published philological opinions supports the authenticity of the stone, but a persistent (though notably back-tracking) minority continues to denounce it as a modern forgery. The center of controversy here lies in the fact that the inscription does not agree on all counts with textbook theory of runology. This fact will be discussed in detail, but here it must be borne in mind that the textbooks are based on what scholars have been able to piece together from medieval records, and that those records were primarily legal documents couched in antiquated formulas while the spoken language must obviously have been changing out from under them. Dialectical differences and the fact that Norse seafarers were not trained clerks will sufficiently account for every irregularity in the inscription. Even now there is no single standard of writing the Norwegian language. Nowhere has local patriotism been more successful in promoting dialectical differences.

Another perennially fascinating and perennially controversial discussion of Norse discoveries in America centers around the stone tower at Newport. It was formerly thought the tower was a windmill built by Benedict Arnold, 17th-century colonial governor, in 1675, but the late Philip Ainsworth Means was the first to upset that theory. I believe the evidence presented in the body of the present study can only lead to the conclusion that it was built as the headquarters of the royal Norwegian expedition of 1355-1364.

There is, finally, a body of cartographical evidence compiled from charts drawn before the time of Columbus. Detailed knowledge of the outlines of a continent cannot be assumed to drift across an ocean by itself: someone must explore the region and return with the information. The details of that information are sufficient to identify with certainty at least some of the areas into which Norsemen penetrated in pre-Columbian time.

The historical record, in fact, indicates that the cartographical information compiled by the Norsemen led step by step to the re-discovery of America by Columbus.

I am indebted to scores of good scholars in this work, to far more than can be mentioned here. I must, however, mention with special gratitude The John Simon Guggenheim Foundation, whose Fellowship, in 1950, enabled me to inspect and measure a number of prototypes of the Newport Tower in Belgium, Germany, England and the Scandinavian countries. I am indebted, likewise, to the Preservation Society of Newport County, which paid my traveling expenses in following the shore line from Manhattan Island to Gaspé in search of possible locations of camp sites of pre-Columbian Norse explorers.

HJALMAR R. HOLAND

Big Maples
Ephraim, Wisconsin

Contents

Illustrations

Introduction

America was visited by many expeditions hundreds of years before Columbus was born. Some of these were larger than Columbus' convoy. We have the record of the adventures of these men and know of their struggles to become permanent settlers in this new land. In this they failed, probably because of the hostility of the natives, just as hundreds and thousands of similar pioneers failed long after Columbus made his voyage. There was still plenty of land in Europe, so it did not seem worth while to cross the sea to fight for it. As late as 1803 American land was still so cheap that the Louisiana Purchase, embracing more than one-third of all the land in the United States, was concluded for only $15,000,000.

The voyage of Columbus became so famous because it was based on a monumental error which promised vast wealth. He accidentally learned that a great scholar in Florence, Toscanelli by name, had declared and demonstrated that the shortest route to the Orient was to sail west. There, only 5000 miles away, it was claimed, lay China and Japan filled with costly spices and gold. Only a few years before this time the sea route around Africa to the East Indies had been opened, and a new and most profitable trade had developed. The lust for gold was then as now irrepressible, and Columbus's discovery of the Caribbean Islands was therefore glamorized as the greatest of all gold strikes. Gold was the motive of Columbus, and gold was the banner of his successors for several generations. Little was found, but a substitute—the capture of slaves—proved highly profitable. Thus, the Spaniards plundered the West Indies and Mexico. While America lost much of its wealth and manhood, it gained almost no settlers because the plunderers took their ill-gotten gains back with them to Spain.

Aside from this ruthless exploitation and devastation, America remained an unknown country for many years. Florida was found as early as 1512, but no settlement was made until 1575. New England was discovered in 1524 and highly praised as a good country, but it had no white settlers until 1620. Then came the Pilgrims, the real pioneers of what is now the United States. They came partly because they were in want of land and partly because they sought religious freedom. And these two objectives remained the chief incentives for emigration for more than two hundred years.

It is a strange fact that the richest landmass of this great spinning globe was the last to be settled by the white race. For thousands of years it lay undeveloped. Then in very few centuries it blossomed beyond all imagination. It is hoped that this book with its review of the voyages of the men who preceded Columbus will clarify a period of American history which is little understood.

The Dawn of
Seafaring Discovery

*F*OR THOUSANDS of years the nations of the Eastern Hemisphere surged back and forth, seeking more and better lands to feed their increasing numbers. Great empires arose and flourished for a time—Egypt, Babylon, Persia, Rome—conquering and annexing the lands around them, but America, the most abundant land of all, lay unknown beyond the western sea. Not until 5000 years of history had been written was America discovered, probably the most important event in the history of mankind.

The early peoples of Europe and the Near East were slow to discover the West primarily because of their fear of the open sea. For them it was no easy thoroughfare, but the domain and embodiment of a dreaded deity, Poseidon, the fierce girder of the land. Homer, in his *Odyssey,* gives many pictures of sea voyages, but they are mere poetic dreams of physical and supernatural dangers encountered by those who ventured out on the waters of the Mediterranean. Evidently the great poet had done very little seafaring. Even more frightful was the Atlantic to those who ventured out upon it. They believed that it was bounded by a rushing torrent that encircled all the lands of the earth. Hopeless, indeed, was the fate of those whose vessel was caught by the suction of that irresistible stream. Moreover, the western sea was believed to be infested by monsters with jaws so big that they could crush the largest ship like an eggshell, and with tails that could demolish the stoutest vessel with a single swipe. There was, therefore, little or no open sea sailing. The knowledge of new lands was gained only by coastwise sailing.

But up along the rock-bound coast of Norway lived a people who to a large extent depended on the sea for their food. To them the sea was less fearful, often even kind, because it filled their nets with cod and herring. It was therefore natural that the first recorded voyage of discovery in the Christian era was made by a Norwegian about the year 870. His name was Ottar, and he became so famous that he was called before the great King Alfred of England to tell the story of his voyage into the Arctic Sea.

He told the King that he lived farthest north of all men in Norway. Once upon a time "he fell into a fancy and wanted to know how far the land extended northward and if there were any habitations of men north of him." So he sailed for six days northward, then four days east, and finally five days south—a distance of more than 2000 miles. Then he came to the mouth of a great river (the Dvina in Russia), and there he found many people. He was not boastful; although he traveled fifteen days, each way through unknown waters, he said nothing about sea monsters. The King recorded his narrative (here much abbreviated) and added it to his translation of Orosius' *History of the World*. And that was all the English knew about the Arctic Ocean for the next six hundred years.

It was this greater intimacy with the sea that made the Scandinavians such a power in the 9th, 10th and 11th centuries. Their swift and sleek ships moved freely and without fear in distant waters, and their boldness enabled their captains to establish kingdoms in England, Ireland, France, Spain and Italy. They were also the first to bring seapower into action for the liberation of Jerusalem and the Holy Land. In 1107, King Sigurd of Norway sailed with sixty ships from Norway to Gibraltar and onward to Palestine. He brought 10,000 warriors eager for battle, and his timely arrival enabled King Baldwin successfully to meet the attacks of the Turks and to establish his kingdom.[1]

In Europe there was no interest in naval exploration, except among the Norwegians, until almost 600 years after the time of Ottar's voyage. Then in 1295 came the Venetian, Marco Polo, after a stay of twenty-four years in China and India. He had marvelous tales to tell of the riches of the East, where the bridges were built of polished marble, and the roofs of the temples were covered with gold. He wrote a book about his travels which was translated into many languages, and his glowing descriptions of riches untold resulted in the creation of caravan traffic across the vast deserts that lay between China and the West. But this was a slow and toilsome traffic. One man believed a better route could be found. This was Prince Henry of Portugal (1394-1460), best known as Henry the Navigator. Although he did not personally lead any exploration, he established a sort of naval intelligence bureau at the harbor of Sagres at the south end of Portugal. Here for forty years he spent most of his energy in promoting and subsidizing expeditions for the purpose of finding a seaway to the Orient. The immediate objective was to circumnavigate Africa.

But in spite of his encouragement, progress was slow. It took twenty years of successive expeditions before Cape Bojador was reached, about a thousand miles down the coast, a considerably shorter distance than Ottar's voyage, made almost 600 years earlier and on his own initiative. As it was a coastwise enterprise, the fears of the seamen were not so much of the monsters of the deep as of the heat. It was an ancient belief that the two temperate zones of the earth were separated by a torrid zone, where the heat of the vertical rays of the sun was so intense as to be beyond the endurance of man. It was therefore with much fear and trembling that the Portuguese seamen met each new day. Having finally reached a few leagues further south than the preceding expedition, each successive captain usually made haste to return.

But strangely the successive expeditions found no greater heat out at sea on their ships when the sun was directly overhead than they had felt on land in Portugal, and the advances became greater. Finally in 1488, after more than sixty years of faint-hearted endeavor, Bartolomeu Diaz rounded the south end of Africa, and the way to the Orient was open. But in the meantime the Norsemen had crossed the Atlantic many times, they had discovered the mainland of America and attempted repeated settlements, and they had established a diocese of sixteen parishes in Greenland. That diocese was almost 500 years old when Diaz reached the south end of Africa.

The First Pathfinder
to the New World

AT THE time Ottar made his long journey into the Arctic Sea, Norway was ruled by a very stern king. He was a son of one of the dozen or more petty kings of Norway, but he had very large ambitions. He resolved to unite all Norway under his own rule and declared he would not cut his hair until that conquest was completed. Twelve years later, in 872, the last resistance was overcome, and the chief earl of the kingdom acted as barber and cut his hair. Thereafter he was known as Harald the Fairhaired, and he enjoyed a reign longer than that of any other monarch, lasting seventy-three years.

But the followers of the vanquished kings and their many connections did not enjoy his reign because he restricted the liberties of all. Worst of all was his annulment of allodial rights. No man was permitted to own land in his own right, but only by permission of the king. Harald's decree was unacceptable to a large part of the proud farmers who had never lived under feudal tenure, and many thousands emigrated to Iceland. In this way King Harald was a remote cause of the early discovery of America.

Among the late emigrants to Iceland was a very promising young man named Erik Thorwaldson, also called Erik the Red.

He was born about 950, a descendant of a wealthy land-owning family in the extreme southern part of Norway. His first appearance in history is as member of the bodyguard of the redoubtable Earl Haakon. The latter disdained the title of King, but he was the firm-handed monarch of all Norway for many years, and the members of his bodyguard, an adjunct of the nobility of those days, were first in line for royal favors and important positions of trust.

But to Erik the door to dignity and riches was suddenly slammed shut. One day a messenger came and told him that his father, 600 miles farther south, had been found guilty of manslaughter and declared an outlaw. Now he had come as a fugitive in his vessel, seeking his son's help. Erik gave it at once. He joined his father and sailed with him to Iceland. They had a few slaves and some cattle, but no home.

Iceland had been discovered by Naddod, a brother of Erik's grandfather's grandfather, but that was a hundred years earlier. All the good land had been taken, and the only place that Erik and his father could find to settle upon was on the north shore of the northwestern corner of Iceland, as bleak and inhospitable a spot as can be found on that rugged island. Here, soon, his father died, broken in spirit. Dissatisfied with the extremely limited opportunities of his surroundings, Erik moved south to Haukedal, in a more favorable part of the island, where he had seen a most attractive young woman to whom he offered his hand. He was accepted by both the girl and the people of Haukedal and obtained a tract of wild land on which he built a small house and began to clear the land.

But bad luck pursued him. One day his slaves through some accident caused a landslide that destroyed some of the buildings of a farmer in the valley below. Terrified, the slaves fled, but were discovered and slain by Eyolf Saur, a relative of the farmer whose buildings had been damaged. Erik resented this violent action against his slaves and went to Eyolf and demanded compensation. A quarrel followed and Eyolf was killed. Shortly afterward Erik was challenged by a professional avenger of wrongs by the name of Ravn, presumably at the instigation of Eyolf's relatives. The hired killer probably did not know that he had challenged one of the most expert swordsmen in the bodyguard of Earl Haakon, and his end came quickly. Eyolf's relatives, their hired champion dead, took the issue to the district court, and since Erik was a stranger without influential friends, the family of Eyolf succeeded in having him declared an outlaw. Erik lost his slaves, his farm, and his liberty to live in the district.

He still had his vessel, however, and he sailed out on Broadfjord, where he took possession of some desert islands which lay in another judicial district. As they were not fit for permanent habitation he built no house. In the meantime he loaned his *setstokkar,* the columns at the back of the high seat of his ancestral house, to a big farmer named Thorgest on the mainland who was building a new house. The latter greatly admired Erik's columns and wanted to make a similar pair. Such carved and painted highseat columns were symbols of dignity in every chieftain's house and were held in great reverence as family talismans. Some of the early chiefs as they approached Iceland tied their *setstokkar* together and threw them out in the sea, so that their guardian spirit through them would choose the proper place for settlement.

Eventually Erik found a spot that suited him for a home and he went to Thorgest to get his columns. But the latter refused to give them up. He had not been able to resist the temptation to build them into his house, perhaps thinking that Erik would not return for them. To pull them out now would invite ridicule. So he chose to be arrogant. Why pay any attention to this landless newcomer who moreover had been outlawed in his own district?

But this was a most flagrant offense, and when Erik declared he would take the columns by force if necessary, there were many who encouraged him. It was, in fact, the only honorable course open to him if he did not wish to be branded a coward. Accompanied by a group of supporters, he went to the house of Thorgest and took his columns by force. They were attacked by a band of Thorgest's men, and in the fight two sons of Thorgest and some other men were killed. After this skirmish both parties were joined by many supporters, and it looked as if the conflict would assume large dimensions. However, the case was quickly brought before the district court. Although Thorgest was married to the daughter of Thord Gellir, one of the most powerful chiefs in Iceland, he won no great victory. Nevertheless, it was decided that Thorgest had suffered a greater loss than was his due under the circumstances, and Erik was declared an outlaw for three years.

Yielding to the decision of the court, most of the supporters of Erik sheathed their swords and went home. But Thorgest did not have the forbearance to let his defeated enemy depart in peace on his banishment exile. Instead he gathered many men with whom he rushed from island to island seeking to kill Erik. But the friends of the latter did not desert him. He and his family were brought to a safe hiding place where they were well guarded, while others put his vessel in good order and provided him with plenty of provisions and supplies for a long voyage. Before long Erik and his wife and small son with a few men went aboard and sailed away toward the setting sun. This was the second purposeful voyage of discovery in the Christian era of which there is any record.

Three years went by, and the lone but intrepid stranger from Norway was almost forgotten. Then one day in the fall of 985 a sail appeared over the western horizon. It was Erik. The sails of his small vessel were black with hard usage and much patched, but he and his wife and son, plus a baby boy, seemed to be in the best of health. Where had he been?

Erik told his story. He had set out to find some islands rumored to have been seen out in the west. He had not found them, but instead he had come to a land rising thousands of feet above the sea. It was covered with ice even in the middle of summer, and outside of it lay a turbulent belt of broken ice twenty miles or more broad. This pack-ice could not be penetrated by boat, nor could it be crossed on foot. He had followed that ice-bound coast southwestward for many hundred miles, and everywhere the barren coast was unapproachable. Now and then he saw icebergs, a mile or two in length, break off from the end of a glacier and tumble into the sea with a splash which threatened his little vessel well out to sea. Finally, after many weeks of storm, fog and drifting ice, he came to the south end of the unknown land. Here the congestion of ice was even worse than farther north, and he lost sight of the land. But by following around the perimeter of the drift ice he eventually reached land and found ice-free harbors. There on the southwest side of the big island he found a region with a far milder climate. He found long fjords extending into the land a hundred miles, bleak with bare mountains near the sea, but green and smiling with fertile meadows in the interior. He had traveled in and out of these fjords, hundreds of miles to the west and north, and everywhere the grass was green, the game abundant, and the reindeer fat and sleek. There were small trees on the banks of the streams and much driftwood for building purposes on the shore. Hunting was much better than in Iceland because there was an abundance of seal, walrus, polar bears and even whales. He called the new land Greenland because it was a very green land indeed. He had selected his own homestead and was going back the next summer.

Here was a tale of discovery, the like of which no man had ever heard, and Erik's fame spread far and wide in western Iceland. Men came from afar to look at this great traveler and to ask questions: How big was that country? Was it inhabited by other people? Was there room for others to settle there? Erik answered that it was bigger than Iceland with room for thousands of people. There were no local inhabitants, and he would be glad to share his possessions with all who wanted to join him.

The result of all these questions and answers was that a large number of Icelanders decided to emigrate to Greenland with Erik. Iceland was crowded, and the prospect of free land in Greenland was tempting. Inventories of needed supplies were made, and ships were overhauled for the great voyage. When finally the day of departure came in the summer of 986, there were so many who planned to emigrate that thirty-five vessels were needed to carry them. As these vessels were small and much of the space was taken up by cattle and horses, feed for the animals, household goods and implements, it is likely that the ships did not average more than thirty persons each. But with thirty-five vessels, this makes more than a thousand participants in this first emigration to the new world. Another report says there were twenty-five vessels.

On the way, however, the expedition was overtaken by a furious storm. Many of the ships were wrecked and their occupants perished. Some of the emigrants managed to return to Iceland. Only fourteen ships reached Greenland. The memory of this storm lingered for centuries through the fact that a Norseman from the Hebrides at the height of the storm composed a metric poem of which the first stanza reads thus:

> Almighty God, to whom alone
> The hearts of all thy saints are known,
> Sinless and just, to Thee I pray
> To guide me on my dangerous way:
> Lord of the heavens that roof the land,
> Hold o'er me Thy protecting hand![2]

The emigrants who reached Greenland were given large tracts of land with which they were well pleased. The colony grew rapidly and soon numbered several thousand people. The settlement was divided into two parts. The principal settlement, which was in the region selected by Erik, was known as the

Eastern Settlement. The other lay about two hundred miles farther northwest in the present Godthaab District and was known as the Western Settlement.

Some commentators have characterized Erik as a brawling troublemaker inclined to bloodshed. This verdict is without basis. Up to the time of his exile, Erik's stay in Iceland had been marked by misfortune and embarrassing situations which were brought about by circumstances that were thrust upon him. The incidents mentioned, therefore, throw no other light on his character or ideals than that he was a brave man not afraid to defend what he thought were his rights, even against great odds. But when he left Iceland behind and sailed out on the open sea, he was freed from these entanglements and could plan his course in life according to his own nature. To the east lay the populous countries of Europe with the sea lanes crowded with merchant vessels. He could have taken his wife and children to Norway and left them with some of his wealthy relatives there while he went out on a viking expedition. This would have been a quick way to recoup his losses and to satisfy his alleged tendency to pugnacity, for at that time such piracy was looked upon as a proper occupation for gentlemen of temporary leisure.

But Erik did not choose this common way of rehabilitating himself. Instead, he turned west into an unknown sea. With amazing fortitude he pushed on in his small vessel with no compass to guide him and explored both the eastern and the western coasts of Greenland—a feat which was not repeated for more than 700 years. He asked no king or corporation for aid, and he found his provisions in the waters that surrounded him. Six hundred years later, when the Danish government endeavored to rediscover Greenland, it took about a hundred years with many well-fitted expeditions before as much was discovered as Erik visited on his one journey. Frithiof Nansen, who was one of the world's greatest discoverers, says that Erik on this journey proved himself to be one of the boldest and most resourceful navigators of all times. It was the most adventurous and fruitful exile in history.

Erik was an uncommonly generous and fair-minded man. Inasmuch as he had found a land to which no one claimed ownership, it was his to do with as he pleased. He could have kept it all and rented parts of it to others as was done by the big landlords of Iceland and Norway, or as the Church did when later by testamentary legacies it obtained possession of about half of the farms in Greenland. But Erik did not do so. He gave the land freely to friends and strangers and levied no taxes upon it. Nor did he set himself up as a titled chief. The Greenland colony was started by him as a republic of the simplest type, and it remained so for almost 300 years. There was no inherited prerogative, no strong arm management, no bureaucracy and no taxes except the Peter's Pence that went to the Pope in Rome. It was started in a spirit of fraternal cooperation, and thus it remained without a civil war throughout its history. Erik's wise planning and kindness were recognized by the people who treated him with the greatest respect and affection. His fame was recognized and praised even in Norway, and many prominent visitors from abroad were entertained in his big house at the head of Eriksfjord, the foundation of which still remains. He died about 1004.[3]

Erik's discovery of Greenland took place in 982, and this is the first authentic date in American history. Like the West Indies, Greenland is a part of the Western hemisphere, and it lies as close to the American mainland as do most of these islands upon the discovery of which the fame of Columbus is founded.

The Discovery of America's Mainland

THE ORIGINAL narratives of the early Norse voyages to America are contained in two collections of sagas, known respectively as the *Flatey Book* and the *Hauk's Book*. Both contain a selection of histories of kings of Norway, but the selections are different. Flatey Book is the largest of all saga collections, and in printed form appears in three volumes containing about 1800 pages. It was compiled and copied by two priests in the latter part of the 14th century. Hauk's Book is much smaller and was compiled by Sir Hauk Erlendson, a learned Icelander and member of the Royal Council of Norway. This compilation dates from the early part of the 14th century.

Included in both collections are many shorter narratives of importance such as the reports on the discovery of America. While there are many minor variations, they supplement each other. The Hauk's Book report apparently represents the Icelandic version and the Flatey Book the Greenland. Both accounts agree that the first discovery of America's mainland was accidental, but the Flatey Book gives a much more circumstantial report. It is here given in translation. The first paragraph is condensed:

Herjulf, the son of Bard, had a son named Bjarni, a capable man who since his youth had been engaged in successful commerce at sea in his own vessel. It was his custom to spend every alternate winter with his father in Iceland.

Bjarni arrived in his ship at Eyrar (on the southwestern coast of Iceland) in the fall of the same year in which his father had sailed with Erik to Greenland (986). He was much concerned to hear the news of his father's emigration and would not unload his cargo. His men then asked him what he meant to do. He replied that he meant to keep to his custom of passing the winter with his father, "and if you will go with me I shall sail for Greenland." They all said that they would abide by his decision; upon which Bjarni remarked, "Our voyage will be considered rash, since none of us have been in Greenland waters." Notwithstanding this they put to sea as soon as they were ready, and they sailed for three days before the land was laid; but then the fair wind ceased, and north winds and fogs came on, and they did not know where they were going, and this went on for many days. Eventually they saw the sun, and so were able to get their bearings, whereupon they hoisted sail, and after sailing that day they saw land. They discussed among themselves what land this could be, but Bjarni said that it could not be Greenland. They asked him whether he would sail to this land or not. "I am for sailing in close to the land," he said, and on doing so they saw that the land was without mountains, well timbered, and there were small knolls on it, whereupon they left the land on the port side, and let the sheet turn towards it.

Then after sailing two days they saw another land. They asked Bjarni if he thought this was Greenland; he said that he did not think this was Greenland any more than the first place, "For it is said that there are very large glaciers in Greenland." They soon neared this land, and saw that it was a flat country and covered with timber. At this point the fair wind dropped, whereupon the crew suggested that they should land there: but Bjarni would not. They considered that they were short both of wood and water. "You are in no want of either," said Bjarni, but he got some abuse for this from his crew.

He ordered them to hoist sail, which was done, and they turned the bow from the land, and sailed out to sea for three days before a southwesterly wind, when they saw the third land: now this land was high and mountainous, with ice upon it. So they asked if Bjarni would put in there, but he said that he would not, since—as he put it—this land appeared to him to be good for nothing. Then without lowering sail they kept on their course along the coast, and saw that it was an island. Once more they turned the bow away from the land, and held out to sea with the same breeze; but the wind increased, so that Bjarni told them to reef, and not crowd more sail than the ship and rigging could stand. They now sailed for four days, when they saw the fourth land. Then they asked Bjarni if he thought this was Greenland. Bjarni replied: "This is most like what was told me of Greenland, and here we will keep our course towards the land." So they did, and they came to land in the evening under a cape, which had a boat on it, and there on that cape lived Herjulf, Bjarni's father, and it is from him that the cape received its name, and has since been called Herjulfsness.

Bjarni now went to his father, and gave up voyaging, and he was with his parents as long as Herjulf was alive, and afterwards he succeeded his parents, and lived there.

Here, more than 600 years before the Pilgrims came to Cape Cod, is a description of the east coast of America with a mention of three headlands spaced certain given distances apart. For the map agrees perfectly with Bjarni's description. Let us assume that the first land seen is Cape Cod. It is described as "a land without mountains, well timbered, and there were small knolls on it." This is a good description of the eastern part of the Cape, and the "small knolls" would correspond to the morainic hills of Cape Cod.

From here Bjarni sailed out into the open sea. We know he did not sail along the coast because he saw no land again for two days. He must, therefore, have sailed in a northeasterly direction because he "left the land on the port (or left) side." After two days' sailing he came to a flat county covered with timber.

The old Norsemen had a nautical unit of distance called day's sailing (*daegr sigling*), equal to about 75 English miles. This was supposed to be the average distance covered in twelve hours of sailing with a fair wind. Later, when twenty-four hour voyages across the open sea became frequent, the same term was used, but the distance was doubled.⁴ When the narrative says that Bjarni sailed "two days," it therefore means that he sailed about 300 miles. Returning now to the narrative, we find that after sailing 300 miles he came to a flat country covered with timber. The map shows that a voyage of 300 miles in a northeasterly direction would bring him to southern Nova Scotia which is flat country, and which was once well timbered.

After waiting for a southwest wind, they sailed out to sea again and did not see land for three days. Three days' sail or 450 miles would bring them up to the south coast of New-foundland. They followed the coast and eventually found that this third land was an island. This discovery could only have been made, if they sailed west and north around Newfoundland. The narrative describes it as high and mountainous, which is very true as some of the islands in the bays on the west coast rise up 2,000 feet and more from the water's edge. The great Long Range also parallels the shore along the west side.

Upon reaching the north point of the island, they again sailed out upon the open sea with a southwest wind which became so strong that it was feared the rigging would break. They may therefore have made much more than the average 150 miles per day. After sailing for four days, they again saw land which proved to be Greenland. Adding the distances as given in the saga, we have nine days at 150 miles or 1,350 miles. To this must be added the length of the coastline on the west side of Newfoundland which Bjarne does not mention, a distance of 317 miles, making a total of 1,667 miles, which is very close to the actual distance by water from Cape Cod to the southern point of Greenland. Here, at his first landing place, Bjarni found his father's house. See page 129.

Some critics have objected that it is absurd to think that Bjarni would be able to sail straight to his father's house, when he knew nothing about the country, nor had any knowledge of his father's place of settlement.

This criticism is without basis. On approaching Greenland from the south or southwest, the first land to be seen is Erssinga mountain, more than 5000 feet high. As Bjarni knew nothing about where his father's home was, he would therefore sail toward this first visible land to make his inquiries. Here, just below and in front of this mountain, lies Herjulfsness, where Bjarni's father had built his home, the most easterly and southerly of all the farms in Greenland. As he arrived late in fall, he would have no difficulty with the icepack as the southern end of Greenland is usually free from ice during the last four months of the year.

It is said that Bjarni saw a *jökull* or glacier on the third land seen by him. This has caused some commentators to bring Bjarni up to Baffin Land or Resolution Island where the most southerly glacier appears at present. They think that the second land he saw was in southern Labrador where there is an area of flat land covered with timber near Sandwich Bay. From here they assume he followed the coast northwestward until he came to Resolution Island close to Baffin Land. But this is contrary to the text. It says that upon reaching the second land, Bjarni "turned the bow of the vessel *from* the land and sailed out to sea for three days." Such a heading would never bring him to Resolution Island. This word *jökull* has several meanings. It is used in the meaning of ice generally and also of drift ice. One of the things that Erik Thorwaldson must have emphasized was that the habitable parts of Greenland lay on the southwest side of it. For this reason we see Bjarni constantly keeping a course to the northeast, a course which would never bring him to Baffin Land. Furthermore, it would have been physically impossible for him to reach Resolution Island at that time of the year (see note 5).

Leif Erikson
Discovers America

THE IMPRESSION one gets of Bjarni Herjulfson is that he was a stolid business man and a good sailor, but without the curiosity of a man of vision. The discovery of a new land was not of sufficient importance to make him delay his journey to his intended destination. Even after he got home safely, the memory of the new lands he had seen did not arouse in him any curiosity to return and explore them. His interest lay in buying and selling, and what lay beyond was immaterial.

But Leif Erikson, the son of Erik the Red, was a man of quite a different type. Just as his father, hunted and exiled, sailed out into the unknown West to see what he could find, so Leif was filled with a curiosity for that which lay beyond his physical and mental horizon. In 999, when he was only about twenty years old, Leif had set out to see the world. Instead of following the old sailing directions by way of Iceland, he boldly set his course directly east to Norway. Who knew what might be seen on that untravelled course? This was the first direct crossing of the Atlantic in history. When his host, the glorious, heroic King Olaf Trygveson, heard of this accomplishment, he was eager to welcome this young man and to give him a place of honor in his bodyguard. But the King was a militant Christian and tolerated only Christians at his court.

To Leif, the man of vision, this new faith was a promise of better things. He not only accepted it, but undertook the task of introducing it to Greenland.

This was a difficult enterprise, but Leif managed it peacefully and successfully. Then, as he visited the various parts of Greenland, he heard of the new lands seen by Bjarni Herjulfson. Here was an enterprise that went right to his heart. He bought Bjarni's ship, hired some of his men and sailed away to see all the lands that Bjarni had glimpsed.

The following is the narrative of Leif's voyage of discovery as told in the old saga.

There was now [after Bjarni's return from Norway in 1002] much talk of exploration. Leif Erikson went to Bjarni and bought his ship and engaged a crew of thirty-five men.

He asked his father to be the leader of the expedition, but Erik said he was now getting too old for such work. Leif insisted that he (Erik) was still the member of the family who would bring the best luck, and Erik finally consented to go. When they were ready to sail, Erik rode from his house on a horse, and when they approached the ship the horse stumbled, and Erik fell off and injured his foot. Then he said, "I am not fated to discover more countries than this in which we are now living, and we will part here." So Erik went home to Brattalid, but Leif went aboard with his companions. Among them was a southerner (German) called Tyrk.

They put out to sea and they found first the country that Bjarni had seen last. They sailed up to the land and cast anchor and went ashore. There was no grass there, and the background was all great glaciers. The land between the sea and the glaciers was like one flat rock, and the country seemed to them destitute of value. Leif said: "We have not failed to land, like Bjarni; now I will give this country a name and call it Helluland (the land of flat stone)."

They now returned to their ship and sailed out to sea and discovered the second land. Again they sailed up to the land, put out a boat and went ashore. This land was low-lying and wooded, and there were wide stretches of white sand, and the slope from the sea was not steep. Then Leif said: "This land shall be given a name from its resources, and shall be called Markland (woodland)." After this they returned to their ship as quickly as possible.

They sailed out again into the open sea with a northeast wind and were out two days before they saw land toward which they turned. They came to an island which lay to the north and landed on it, the weather being fine. There was dew on the grass, and it came about that they put their hands on the dew and carried it to their mouths, and they thought they had never known anything so sweet as that was. Then they went back to the ship and sailed into the sound which lay between the island and the ness which ran north from the land. They steered a westerly course past the ness. It was very shallow there at low tide, so that their ship ran aground and soon it was a long way from the ship to the sea. But the men were so eager to get to land that they did not wait for the tide to rise under the ship, but hurried ashore where a river came out of a lake. Then when the tide returned they rowed back to the ship and took it up the river, and afterwards into a lake where they cast anchor. Then they carried their kitbags ashore and put up shelters. Later they decided to spend the winter there, and they built large houses.

There was no lack of salmon, both in the river and the lake, and bigger salmon than they had ever seen before. The climate was so mild, it seemed to them that cattle would not suffer from lack of fodder in winter. There came no frost during the winter, and the grass did not wither much. Day and night were more equally divided than in Greenland or Iceland. On the shortest day of the year they had sunlight both at breakfast time and at their afternoon meal.

When they finished the building of their houses, Leif said to his men: "Now I will divide our group in two and explore this country: half of the men shall remain in the camp while the others explore the country, and they must not go farther than they can return by evening, and they must not separate." For a time they did this, Leif sometimes going with the explorers and sometimes staying at home in the camp. Leif was big and strong, the handsomest of men in appearance and clever. In fact, he was in all respects an excellent commander.

It happened one evening that a man was missing; it was Tyrk the southerner. Leif was much disturbed over this, because Tyrk had been with Leif and his father a long time, and he had been very fond of Leif as a child. Leif reproached his men and, taking a dozen of them with him, he set out to search for Tyrk. But they had gone only a short distance from the camp when they were greatly pleased to see Tyrk coming toward them. Leif saw at once that he was in high spirits. Tyrk was a rather small man with a projecting forehead and a small face with roving eyes; but he was very handy in all sorts of craftsmanship.

Leif said: "Why are you so late foster-father, and how did you get parted from your company?"

Tyrk talked for a long time in German, rolled his eyes and was much excited. They did not understand what he said. Finally he spoke in Norse and said: "I did not go very far beyond the others, but I found something new. I found grape vines and grapes!"

"Is that really true, foster-father?"

"Certainly it is true," he answered, "for I was born where there was no lack of vines and grapes."

Now they slept that night, but in the morning Leif said to his men: "We shall now have two jobs on our hands. One day we shall gather grapes, and the next we will cut vines and fell trees to make a cargo for my ship." This plan was carried out. It is said that they filled the afterboat with grapes, and the ship itself with a cargo of timber. In the spring they made ready and sailed away, and Leif gave the country a name according to its resources, and called it Vinland (Wine land).

They then sailed away with favorable winds behind them until they sighted Greenland and the mountains under its glaciers. While Leif held the rudder one of the men spoke up and said: "Why are you steering the ship so much into the wind?"

"I am watching my course," said Leif, "and something else also. Do you see anything yonder?"

They said they could see nothing remarkable.

"I am not sure," said Leif, "whether I see a ship or a reef."

Then they saw it and said it was a reef. But Leif's vision was so much better than their's that he could see men on the reef.

"Now," said Leif, "we shall beat up into the wind so as to reach them if they need our help. If they are not peaceably disposed, we shall be masters of the situation and not they."

They came up to the reef, lowered the sail, cast anchor, and launched another small boat that they had. Leif asked who was the captain (of the shipwrecked party). One of them spoke up: "My name is Thori, I am a Norwegian. What is your name?"

Leif told his name.

"Are you the son of Erik the Red of Brattalid?" asked Thori.

"I am," answered Leif, "and now I will take all of you on my ship and as much of your cargo as the ship will hold."

They accepted this offer and sailed to Eriksfjord. Leif invited Thori and his wife Gudrid and three of the men to make their home with him, and he also found lodgings for the others.[6] Leif rescued fifteen men from the reef and was later called Leif the Lucky.

So Leif gained both wealth and honor. But the following winter Thori's people were attacked by sickness, and Thori and a large part of his crew died. Erik the Red also died that winter.

The question arises, when did this voyage take place? It could not have been in the year 1000 on Leif's return from Norway, because it is recorded that he reached Greenland the same summer, in which case he could not have taken his observation on the length of daylight on the shortest day of the year which required his presence in Vinland in December. Nor could it have taken place in 1001 because the saga says that he made the voyage in Bjarni's ship, and Bjarni used it in sailing to Norway in 1001. Nor could it have been in 1002 because Bjarni did not return from Norway until the late summer of that year. As the southern harbors of Greenland usually are inaccessible until some time in August because of the accumulation of field ice, his return was hardly possible until then. After this, some time must be allowed for the news to spread about Bjarni's earlier voyage, as mentioned in the previous chapter, and for the purchase by Leif of Bjarni's vessel. It would also take some time to gather together the necessary supplies for a possibly lengthy voyage and for hiring the crew. As this would advance the possible date of departure pretty well into the autumn when storms are very frequent, it is highly unlikely that Leif would set out on a long voyage to an unknown country so late in the year.

The earliest reasonable time of departure would therefore be in the summer of 1003. This conclusion is further supported by the fact that the voyage must have taken several weeks, after which the travelers had time to build permanent houses and spent some time in exploring the country before the grape vines were discovered. The wild grapes of New England are ready for picking in September. Allowing three weeks for building the houses and exploring the country, Leif Erikson's arrival in Vinland could not have been later than September first. Very likely it was a couple of weeks earlier. The date, October ninth, which is called Leif Erikson Day, is therefore much too late in the season.

It is evident that Leif, when he built his houses in Vinland, planned to settle there permanently. His father had gained prosperity and great fame in discovering Greenland, but it was a very poor country compared to the one that Leif had found. Its possibilities were wonderful and inexhaustible. But his father died the following winter, a victim of the same pestilence that took the lives of Thori and of half his crew. Leif's new obligations as chief of the colony in addition to his work of establishing Christianity in Greenland therefore prevented any immediate plan to emigrate to Vinland, but he was still looking forward to making his home there, because he would not sell his houses. To each new leader who sailed to Vinland and asked to buy his houses, the answer was always the same: "No, you can use the buildings, but they are not for sale."

Leif Erikson seems to have been one of Nature's noblemen. With fine physique and charming address, he was popular with everyone. On his arrival at the court of Olaf Trygveson, the most regal and respected of all the kings of Norway, both in life and after death, he was immediately accepted with the greatest courtesy and made a member of the King's very aristocratic body-guard. When he returned to Greenland with a new faith and told the people to throw their idols into the sea, these common people were so captivated by his personality that he had no trouble in introducing Christianity. He seems to have possessed true courtesy, even to the extent of being gentle to a slave who had annoyed him. When that poor servant and foreigner, Tyrk, appeared after an annoying delay, no doubt fearful because he had disobeyed orders, Leif did not scold him but merely said: "How did you become separated from the others, foster-father?" Tyrk, of course, was not Leif's foster-father, being only a humble slave without property. But the word was often used as a term of endearment, and Leif used it to reassure the old man. And Tyrk, delighted with his discovery of the grapes and happy that his young master was not angry, danced about in uncontrolled joy.

Where Was Leif Erikson's Vinland?

W HEN LEIF ERIKSON made his voyage of discovery to America, he reversed the voyage of Bjarni Herjulfson. The last land seen by Bjarni was therefore the first seen by Leif, and he called this land Helluland. The identification of the other lands Leif visited in America must, therefore, depend primarily upon the identification of Helluland.

Some writers have claimed that Helluland was up in Baffin Land which lies northwest of that part of Greenland where Leif and Bjarni lived. But we have already seen that Bjarni's voyage cannot be made to harmonize with this conclusion. Bjarni kept a continuous course toward the northeast throughout his return voyage, because he knew that Erik Thorwaldson's part of Greenland had a southwestern exposure. He repeatedly sailed away from the coasts or lands facing eastward and he would therefore never reach Baffin Land far northwest of the settled parts of Greenland. Finally we have the fact that whenever the location of Helluland is mentioned in the old writings it is always described as lying south or southwest of Greenland.[7]

Helluland is described as marked by three characteristics: (1) There was a large expanse of low flat rock. (2) There was no vegetation in sight. (3) There was an anchorage. The last implies that Leif Erikson entered a good harbor, because the smooth granite bottom off the shore would not provide holding ground for the anchor, except in landlocked harbors, where the silt would not be carried away.

There are only a few such harbors protected by a large area of flat rock. In Notre Dame Bay, halfway up the east coast of Newfoundland, there are several flat rock formations with a harbor inside, but as this part of the coast is well wooded, Leif would not call such a timbered region "good for nothing." But about fifteen miles north of St. Johns, there is one spot that fills all requirements, and, most fittingly, it has the same name (in meaning) as Leif gave it almost a thousand years ago. It is a low flat ledge of rock, several thousand feet long, behind which is a well-protected harbor. The early fishermen called it Flat Rock Point, and the harbor within, Flat Rock Cove. This spot is on the extreme eastern projection of the big island, and Black Head and other bald, precipitous mountains make this the most conspicuous landmark for north-south traffic. For Leif, coming from the north and a little to the east, this point, under any normal sailing conditions, would be the first land to be raised.

The probability that Leif's first landing place was at Flat Rock Point is supported by the next sentence in the saga: "Thereupon they sailed out to sea until they came to the second land." As it is not likely that they would have discontinued following the coast unless it turned away in a wrong direction, the narrative implies that their landing place was near the southeastern corner of the island. Since Leif was reversing Bjarni's course, he would, therefore, head southwest across the open sea, and not see land again for several days. This gulf, several hundred miles wide, is the Gulf of St. Lawrence. With the identification of Helluland as southeastern Newfoundland, it follows that the next projecting land, Nova Scotia, would be Markland.

All that we hear about Markland is that "it was low-lying and wooded, and there were wide stretches of sand, and the slope from the sea was not steep." This description excludes the shore northeast of Halifax. When I was there in the summer of 1951, I found this shore bold and rocky, and with no wide stretches of sand. But southwest of Halifax there are many places which fit Leif's description. Six hundred years later Henry Hudson passed the same way, and he describes the southwestern shore of Nova Scotia, facing the Atlantic, in almost the same words: "The land by the water-side is low, with white sandy banks rising, full of little hills."

When Leif Erikson left Markland he put out to sea and did not see land again for two days and nights. This was a voyage of about 300 miles according to the reckoning used at that time. Then he saw land and on approaching nearer he saw a ness (a pointed headland), extending northward from the land. North of this ness was an island.

At first reading this suggests Cape Cod, but there is neither ness nor island north of it. However, just south of the elbow of the Cape are conditions precisely as described by Leif. There lies Nantucket Island with hills more than a hundred feet high. A long ness extends northward for about five miles from the eastern end of the island, and Leif would be able to see it was a point because it is a low sand spit. North of this ness was formerly an island as shown on Captain Southack's chart of 1694 (see Fig. 4). On the chart it is shown as being about ten miles long and almost as wide. It is marked dry. As Leif and his men arrived at the island so early in the morning that the dew was still on the grass, it is likely that he passed Cape Cod well to the east in the night. When morning came he saw in the distance Folger Hill, a conspicuous landmark more than a hundred feet high in the eastern part of Nantucket. Many commentators have become confused because they have assumed that *land,* the word in the saga, refers to the mainland, and there is no island lying north of any mainland until Cape Breton is reached, north of Nova Scotia. But in Old Norse the meaning of *land* is opposed to water. The explorers saw dry land and were not yet in position to determine its extent, and therefore used the comprehensive term *land*. The word for mainland in Old Norse is *meginland*.

After they had landed on the island "they sailed into the sound which lay between the island and the ness which ran north from the land." Such a heading would indicate that the wind was from the southeast. With wind from that quarter they would soon see the mainland to the north. Nothing is said about how long they sailed, but the water was very shallow, and when the tide went out their ship ran aground. They were now near a place where a river issued. It must have been quite a large river because when the tide turned they sailed or towed their ship up this river to a body of water where they anchored and built their camp. The presence of this tidal river indicates that the camp was located on the south shore of Cape Cod, because there is no such inlet big enough to take a large ship on any of the islands. It is here also that most commentators have located Leif's Vinland for various reasons.[8] See Fig. 3.

At my suggestion, Mr. Frederick J. Pohl, who has been of much assistance in this research, made a search along the south coast of the Cape for a river coming from a lake big enough to accommodate an ocean-going ship of that time. He found there was only one such river and lake. This is Bass River and Follins Pond. This river at high tide is a fine, large waterway, somewhat reminiscent of the Merrimac or the Penobscot, several hundred feet wide. As there is considerable tidal current up and down the river, mooring stones would be necessary for safe anchorage, and there are several. One, in Follins Pond, was apparently intended for the mooring of a large boat or vessel because it is about fifty feet from the shore. Another is a mile or two down the river. From the latter down to the sea, the river is easily navigable for vessels of shallow draught; above this the waterway is somewhat obstructed by shallows and rocks. It is probably because of these conditions that a mooring hole was drilled in the rock in the river. It might be objected that both of these holes may have been drilled for the purpose of blasting stones. Against this argument, however, is the fact that the big rock in the pond is more than fifty feet from the shore and is inaccessible by land. The rock in the river is also inaccessible by any land vehicles. Besides these two holes there are also a number of other mooring holes, the origin of which is doubtful. These mooring stones may have been made by successive parties of Norse visitors or they may have been drilled by settlers in colonial times.

The question of the origin of the mooring holes, however, may be put aside in favor of the more positive evidence of the topography itself. I have inspected the river and the pond twice, and they appear to fit the conditions mentioned in the original narratives perfectly. There remains the possibility that other locations might fit Leif's description equally well. Some scholars, moreover have identified Leif's Vinland as being in Nova Scotia, or New Brunswick or the Gulf of St. Lawrence. In 1951, therefore, I made a search along the entire shore from Manhattan Island to the Gaspé Peninsula and westward into the St. Lawrence as far as Quebec. I found only three places whose topography agrees with the description in the saga. These were at Boston, Kingston, and Bass River, all in Massachusetts. The locations at Boston and Kingston do not fit, however, because they do not lie on a shore running east and west, a point plainly emphasized in the narrative about the voyage of Thorwald Erikson who occupied Leif's camp for three winters. I therefore believe that Mr. Pohl's identification is correct.

Leif mentions many other characteristics of Vinland besides its physical features. He said the climate was so mild it seemed as if cattle could graze all winter. This implies a location far south of both Newfoundland or Nova Scotia.

So also does the presence of abundant grapes. For some reason several writers have claimed that the "grapes" found by Tyrk were some variety of cranberry or other northern berries. But why should Leif and his men be excited about such a discovery? When Tyrk mentioned that he had found grapes, Leif was incredulous. "Is that really true?" he asked. And Tyrk answered: "Certainly it is true because I was born (in the south) where there was no lack of grapes." It was the discovery of grapes which prompted the name, *Wineland the Good.* As an agricultural area the sandy soil of Cape Cod gave little promise.[9]

The mild climate and the abundance of grapes indicate a southern location. But Leif mentions another find which limits the southern position: He found salmon. This is a cold water fish whose southern limit is Nantucket Sound and Hudson River. Vinland could not therefore be farther south than the Forty-first parallel.

Finally, we have an important observation made by Leif Erikson which in another way fixes the approximate latitude of his temporary habitation in Vinland. He noticed that the days in Vinland in winter were much longer than in Greenland. To make this matter clear, he made the following statement:

> The days and nights were of more equal length than in Greenland or Iceland. The sun was shining at *dagmalastad* and *eyktarstad* on the shortest day of the year.

Leif is here referring to the sun's position on December twenty-first at two definite times of the day, and is therefore pointing out the latitude of his camp in Vinland.

These two terms, *dagmalastad* and *eyktarstad,* refer to two of the four or five daily mealtimes in vogue in Iceland and Greenland. The former was the forenoon meal, the latter the afternoon meal, corresponding to the English tea time and the Norwegian *eftasverd,* (*eyktarstadverd*). We do not know the precise time of *dagmalastad,* but *eyktarstad* was at 4:30 P.M., a determination for which we have the authority of the historian, Snorri Sturlason, who (in Snorri's *Edda,* I, 510) writes: "*From the (September) equinox is fall until the sun sets in Eyktarstad. Then is winter until the (spring) equinox.*"

It is well known that the winter was reckoned from the Saturday preceding October 18th (old time), and observations have shown that the sun at that time at Snorri's home set at 4:30 or very close to it. This hour therefore was the old Icelandic *eyktarstad*. As most, if not all, of the first settlers in Greenland, including Leif Erikson's family, came from the same part of western Iceland where Snorri's home was located, there is no reason to doubt that their *eyktarstad* meal came at the same time. It was an ancient custom which grew out of conditions that existed on all farms. The greater part of the afternoon was spent in the fields, and the workers would return hungry. After *eyktarstad,* followed the multitudinous domestic chores—milking, feeding, and repairs—until about eight o'clock, when the evening meal was eaten. Even now, this custom and the timing are followed almost everywhere in the Scandinavian countries and in rural Great Britain.

More than a century after Leif Erikson's time, an attempt was made by two bishops in Iceland to identify *eyktarstad* with *non,* the ninth hour (3 p.m.), which had a religious dignity because all work should end at that hour on all days preceding holy days, including the sabbath. These two bishops compiled a small treatise dealing with the duties of church members, and in this compendium, known as *Kristinret* (The Christian Law), they give the same hour for both *non* and *eykt.* Following this interpretation blindly, the learned Vigfusson, in his dictionary, defines *eyktarstad* as being the same as *non,* 3 or 3:30 P.M.

But there are two reasons why *eyktarstad* was not 3 or 3:30 P.M. If Leif saw the sun set at that hour, he must have had his camp in the northern part of Labrador, a location which no one will claim fits Vinland. Moreover, there is only a few minutes' difference in the time of sunset in northern Labrador and southern Greenland. It should be noted that Leif does not say that the days were a *little* longer than in Greenland or even *much* longer. He goes much further than that. He says that the *days and nights* were of more *equal length.* To justify the use of such a comparison, he must have been at a much more southern latitude.

This observation was made by Leif in 1003, before Christianity had been established in Greenland, and before he could have learned much about ecclesiastical terminology. It must be viewed in the light of the time in which it was written, and this brings us back to the native customs of Greenland and Iceland, and the *eyktarstad* time of 4:30, the hour when the afternoon meal was eaten. The sun sets at 4:30 at latitude 42° 30′, which parallel runs a short distance north of Boston. However, as Leif says that "the sun was shining at *eyktarstad*," that is, it had not yet set below the horizon, the true sunset was a few minutes later, which means that his camp was a little farther south. Only the south coast of New England would correspond reasonably to such a latitude and to the general description of Leif's voyage.

Just as this book went to press, a new book has appeared which deals with the significance of Leif's observation in Vinland that the sun was shining at *eyktarstad* on the shortest day of the year. It is written by Almar Naess, Professor of Mathematics at the University of Oslo, Norway. It is entitled *Hvor Lå Vinland?* (*Where Lay Vinland?*) This is a scientific work of much merit dealing with every factor involved in this astronomical observation, and Naess shows conclusively that Leif's observation was made about 4:30 P.M. The latitude would therefore be at approximately 41 degrees, depending on whether the sun was just disappearing or was visible for some time later.

However, Naess makes one mistake. As the Atlantic coast faces east, he assumes that Leif, no matter where he was, saw the sun setting behind a horizon of hills. The true sunset, he thinks, would thus come somewhat later, and the latitude would be two or three degrees lower. He is therefore inclined to place Leif's landfall at or near Chesapeake Bay.

This assumption that Leif saw the sun set beyond a horizon of hills is erroneous. While the Atlantic coast has a general eastern exposure, there is one stretch of shore two hundred miles long where a sunset in December would be visible over the open sea. This is the south shore of New England from the elbow of Cape Cod to Manhattan Island.

America's
First Homesteader

W HEN LEIF ERIKSON returned to Greenland in 1004 and told about the new lands he had visited, he must have created a great sensation. Not only was this land far superior in climate and products to Greenland—it excelled even Iceland and Norway. Moreover, it had been a most profitable trip. He brought home a large cargo of timber for housebuilding and furniture, and vines (withes), much in demand for bindings, baskets and shipbuilding. On top of that he had rescued a shipwrecked crew. He was therefore given a new title of honor: he became known as Leif the Lucky.

However, there was one man who was not satisfied with Leif's achievement. This was Leif's brother Thorwald. He thought that Leif had neglected a very important part of his enterprise—he had not explored these new countries sufficiently. Leif had not permitted any of his men to go farther than a few miles from camp, and they were required to return before nightfall. Thorwald thought this new land should be widely explored in order to make available a comprehensive knowledge of its extent, character and population. Leif evidently agreed with him because he offered Thorwald the use of his vessel to make a voyage. The following is the saga narrative of Thorwald's voyage.

There was now [after Leif's return] much talk about Vinland, and Thorwald, his brother, thought that the new land had been insufficiently explored. So Leif said, "If you would like to do better, brother, you can take my vessel and go to Vinland. But first I would like to use the vessel in fetching home the timber which Thori had on the reef."

This was done, and Thorwald made his preparations with the help of Leif. He hired thirty men, [among whom he naturally chose many who had accompanied Leif]. When they were ready they held out to sea, and there is no report of their voyage before they came to Leif's camp in Vinland. There they laid up their ship and remained quiet that winter, catching fish for their food. In the spring the ship was made ready, and Thorwald took a part of the crew in the afterboat to explore the coast to the west. It seemed to them a fine timbered country, the woods coming down close to the sea, and there were white sandy beaches. There were many islands and many shoals. They found no trace either of man or beast, except that on an island in the west they found a corncrib (kornhjalm).[10] Finding no further human handiwork, they returned to Leif's camp in the autumn.

The next summer Thorwald took his ship and sailed east and northward along the land. There a sudden storm arose off a cape and flung their ship on the shore, breaking the keel. Here they were delayed a long time repairing the vessel. Then Thorwald said: "Now I suggest that we raise the keel here on the cape and call it Keelness," and so they did.

They then sailed away from the land and then eastward along the coast, and into some fjord openings to a headland which ran out; it was covered with timber. Here they moored their boat and went ashore. Then Thorwald said: "Here it is beautiful! Here will I build my home!"

After a time they went back to the ship and sailed farther in. Here they saw three little mounds on the sandy shore inside the headland. When they got closer to them they saw three skin canoes with three men. They divided their party and seized all of them except one who escaped in a canoe. They killed the eight men and then returned to the headland. From here they saw a number of mounds farther up in the fjord which they took to be human dwellings.

After that they became very drowsy and they all fell asleep. Then they heard a voice above them so that they all awoke, and it cried: "Awake, Thorwald, and all your company if you value your life. Return to your ship and hurry away from this land with all your speed!" They now saw countless canoes coming toward them from within the fjord. Then Thorwald said, "We must set up battle-flakes [a hurdle of wicker work for protection against arrows] and defend ourselves as well as we can, but do as little killing as possible." So they did, and after the savages had shot at them for a while, they hurried away as fast as possible.

Then Thorwald asked if any of his men were injured, and the answer was no.

"I got a wound under my arm," said Thorwald; "an arrow flew between the gunwale and the hurdle and hit me under the arm. Here it is and I fear it will be my death. Now I advise you to leave this place as quickly as possible. Take me to the headland which I found so pleasing for a home. It seems I spoke the truth when I said I would stay here. Bury me there and place a cross at my head and at my feet and call it Crossness hereafter."

So Thorwald died and he was buried as he had instructed them. The others returned to their companions [at Leif's camp] and stayed there the following winter gathering grapes and vines for their ship. The following spring they sailed away to Greenland and arrived in Eriksfjord with an account of what had happened for Leif.

THORWALD ERIKSON'S EXPLORATIONS

The old saga narrative about Thorwald's explorations is most clear and graphic. He arrived at Leif's camp in the fall, too late for any explorations that year. The next spring he started on a long trip westward, using the yawl, presumably because the water in the sound was shallow. As they were away all summer, they probably continued at least up to the head of Long Island Sound. "They found a pleasing timbered shore, the woods coming down close to the sea, and there were white sandy beaches. There were also many islands and many shoals." This is about as concise and correct a description of the south shore of New England as can be given in so few words. Furthermore, it definitely fixes the location of Vinland, because nowhere else on the Atlantic coast is it possible to travel for a long distance westward with such particular surroundings. See Fig. 2, page 130.

The next year Thorwald took his ship and part of his crew and after sailing east proceeded northward along the coast until they came to a cape. This description of the shore in addition to his sailing directions also shows that his (and Leif's) camp was on the south shore of New England. There is no other point on the Atlantic coast from which one could sail any considerable distance west on one side, and any considerable distance east and then north on the other. One could sail west from a point on the south side of Long Island, but not east and then north without soon running out of land. On approaching the north of the cape they were caught in a storm, the vessel was thrown ashore, and its keel was torn away. After the labor of putting in a new keel, Thorwald and his men raised the old keel on the head of the cape as a landmark.

This keel apparently stood near the north end of Cape Cod because they would not know that they were on a cape until they saw its end. From this cape they sailed out "away from the land." The mainland of Massachusetts would be visible, and they then continued *eastward* along the coast until they came to some fjords.

The Norsemen with thousands of miles of sea shore had eight designations for different kinds of inlets from the sea. A *fjord* is a long and narrow waterway with considerable depth, and flanked by steep, rocky banks or mountains. On the Atlantic coast of the United States this type of waterway is extremely rare. From the southern end of Florida to Portland, Maine, there is only one true fjord—the lower end of Hudson River, including Harlem River. From Portland, eastward, the coast is cut with long bays, but they are shallow and without precipitous banks. It does not seem likely that anyone from Greenland would think of calling these inlets fjords. Moreover, the approach to them is so obstructed by islands, skerries and tidal currents that a seafaring man, coming there for the first time, would hesitate to risk his vessel into those dangerous waters. The *U. S. Coast Pilot* says: "The coast (of Maine) is subject to severe fogs, the tidal currents are strong, and small crafts must go miles off shore to avoid the turbulent seas at the mouths of the rivers during strong offshore winds."

This phenomenon continues for about two-thirds of the coast of Maine, but on arriving at Mount Desert Island conditions are different. The waters off shore here are fairly clean, and the island is the most imposing landmark along the entire Atlantic coast. It is about fifteen miles long and ten miles wide, and its area is mostly taken up by fifteen imposing mountain tops, from seven to seventeen hundred feet in height.

This island is almost bisected by a straight fjord about eight miles long and flanked by precipitous walls. It is known as Some's Inlet and enters the island from the south, where its harbor is well-protected by a number of islands. Near the mouth of this narrow fjord is a timbered promontory, which terminates in a sloping meadow called Jesuits Field.[11] Behind the promontory is a small sandy cove called Valley Cove where there is a spring. The topography of this part of Mount Desert corresponds perfectly with the description in the narrative. It was Frederick J. Pohl who first called attention to the exact correspondence of this topography to the saga description.

Another unusual characteristic of the site selected by Thorwald was its beauty. If this young man from Greenland saw the panorama of the island from the promontory in the fjord, he had abundant reason to exclaim: "Here it is beautiful! Here will I build my house!"

But like Moses on Mount Nebo, Thorwald was not permitted to enjoy the promised land. There was immediate trouble with the Indians. There seems to be something wrong with the passage about the killing of the eight Indians. As it stands we get a picture of nine Indians, dozing under their canoes, being suddenly attacked and murdered by the white men. The action is unmotivated and therefore unreasonable. Moreover, as told, it seems so imprudent that no man of sense would have ordered his men to do it. Furthermore, Thorwald was not a blood-thirsty brute. Later in the day when the white men were attacked by Indians in "countless canoes," Thorwald tells his men to defend themselves, but to "do as little killing as possible." Perhaps the old manuscript that the clerk was copying was defective here, and all he could make out was that eight *skrellings* were killed.

The true happenings may possibly be conjectured thus: These Indians were not sleeping, but were lying in ambush under their canoes, waiting for some game to come down to the spring to drink. There is an easy approach to the spring from the hills above. When the Indians saw the white men making a landing, they naturally expected trouble and immediately attacked with bows and arrows. In the fight that followed all the Indians but one were killed.

The narrative mentions *hide boats,* and this has made some commentators ponder the possibility that these natives were Eskimos. But there is no probability that Eskimos ever inhabited a region as far south as Maine. A more reasonable possibility is that the Indians a thousand years ago used hide boats. We have no knowledge of their arts that long ago, but it is known that they sometimes used skin boats within historic times. Baron Lahontan mentions that in 1683 a group of Outagami Indians in Wisconsin made skin boats to keep a war party of Iroquois from escaping from an island. When the first white men came to the Mandans, who were perhaps the most advanced in culture of all the tribes north of Mexico, they found that these Indians used wicker coracles covered with hides. Professor F. G. Speck mentions that the Penobscots of Maine used canoes of moose hide.

The memory of this first homesteader in America is one of tragic dignity. He evidently was a thoughtful young man, because when Leif returned to Greenland and reported his great discovery, Thorwald at once put his finger on the weak spot in his enterprise: while Leif came back with a rich cargo, including many casks of red wine, his knowledge of the new country was slight—he had been more interested in immediate profits than in exploration.

To fill this deficiency, Thorwald set forth to Vinland, but when he arrived there he did not precipitately start his explorations. He had to provide food for thirty men, and as conditions in winter in this new land were unknown, he devoted all his attention the first fall to providing supplies for the cold weather. When spring came he took cognizance of the shallow waters in the Sound and did his exploring in the pinnace which, with a mast and sail as well as oars, was better suited than a ship for such waters.

After spending a whole season in exploring the coast westward, he set out to investigate the land to the north. The desolate shore of the cape to the northeast, later called *Furdustrandir,* needed no exploring, but beyond lay an unknown gulf (the Gulf of Maine) where a ship was required. However, the northern extension of Cape Cod was not to be lightly passed by. Thorwald's vessel was caught in the grip of a storm and flung on the shore, the keel breaking in two. It must have been a most difficult task to replace this main timber of the ship, on which all its ribs are based, with a new keel cut from the woods of the cape, but eventually it was done. In this work Thorwald was probably more a spectator than a leader, because Greenland was treeless, and he could have had no experience in shipbuilding.

The ship Thorwald was sailing was a famous traveler. It had belonged to Bjarni Herjulfson who for years had sailed it in many European waters on his trading trips. Each alternate year he had gone to Iceland to spend the winter with his parents. This was the ship in which he had been carried in successive autumn storms far down south when he accidentally discovered the new lands in the West, and in this ship Leif had made his successful voyage to Vinland. As Thorwald looked on that broken keel which had cleaved so many thousands of miles of the great ocean, he evidentally felt that it possessed a dignity far above the flotsam of the sea. It was a memorial of sturdy achievement and great adventure, and he decided that it should stand as a monument to the sailors of Greenland. So he raised it on the beach above the angry waves, fixed firmly in the ground, the first landmark in America constructed by a white man.

Then along the shores of the Gulf of Maine he sailed, past many harbors where now stand great seaports. But to one who has lived among mountains, this coast would seem rather insipid. Thorwald, born on the shore of a fjord, as were most of his ancestors, felt the need of something different. And he found it! Coasting eastward along the shore, his eyes were pleased to see the mountain tops of Mount Desert Island, rising upwards of 1700 feet above the sea. Here was something that conformed to the images that not only had been built up within him throughout his own life, but had also been inherited from his fathers, and when he entered into this dreamland by way of the narrow fjord, his enthusiasm was unbounded. Over the lapse of many centuries we can hear him rapturously exclaiming, "Here it is beautiful! Here I will build my home!" He had found his El Dorado, his Garden of Eden!

But on that day of infinite satisfaction the bell tolled for Thorwald Erikson. In the afternoon the Norsemen were attacked by "countless canoes" of natives, the avenging war party. Safe against arrows behind their protecting shield of wickerwork, the men were unharmed with one exception, Thorwald. He felt it was his death, but there was no repining. He told his followers to carry his body back to the headland he had selected for his home and gave directions for his burial. Then he closed his eyes with a mild jest: "It seems I spoke the truth when I said that here I would remain."

Thorwald's expedition appears to have spanned the three years from 1004 to 1007. It is natural that such a great discovery as Leif had made would arouse the greatest interest, and the Greenland saga says that there was much talk about it. Thorwald criticized his brother for not having explored the new land more thoroughly, a charge Leif seems to have admitted. He offered Thorwald the use of his vessel as soon as he had salvaged the lumber and logs from Thori's wreck. Lumber was of great value in treeless Greenland, and Leif lost no time fetching it. While the harbors of Greenland most often are inaccessible until August because of the accumulation of the field ice outside, this is not always the case. As Leif left Vinland in Spring, it is possible that he returned to Eriksfjord in summer. Salvaging the timber would not take long, as the wreck was on a skerry near Greenland, and Thorwald would have been able to start for Vinland the same fall. A fall sailing date is also indicated by the fact that Thorwald attempted no exploration on reaching Vinland, presumably because of his late arrival. The narrative states that on arriving at Leif's camp "they laid up their ship and remained quiet that winter, catching fish for their food." In the summer of 1005, Thorwald made his explorations westward, and in 1006 he went north and east to the spot where he was killed. He urged his men to return to Greenland without delay, but the prospect of gathering grapes, making wine, and cutting vines and logs induced his men to remain in Leif's camp until the following year. Thus, if this chronology may be accepted as reasonable, the expedition would have returned to Greenland in 1007.

It was a great shock to the sons of Erik when the news came that Thorwald had been killed in Vinland. Thorstein, the youngest son, was very religious and he determined to make a voyage to Vinland to get his brother's body and bury it in consecrated ground by the church near Brattalid which his mother had built, the first church in Greenland. While Thorwald was in Vinland, Thorstein had married Gudrid, the daughter of Thorbjorn Vifilson, and the next summer (1008) he set out with his bride and thirty men in the vessel of his father-in-law, Thorbjorn. Gudrid is described as "a fine-looking, intelligent woman, with a gracious manner toward strangers."

But Thorstein's expedition was ill-fated and never came near Vinland. All through the late summer and early fall the ship was driven about by contrary winds, first toward Iceland, then south to Ireland, and then northward again. Thorstein finally arrived in the Western Settlement of Greenland, 200 miles north-west of his starting point. Here trouble continued; the crew was smitten by an infectious disease, and Thorstein and many of his shipmates died. Eventually Gudrid arrived with her husband's body at Brattalid in 1009, where she became the ward of Leif.

Thorfin Karlsevni
Sails to Vinland

T HE STORY of the Norse discovery of America, despite a few superstitious embellishments characteristic of the times, is told in a clear and graphic way in the old narrative. First we have Bjarni's accidental discovery. Then we have Leif Erikson's quick and purposeful voyage, followed in turn by Thorwald's more comprehensive exploration. When Thorwald's companions returned and made their report, the people of Greenland, or at least many of them, should have had a reasonably clear conception of a substantial part of America, a shore a couple of hundred miles in length, with its physiography, climate and flora. As this known part of America was highly pleasing, attempts at colonization would naturally follow.

It was at this stage that Thorfin Karlsevni came to Greenland. Thorfin was a very promising man, a successful trader and an experienced sea captain. The following is the account of his great voyage, given in *Hauksbok*. Throughout this saga Leif Erikson is referred to as Erik.[12]

> There was a man named Thorfin Karlsevni (the promising),
> a son of Thord Horsehead, who lived in the north of Iceland
> at Reyniness in Skagafjord. Karlsevni was a man of good stock
> and very well-to-do. His mother's name was Thorun. He sailed
> on trading voyages and was considered a successful merchant.

One summer he made his ship ready for sailing to Greenland. Snorri, a son of Thorbrand from Alptafjord, joined him, and together they had a crew of forty men. That same summer two other men, Bjarni Grimolfson from Broadfjord and Thorhall Gamlason from Eastfjord, also fitted out a ship to sail to Greenland with forty men on board.

Both ships sailed out to sea as soon as they were ready. We are not told how long they were at sea, but in the fall they both arrived in Eriksfjord. Erik,* and other settlers rode down to the ships to meet them, and at once began bartering for the goods they had brought. The skippers told Erik to help himself to all he wanted. Erik showed his generosity in turn by inviting all the men to Brattalid for the winter. Later their wares were carried to Brattalid, where there was no lack of fine, roomy outhouses to store them in.

The traders had a merry time of it at Erik's home that winter. But as it drew toward Christmas, Erik became silent and moody, very different from his usual cheerful self. One day Karlsevni got to talking with him and said, "Are you troubled about something, Erik? It strikes us that you are rather less cheerful than you have been. You are treating us so royally here that we owe you whatever returns we can give. Now tell me what makes you so gloomy."

Erik replied, "You are fine, courteous guests, and nothing is farther from my thoughts than any unpleasantness between us. It is simply that I should feel deeply shamed if it came to be said that you had never had so bad a Christmas as the one you spent at Erik the Red's house in Greenland."

"There is no need of that," answered Karlsevni. "On our ships we have malt and flour and grain, and you are welcome to take as much as you wish, and hold whatever kind of celebration your generosity may dictate."

Erik accepted the offer and made ready for the Christmas feast, and it turned out so well that people could hardly recall a better one in a poor country.

After Christmas, Karlsevni asked Erik for Gudrid's hand, since it appeared that Erik had the legal right to marry her off. Erik answered that he would be glad to advance his cause, and he added that she deserved to be well married.

---

* This should be Leif because Erik died in 1004.

"She will have to follow the fate that is cut out for her, and we have heard nothing but good about you." The question was then put up to her, and she said that her wishes agreed wholly with Erik's. They wasted no time carrying out the plan, and extended the Christmas feast into a wedding party. It was a jolly winter in Brattalid that year, with much chess-playing, saga-telling, and everything that might contribute to their good cheer.

There was much discussion at Brattalid that winter about going to Vinland the Good, for it was agreed that the country must have valuable resources. For this reason Karlsevni and Snorri decided to go exploring in the spring. Bjarni and Thorhall, who had outfitted one of the two ships, made ready to join them with their ship and crew.

There was a man named Thorvard, who was married to Freydis, an illegitimate daughter of Erik. He also decided to go along. With him came Thorhall, who was nicknamed "The Hunter." He and Erik hunted and fished together in the summer, while in the winter he was Erik's overseer and trusted man. He was a huge fellow, dark and glowering, rather beyond middle age; however, he was a hard man to get along with, mostly taciturn, but also abusive and underhanded, and he was a bad adviser to Erik. He had refused to adopt the new faith when it came to Greenland. He had few friends, but Erik had high regard for him, and he was taken on the voyage because he was acquainted far and wide with the unsettled regions of the country. They sailed the ship that Thorbjorn, Gudrid's father, had brought out from Iceland, and most of the men aboard were Greenlanders.

Altogether there were a hundred and sixty men aboard the three ships. They sailed first to the Western Settlement and then out to the Bear Isles.[13] From there they sailed for two days, accompanied by a northerly wind, before they sighted land. They rowed to shore in their boats and explored the country; here they found huge slabs of stone, many of them twenty-four feet across (the Greenland Saga says that two men could easily lie outstretched on them with their soles touching). Here, they saw many arctic foxes. They named the country Helluland (the land of flat rocks). Then they sailed for two days more, changing their course from south to southeast, and then there was a land before them on which were great forests and many animals. Off the shore to the southeast lay an island, and here they killed a bear. For this reason they called it Bear Island, while they named the country itself Markland (forest land) because of the woods.

Then they sailed southward a long time along the coast and came upon a cape. They tacked along the coast, which was on their starboard. It was an open, harborless shore, with long, sandy beaches. They put out their small boats and rowed ashore. On the cape they found the keel of a ship, which they called Keelness. The sandy beaches they called Furdustrandir (the strange and weary shore), because it took so long to sail past them. Then the coast grew more indented with bays, and they steered the ship into one of these.

When Leif Erikson had been at the court of Olaf Trygveson, and King Olaf had asked him to proclaim Christianity in Greenland, he had given Leif two Scottish (Gaelic) slaves, a man named Haki and a woman named Hekja. The king suggested that if he needed speed, he might use them, for they were swifter than deer. Leif had turned them over to Karlsevni for the voyage. When they had sailed past Furdustrandir, they landed the Scots and told them to run southwards and see what the country had to offer, but to return before three days had past. They were dressed in garments which they called "kjafal" (Irish *cabhail*). These were made with a hood on top, were open on the sides, sleeveless, and fastened between the legs with a button and a loop. Otherwise the Scots were naked. They cast anchor and lay there in the meanwhile. When three days had passed, the Scots came running down to the shore. One of them bore a bunch of grapes in his hand, the other an ear of wild wheat. Karlsevni remarked that they seemed to have found a country rich in resources, and took them back on board.

Then they sailed away on their course, until they reached a place where the shoreline was indented by a fjord, and they sailed into this fjord. At the mouth lay an island, washed by swift ocean currents; this they called Stream Isle. There were so many eider-ducks there that it was hardly possible to step between the eggs. Sailing up the fjord, they called it Streamfjord.

Here they unloaded their cargoes and set up camp. They had brought along all kinds of livestock, and now they turned them out to graze in the tall grass. There were mountains there, and the country was beautiful to see. The men spent all their time exploring. They stayed throughout the winter, which turned out to be a severe one. They had not provided for it during the summer, and so they ran short of food, and had trouble finding any game or fish.

They went out to the island in the hope that something would turn up—either wild life or flotsam from the sea. But there was little that one could eat, even though their cattle were getting along fine. Then they prayed to God, and asked that He send them some food, but their prayers were not answered as quickly as they had need of. Meanwhile Thorhall the Hunter disappeared and the men made a search for him, keeping it up for three days. On the fourth day Karlsevni and Bjarni found him on top of an overhanging cliff. He was staring up in the air, with his eyes and mouth and nostrils wide open, while he scratched and pinched himself, and mumbled something. They asked why he had gone there. He told them it was none of their business, that they had better not bother about his actions, and that he had lived long enough so that he needed no advice from them.

They told him to come home with them, and he did so. Soon afterwards a whale drifted in, and the men rushed at it and cut it up, but they did not know what kind of whale this was. Even Karlsevni, who was an expert on whales, could not make out what kind it was. When the cooks had boiled the whalemeat, they ate some of it; but all of them got sick from it. Then Thorhall walked over and said to them, "Isn't it so that the Redbearded One [Thor] turned out to be stronger than your Christ? This is my reward for the chants I made to my trusty friend Thor; he has rarely failed me." When the men learned this, none of them would touch the meat, and they threw it over a cliff into the sea. They lifted up their voices and asked for the mercy of God. Then the weather got better, so they could row out to sea, and now they were able to find plenty of food. In the spring they went back to Stream-fjord and gathered supplies along the shore. There was game on the mainland, birds' nests on the island, and fish in the sea.

Now they began to discuss the future course of their journey. Thorhall the Hunter wanted to sail north of Furdustrandir past Keelness and look for Vinland in this direction, while

Karlsevni wanted to sail southward along the coast and to
the east of it, for there seemed to be better land the farther
south they got, and it seemed to him more advisable to explore
in both directions. Thorhall rigged up his ship off the island,
but only nine men went with him. All the rest joined Karlsevni.
One day, as Thorhall was carrying water on board his ship,
he took a drink and recited this verse [translated by G. M.
Gathorne-Hardy]:

> They flattered my confiding ear
> With tales of drink abounding here:
> My curse upon this thirsty land!
> A warrior, trained to bear a brand,
> A pail instead I have to bring,
> And bow my back beside the spring:
> For ne'er a single draught of wine
> Has passed these parching lips of mine.

After this they sailed away, and Karlsevni followed them
out to the island. Before they hoisted sail, Thorhall recited
another ditty:

> Now let the vessel plough the main
> To Greenland and our friends again
> Away and leave the strenuous host,
> Who praise this god-forsaken coast,
> To linger in a desert land,
> And boil their whales on Furdustrand.

Then they parted company, and Thorhall and his crew
sailed north past Furdustrandir and Keelness. There they tried
to tack to the west, but a storm struck them and blew them
east as far as Ireland. Here they were beaten up and thrown
into slavery, and Thorhall lost his life, according to stories
told by traders.

Karlsevni sailed south along the coast with Snorri, Bjarni,
and the others. After some time they came to a river that
first ran down into a lake, and then out to sea. There were
great sandbars outside the river mouth, and they could only
enter the stream at high tide. Karlsevni sailed into the river
mouth and named the country Hop [a small, landlocked bay].
Here they found self-sown wheat fields in the lowlands, and
grapevines wherever there were hills. Every creek was full

of fish. They dug pits at the point where land and sea met at high tide, and when the tide went out, there were halibut in the pits. The woods teemed with all kinds of animals. For half a month they stayed there and enjoyed themselves, without being aware of any danger. They had their livestock with them.

Identification of
Thorfin Karlsevni's Route

*A*PPARENTLY Hauk Erlendsson used a defective manuscript in compiling the beginning of Thorfin Karlsevni's saga because the sailing directions are very confusing. This confusion at the beginning of the saga, however, need not seriously effect the identification of Thorfin's route. During his winter's visit with Leif Erikson, Thorfin had heard very complete accounts about "Vinland the Good" and how to reach it. As his purpose was to find the same land, he would certainly follow the now well established course. Moreover, he would no doubt include in his company as pilots some of the men who had already made the journey. We may therefore ignore the sailing directions recorded by Sir Hauk, especially since they lead nowhere. It is a mistake to think that a series of more or less faded and defective manuscripts could be successively copied without errors. As long as the main trend of the narrative is intelligible, minor errors in distance and direction are immaterial.

Karlsevni's sailing directions are not too bad; he states that after sailing south some days he came to Helluland. Then, he continues, after leaving Helluland, the expedition sailed south for two days, "changing the course from south to southeast," whereupon they came to a land with great forests—Mark-

[65]

land. The implication is clearly that there was an open sea
between Helluland and Markland—just as is mentioned in
Leif's sailing directions. But while a southeastern course might
bring them to Africa, it would never bring them to Markland.
In all probability, therefore, the word *southeast* is a clerical
error for *southwest*. Their course is further determined by the
statement that off (some distance) to the southeast of Markland
lay an island. Sable Island, twenty-five miles long, lies southeast
of Nova Scotia, which, as already discussed, offers itself as the
only reasonable identification for Markland.

Erik's Saga which is a close variant of the narrative in Hauk's
Book, but a hundred years older, says that after leaving Markland:

> When two dægr had elapsed they saw land and sailed to
> it. There was a cape to which they came. They beat into the
> wind along this coast, having the land upon the starboard
> side. It was an open, harborless shore with long and sandy
> beaches. They went ashore and found the keel of a ship,
> which they called Keelness. They likewise gave a name to the
> beaches and called them *Furdustrandir* because they were
> so long to sail by.

According to Vigfusson's *Icelandic Dictionary, furdu* means
a specter, an ominous appearance; *strandir* means a strand, a
beach. *Furdustrandir* therefore means a very strange shore with
the connotation of something ominous. Some writers have translated it "a wonderful shore," which has an entirely different
implication. It must have seemed ominous to these Norsemen
because a sandy shore having a convex shape toward the sea
was unknown in Iceland or Greenland. This inhospitable shore,
continuously entering on the horizon in front and vanishing
behind, would have been new to them and therefore uncanny.

The first desolate monotonous shore without harbors, but
with long sandy beaches, that the explorers would find in sailing down along the Atlantic coast is the shelterless eastern shore

of Cape Cod. The shore of Nova Scotia cannot be called desolate
because it has many bays, harbors and timbered islands.

Another evidence that this was Cape Cod is the keel which
they found. This can only have been the keel left by Thorwald
Erikson a few years earlier. The voyage, it must be remembered,
took place many years before there was any traffic in ships along
the eastern coast of America. The possibility that the keel they
found was any other than Thorwald's is too slight to merit
serious consideration. Moreover, the cape is so exposed because
of its convex outline, that no flotsam remains.

Finally they came to an inlet, perhaps the present Nauset,
and put in here.

It is at this point that the episode of the two runners, Haki
and Hekja, is introduced. It is generally believed that this is
an interpolation by some copyist who had heard of such runners
and thought that they would make a picturesque addition. All
commentators are agreed that the two verses recited by Thorhall
the Hunter a short time after this (see page 63) are survivals
of the most ancient form of the narrative. But these verses owe
their existence to the fact that no grapes had been found up
to the time they were recited. It is said that these runners were
a gift of King Olaf to Leif, and if this is true, one would
expect them to perform their act when Leif or Thorwald made
their journeys and not many years later when Thorfin Karlsevni
set out to visit Vinland.

Before leaving Greenland, Thorfin had offered to buy Leif's
property in Vinland, but the latter refused to sell. Leif's refusal
indicated that he intended to make use of his possessions, and
Thorfin would not therefore select any land close to Leif's
houses because the latter might think it an encroachment on
his domain. The narrative therefore continues as follows:

> Then they sailed away on their course, until they reached
> a place where the shoreline was indented by a fjord, and into
> this fjord they steered their ships. At the mouth lay an island,

washed by swift currents. This they called Stream Island. They sailed along the fjord and called it Streamfjord. Here they unloaded their cargo and set up a camp. They had brought along all kinds of livestock, and now they turned them out to graze in the tall grass. *There were mountains there,* and the country was beautiful to see. The men spent all their time exploring. They stayed throughout the winter, which turned out to be a severe one.

This is a perfectly clear narrative telling of an apparently uninterrupted journey from *Furdustrandir* (Cape Cod) into a fjord having a swift current. Where is this fjord? As this was the place where a large company of pioneers attempted for three years to make a permanent settlement, its exact location is of much interest.

Gathorne-Hardy believes that this fjord was Long Island Sound, and he identifies Fisher's Island at its east end as Stream Island because at certain hours of the day there is a very rapid current, known as the race, between it and the Gull Islands to the south. He places the camp near Fisher's Island.

While this island would do for Stream Island, the Sound cannot be called a fjord. It is shallow and quite wide (twenty miles wide in the middle), and has low shores and very little current. In other words, it is a sound. A fjord on the contrary is deep, narrow, and enclosed by high rocky banks. Still more important is the mention of mountains. These are mentioned twice in the description. We must seek the camp at a place where high rocky hills or mountains were near by because the narrative says that they stayed *along the fjord* before they built their camp.

Such a fjord with swift currents and mountains near by we find at the western end of Long Island Sound. Here is the Harlem River, a true fjord, with steep cliffs rising hundreds of feet from the water's edge and still higher mountains in the background. At the mouth of the Harlem River is an island and the entrance was called Hell Gate, which name is reminiscent of the ancient terrors of its waters. We have several descriptions of this area from the XVII century, before the builders of Manhattan blasted the hills and cleared the waters of obstructions (see note 14).

Here, apparently, on the banks of the Harlem River, "one of the sweetest streams that ever gave a charm to landscape," was their camp; but it is also possible that the camp was at the south end of Manhattan Island and the fjord was the Hudson River, because the saga says that the Norsemen lived "above the lake," which may mean upper New York harbor. Verrazano in 1524 also called this upper harbor a lake. Here, then, probably somewhere on Manhattan Island, in the autumn of the first year, was born the first white child in America. His name was Snorri, the son of Thorfin Karlsevni and Gudrid, and he grew up to become the ancestor of three bishops and of other eminent men in Iceland.

It took a large amount of food to provide for the 160 men, and as they had neglected to lay in supplies in fall, the winter was a hard one. For this reason they moved out to one of the islands. The cattle did well on the island, but human sustenance continued to be scarce. In addition, Thorhall, the Hunter disappeared, and the men searched for him in vain for three days. Finally, on the fourth day they discovered him. This long search by many men indicates that the island was large, and once more suggests Manhattan Island or Long Island.

Fortunately a whale was found stranded on the shore, and this provided food for some time. Thorhall, the Hunter, who was a disagreeable old heathen, claimed that Thor had sent him this whale in answer to his prayers, whereupon the men found that the whale meat made them sick. This incident is probably an embellishment of some pious copyist who wanted to show that nothing good can come from a heathen god. According to the

Greenland version the whale meat did not make them sick, and it appears from Thorhall's second verse that they subsisted on it for some time.

Thorhall was greatly disappointed in not finding the grapes from which to make wine. The following year, therefore, he decided to go north and west to look for grapes. He probably intended to find the fjord which Thorwald had found so pleasing. Thorfin, however, did not favor Thorhall's plan, believing that conditions were better toward the south. The result was that nine men decided to go with Thorhall. Thorfin accompanied them past the islands. The saga says: "They sailed north past Furdustrandir and Keelness, and planned to bear westward." Here is another proof that Keelness and Furdustrandir were on a projecting land mass, to the west (and northwest) of which was an unexplored body of water (Cape Cod Bay and the Gulf of Maine are the only such bodies of water so situated in relation to the land within the latitudes prescribed by the other evidence of the sagas) which Thorhall wanted to explore. But they were caught by a storm and driven across the Atlantic to Ireland where they were enslaved. Their arrival in Ireland is probably hypothetical.

_____

The Norsemen Fight
with the Indians*

_____

*E*ARLY ONE morning, as the Norsemen were looking around, they caught sight of many skin-covered boats. The men in the boats were waving wooden sticks at the ships, and they were waving them in the direction of the sun. It sounded very much as if they were threshing grain. Then Karlsevni exclaimed, "What can this mean?"

Snorri Thorbrandson answered, "It may be that this is a signal of peace, so let us take a white shield and lift it up before them."

So they did, while the others rowed up to them, gazed at them with astonishment, and then went on land. They were dark men and ugly, with unkempt hair on their heads. They had large eyes and broad cheeks. After they had stayed a while and marvelled, they rowed off to the south of the cape.

Karlsevni and his men had built their shelters above the lake, some of them close to the water, others farther away, and here they stayed that winter. There was no snowfall whatever, and all their cattle grazed by themselves in the open.

_____

* From the Icelandic version in Hauk's Book.

But early one morning, as spring drew near, they were confronted by a vast number of skin boats being rowed around the cape from the south. The bay was dotted with them, as if strewn with pieces of charcoal, and on every one the sticks were waving. Karlsevni's men raised their shields, and when the two parties met, they started trading with each other.

These people wanted most of all to buy red cloth. They also wanted to buy swords and spears, but that was forbidden by Karlsevni and Snorri. In exchange for the cloth they offered untanned furs and grey pelts, and for each fur they got a span's length (about nine inches) of the cloth, which they tied around their heads. This went on for a while, until the Norsemen began to run short of cloth. Then they cut it into smaller strips, until each was no more than a finger's width, and yet the Skrellings (as the Norsemen called the savages) gave just as much for it or even more.

In the Greenland Saga it is told that the Norsemen sold the savages milk. Karlsevni asked the women to carry out vessels of milk and other dairy products. At once the savages wanted to buy this and nothing else. Thus the trading found the savages carrying their purchases away in their stomachs, while Karlsevni and his men obtained their furs.

At one meeting a bull belonging to Karlsevni and his people ran out of the woods bellowing furiously. The savages were so terrified that they ran to their boats and rowed along the shore to the south. For three weeks there was no trace of them. Finally, a vast fleet of Skrelling boats hove into sight, rushing from the south like an angry torrent. This time the savages were waving their sticks in a counter-sunwise direction, and were yelling at the tops of their voices. Seeing this, Karlsevni and his men took their red shields and held them aloft. The savages leaped from their boats; the two parties met and started fighting. It was a furious battle, for the savages had war slings to help them. Karlsevni and Snorri watched them lift up a pole with a huge knob on the end, black in color, and about the size of a sheep's belly, which flew up on land over the heads of the men, and made a frightening noise when it fell. At this a great fear seized Karlsevni and his followers, so that they thought only of flight, and retreated up the stream. It seemed to them that they were being attacked by savages on every side, and this did not let up before they got back to some cliffs, where they fought a hard battle.

Freydis came out and saw them retreating. She shouted to them, "Why are you running away from these worthless fellows, fine men you are! It looks to me as if you should be able to cut them down like cattle. If I had weapons, I think I could fight better than any of you!"

They paid no attention to what she was saying. She tried to follow, but had trouble keeping up with them, for she was with child. She went after them into the woods, and the savages started towards her. In front of her lay a dead man, Thorbrand, Snorri's son, whose head had been crushed by a flat rock. Beside him lay his sword, and she picked it up to defend herself. When the savages approached, she pulled out her breasts from under her dress and slapped them with the naked sword. At this the savages were so appalled that they ran down to their boats and rowed away.

Karlsevni and his men now came up to her and praised her good fortune. Two of Karlsevni's men had fallen while a great many of the savages were killed, although the latter were far superior in number. They now returned to their camp, dressed their wounds, and talked over who the men might be that had attacked them on land. It had seemed to them as if there were two attacking parties, but now they saw that one of these must have been a delusion.

The savages found one of the dead with an axe beside him. One of them picked up the axe and hewed at a tree with it; one after the other tried it, and it seemed to them a great treasure because it cut so well. Then one of them took and struck a rock with it, so that the axe broke. They decided then that it was useless, since it could not withstand stone, and tossed it away.

Karlsevni and his men were now convinced that even though the country was richly endowed by nature, they would always live in dread and turmoil because of the enmity of those who already lived there. Thus, they made ready to break up and return to their own country.

Karlsevni set out with one ship to search for Thorhall the Hunter, while the others stayed in Streamfjord. They sailed north of Keelness, and then headed west, with the land on their port side. They found nothing but a forest wilderness, with hardly a clearing among the trees. When they had sailed a long time, they found a river running from east to west into the sea. Here they steered for the river mouth and landed on the southern bank.

(The remainder of the narrative concerning their last winter in Vinland is of minor value, historically or geographically. They returned to Greenland the next summer. A son named Snorri was born to Karlsevni the first autumn, and he was three winters old when they left.)

SOME COMMENTS ON THE ABOVE NARRATIVE:

In this narrative there is one important incident which gives additional information about the approximate location of Streamfjord. It is said that after the second winter in Streamfjord, Karlsevni set out with one ship to search for Thorhall the Hunter. He sailed north to Keelness and headed west, with the land on the port side. Here he found a river running from east to west into the sea. This description has puzzled many writers because they could not see how a coast facing east could have a river flowing westward.

However, there are several rebuttals to this theory. A river running into the sea from the east calls for a shore running in a general north-south direction, and this is what Thorfin would find after rounding Keelness and keeping the land on the port side—the west side of Cape Cod. Here are at least three tidal inlets which, like Bass River on the south side, look so much like true rivers that they are still so called. One is Pamet River near the end of the cape. As it is said that Thorfin searched for a long time, it could not have been Pamet River where "he lay his ship on the south side." But near the base of the peninsula is Chase Garden River which also flows from the east to the west, a wide waterway. There was also a big "river" west of Nauset. Captain Southack's map of 1696 shows a wide waterway bisecting the cape at this point (See Fig. 4). The Captain says he went through this passage in a whale boat. As it would be necessary to use a row boat in examining the shore for signs of Thorhall's camp, Thorfin's progress would be slow, which probably explains the use of the term "a long time" in the narrative whose detailed agreement with the physical features of the Cape Cod Peninsula would, accordingly, indicate that Streamfjord lay a considerable distance to the west or southwest of the cape.

Finding no trace of Thorhall, Thorfin returned to Streamfjord, and after spending another winter there, he and his companions returned to Greenland. While this new land was excellent, the natives were too formidable for a small company of settlers.

As stated above, Gudrid brought the body of her husband Thorstein back to his old home, Brattalid, in 1009, and she became a ward of Leif. That fall Thorfin Karlsevni came to Greenland. The following winter he and Gudrid were married, and in 1010 they set out with the large expedition to Vinland. They returned in 1013 and made their home in Iceland. Some years later when Thorfin died, Gudrid is reported to have journeyed to Rome.

Grönlendinga Saga in Flatey Book tells of one more expedition to Vinland in this period. This account, however, adds nothing of value to the report of the discoveries and seems to be founded on only a confused retelling of the adventures of Bjarni Grimolfson and Thorhall Gamlison. The only reason it has been preserved is that it is a tale of most revolting murder on a large scale, and such morbid stories have a fascination for many people. Briefly summarized, it runs as follows:

The same year that Thorfin Karlsevni returned to Greenland, a ship arrived in Eriksfjord. It belonged to two brothers named Helgi and Finbogi who were from the eastern part of Iceland. They remained in Greenland that winter, and on the initiative of Freydis they agreed to join her and her husband Thorvard in an expedition to Vinland. Each of the two parties was to bring thirty fighting men, and the profits were to be equally divided. When they sailed the next summer, Freydis managed to smuggle five extra men into her ship.

On arriving in Vinland, Freydis took possession of Leif's houses and the two brothers built new quarters. When winter came with much idle time the two groups were on good terms, but this friendship later cooled. Towards spring Freydis got up very early one morning and went barefooted over to the house of the brothers. The door was slightly ajar and she pushed it open. Finbogi was awake and went out to see what was on her mind. She told him she wanted to buy the brothers' ship because she planned to return to Greenland with a large cargo of timber, and their vessel was bigger than hers. Finbogi told her he was willing to trade ships, whereupon she returned to her own house.

When Freydis got into the bed with wet and cold feet her husband awoke. He is reported to have been a man of "no account," but was reputed to be rich. He asked what she had been doing, upon which she broke into a torrent of abuse against him and the brothers. She said she had gone to them with an offer to buy the ship, but they had reviled her and beaten her. "But you," she said, "are such a spineless man that you would never avenge either my disgrace or your own.

I am certainly finding out that I am far from Greenland. But if you do not avenge this, I shall leave you."

She kept this tirade going till he got up and told his men to arm themselves. Then they went to the other house and seized the men while they were still asleep. They led them out, one by one, and killed them. But there were five women and none of Thorvard's men would raise his hand against them. Seeing this, Freydis took an axe and killed all the women.

This tale is extremely crude and entirely improbable. The originator of the story knew so little about these two brothers that he did not even know their surnames, a fact which may well make the whole thing suspect. The conversation between Freydis and Finbogi is quoted verbatim although there were no witnesses. Only she could have quoted it. But if so, she would have made Finbogi's remarks offensive, which they are not. There was no motive for the killing, because Freydis had everything her own way and had been promised the ship belonging to the brothers. It is also contrary to all we know of Norse manhood that Thorvard's men would attack these sleeping men who had done them no bodily harm. Finally the result of the battle is beyond belief. These men were presumably sleeping with their clothes on as was customary in the wilderness, and they all had their hunting knives in a sheath on their hips; and as they were camping in a land of dangerous savages, most of them probably had axes under their pillows, so that the battle would not have been so entirely one-sided. Nor is it thinkable that the five women would meekly stand waiting for Freydis' axe. More likely they would have torn her to pieces.

If we ignore this wild tale of human butchery, we find the original of the story in Thorfin Karlsevni's Saga (see page 59). It is recognized by all commentators that this version is more dependable than the Grönlendinga Saga when it deals with Thorfin's own voyage and with Icelandic persons. It is expressly stated in Hauk's Book that Freydis and Thorvard went to Vinland in Thorfin's vessel. As this story about Freydis says that the two Icelanders went to Vinland the same year as she did, they must have accompanied Thorfin in their own vessel. In Thorfin Karlsevni's Saga we find two Icelanders, Bjarni Grimolfson and Thorhall Gamlison. The latter is said to have come from the same distant eastern shore of Iceland as did Helgi and Finbogi. We know that Thorhall and Bjarni, like Helgi and Finbogi, did not return. Finally, Thorfin's saga says that one vessel was lost.

It is easy to understand how the confusion arose. Freydis was probably hated by many people whom she had plagued and persecuted. When nothing was seen or heard of Bjarni and Thorhall on Karlsevni's return to Greenland, it was easy to assume that they were the victims of foul play. After all, who was better at that than Freydis? And thus this old wives' tale, false and crude in every detail, was built up by those who had reason to hate the abnormal Freydis.

Of similar doubtful value are the reports of the accidental discovery of America by Ari Marsson, Bjorn Asbrandson and Gudleif Gudlaugsson, each in turn. The story of Bjorn is highly romantic and unrealistic, and as all three of these narrations lack supporting evidence, it is probable that they are later inventions added to magnify the reputation of popular men who sailed out to sea and were never heard from again.

America Visited 1047

THE NEWS of the discovery of Vinland the Good quickly spread to Iceland, Norway, Denmark and other countries. The earliest existing record of the discovery is not from Greenland or Iceland, but was written in Latin by a German scholar, Adam von Bremen, the rector of the Cathedral school in Hamburg. About 1070 he wrote a history of the Archbishopric of Hamburg and traveled widely to obtain his information. Among those he visited was King Swen Estridson of Denmark who told him much about the Church in the Scandinavian countries. The King also told him of the discovery of Vinland far off in the western ocean, which Magister Adam recorded as follows:

> He (King Swen) told me of yet another island, discovered by many in that ocean, which is called Wineland from the fact that there grow vines, producing the best of wines. Moreover, that grain abounds there without sowing, we have ascertained, not from fabulous conjecture, but from the reliable reports of the Danes.

In this way the news of the discovery reached Rome, where it perhaps was already known from the personal report of Gudrid, the wife of Karlsevni and the mother of the first white child born in the western hemisphere. As already noted, Gudrid is reported to have journeyed to Rome after Karlsevni's death.

The discovery of Vinland was also known to King Harald the Ruthless, of Norway. That famous King was a great traveler, having been the Commandant of the Imperial Guard at Constantinople for many years. The news of Vinland the Good interested him, and about 1050 he set out "to explore the western sea." Because he was a very capable man of wide experience, the thought of having a rich colony in the far west would strongly appeal to him. However, he almost lost his life in the attempt. Here is what Magister Adam, who was a contemporary, says of his voyage:

> King Swen said that beyond this island (Wineland) no habitable land is found in that ocean, but all that is beyond is full of intolerable ice and utter darkness. . . . This was lately tested by the most enterprising Harald, Prince of the Norsemen, who, when exploring with his ships the breadth of the northern ocean, hardly escaped with safety from the awful gulf of the abyss by turning back, when at length the bounds of the earth grew dark before his eyes.

It is probable that King Harald had an additional purpose in his western voyages. Somewhere out in the northern ocean there was a potential rival to his throne whom he wished to find and destroy. Harald was not popular in Norway because he was vindictive and ruthless. Among those who opposed him was his own nephew, Thrond Halfdanson, who had sought temporary shelter in Greenland. The story of their conflict and of how it led to Vinland is as follows.[15]

The earliest mention of Vinland is not found in the sagas of Iceland, but on a stone inscribed with runic characters unearthed in Norway. In 1823, Major L. D. Kluwer, an antiquarian, was shown this stone on the farm of Hönen in Ringerike. It was a neatly chiselled stone four feet long, eight inches wide, and four inches thick. The inscription was carved on the narrow edge. The major made a careful copy of the inscription, but did not attempt a translation. In fact, it does not seem to have been translated until 1902 when Professor Sophus Bugge published a monograph in which he discusses the inscription in much detail. According to Bugge, the inscription constitutes a six-line stanza in the old *malahattr* meter as follows:

> Ut ok vit ok thurba
> therru ok ats
> Vinlati a isa
> i ubygd at komu
> Aud ma ilt vega
> (at) döyi ar

The following is a Norwegian translation conforming to the alliterative characteristics of the old meter:

> "Ut og vidt de for,
> fristed sult og væde;
> drev fra Vinlands kyst
> op til Ubygds-isen.
> Vanheld vender lykken
> volder tidlig död."

In English prose this is: "Far and wide they were driven from the coast of Vinland, and were cast on the ice of the uninhabitable regions, needing food and clothing. Evil fate may overtake one so that he dies early."

As Bugge says, this is an epitaph over a young man of good birth, otherwise a memorial in verse would hardly have been raised to him. This indication of family eminence is supported by the still existing local tradition that the estate of Hönen, formerly much larger, was in olden times a royal seat (*Kongsgaard*). Bugge fixes the date of the inscription at about 1050 for linguistic and runological reasons.

But this inscription has several other points of interest. As already mentioned, it contains the earliest use of the name of Vinland. Furthermore, it is the only mention of any journey from Norway to Vinland in Viking times. Who was this lone explorer from Norway who lost his life on the journey, but who evidently was brought back to his own country and buried on his own estate? No one has attempted an identification, and the attempt may seem futile in view of the fact that no names are mentioned. The inscription is incomplete, the stone being broken in two across the first remaining rune.

But perhaps an identification is not impossible. Perhaps there are facts mentioned or implied in the inscription which, when viewed in the light of the history of Ringerike, are sufficient to enable us to identify the person in whose memory the inscription was made. I believe this can be done.

Now what facts do the inscription and the place where it was found reveal? First, that the deceased was a young man; second, that he was from Ringerike; third, that he was of a prominent family; fourth, that he had lived on an estate which according to tradition was an ancient royal manor; fifth, that about 1050 he made a voyage into the American waters of Vinland; and sixth, that he did not return alive. Most of these circumstances are quite definite, especially as journeys across the Atlantic were very rare in the 11th century.

There was one man of wealth whose age, social standing, and place of residence agree with the facts revealed in the inscription. In 1047 he was impelled by political reasons to seek temporary refuge in Greenland. The following is a brief synopsis of the circumstances which drove him to the western world.

In 1046, Norway was ruled jointly by two kings. One was Magnus, later called the Good, who was the son of King Olaf, the later patron saint of the North. The other was Harald the Ruthless, so called because of his grasping, perfidious, and vindictive temperament. This is the same King Harald who in 1066 invaded England and met his fate in the battle of Stamford Bridge. He was the son of King Sigurd Syr of Ringerike and half brother to King Olaf. When Harald in 1045 returned to Norway laden with riches, the proceeds of ten years' plunder as captain of the Imperial Guard of Constantinople, his ambition was to become the sole ruler of Norway. He therefore first went to Ringerike, his father's old kingdom, and asked the people there to accept him as king. But the people refused to give up their allegiance to King Magnus, and not even Harald's own relatives would give him any encouragement. Greatly embittered by this and other rebuffs, Harald joined forces with Earl Swen, later King of Denmark, to make war against Magnus. Shortly afterward, however, Magnus magnanimously offered to share the kingdom with his uncle.

Some time after this King Magnus came to Oplandene, the collective name of the six prosperous districts of south-central Norway, of which Ringerike was one, to hold a *Thing* or official assembly with the people. While Ringerike had always been loyal to King Olaf and his son, the other five districts had been more than unreliable in their allegiance, as their five kings had been among the first to turn against King Olaf. Here, Magnus made a speech and said he would not press his charges against them for their enmity toward his father, provided they would give him their good will and sincere cooperation.

When the King ceased speaking, a distinguished looking young man named Thrond, very richly dressed, arose to answer. He said in effect that while many of the people of Oplandene had been unfaithful to King Olaf, a new generation had now grown up which had taken no part in the defeat and death of King Olaf, and this generation desired only to serve their present king, Magnus. As a sign of his trust and devotion, the speaker expressed a desire to exchange clothing and arms with the King. Magnus courteously agreed to this especially, he said, since Thrond's raiment and equipment was much better than his own. Such exchange of clothing was in the Viking Age a ceremony indicative of perfect trust between the two parties, their act symbolizing that each was giving to the other something that partook of his own personal self. Thereupon Thrond invited the King and his numerous retinue to be his guests, and he entertained them sumptuously and gave the King more valuable gifts.

The scene mentioned above shows that Thrond was a wealthy and prominent chief, perhaps the ranking chief of Oplandene, because custom decreed that the most important men at the *Thing* should be given priority in addressing the king. It also indicates that he must have been connected with the family of the former King Sigurd Syr of Ringerike, because all the other kings of Oplandene had been tortured and banished by King Olaf and their estates confiscated. If Thrond had been connected with any of these five kings who had been thus treated, he would have felt no urge to support the son of his family's oppressor. Moreover, in such case he could not have become a wealthy man a few years after his family had lost all its possessions. The most probable conclusion is therefore that he was a grandson of King Sigurd Syr, King Olaf's stepfather, who had always supported his stepson. This conclusion is supported by the statement in two old sagas that Thrond was a *fraende* (kinsman) of Kalf Arneson who both before and after this time was the most important uncrowned man in Norway. While Kalf Arneson and his immediate relatives were from distant parts of Norway, his brother, Finn Arneson, was married to Bergliot, the daughter of Halfdan, the son of King Sigurd of Ringerike. Thrond was, therefore, her brother, and his full name was Thrond Halfdanson.

When King Harald a short time later heard of Thrond's reception of King Magnus, he became furious. This reaction at first sight seems strange. Both King Magnus and King Harald spent much time in visiting various parts of their joint kingdom, sometimes together, but more often separately, and it was customary for the leading men at such times to entertain them lavishly with the usual assurances of unswerving loyalty. Thrond had done nothing more than what scores of other men had done when entertaining either king, and their actions had caused no offense. There must have been some special reason for King Harald's wrath.

This reason we find in the fact that Thrond was a son of Harald's brother Halfdan. The King would consider it bad enough that strangers were unwilling to recognize his merits, but the fact that his own kinsman took a leading part in bolstering the royal power of his rival would certainly seem intolerable. Such an act would be to him a treacherous breach of the bonds of family loyalty. Nor did King Harald shrink from a family quarrel. In the preceding year he had waged war against his nephew, King Magnus, to gain the kingdom. Now he plotted the destruction of another nephew, Thrond, because the latter preferred Magnus to him. He instructed a dependable lieutenant of his earlier adventures to take twelve men, dress them in monks' cassocks, and in this disguise to seek admission to Thrond's house and to kill him.

Early one morning these knaves approached Thrond's house and meeting some of the workmen on the farm, they inquired if Thrond was at home. The answers were unsatisfactory and, being short of temper, the lieutenant had the workmen beaten unmercifully. A foster-brother of Thrond, named Sigurd, saw this strange behavior on the part of the black-robed visitors and hastened to tell Thrond that these monks acted very suspiciously.

Thrond agreed, but being unwilling to take harsh measures against possibly godly men, he decided to test them. As it was early in the morning, he had not yet left his *skemma* (a small detached building used for sleeping). "Let them come without hindrance," said he. "When they come, I will speak to them from a window and ask them to step into the *stofa* (the main hall or dwelling house) until we get the sleep out of our eyes. If they are holy men begging alms for a good cause they will do so. But if they are bent on mischief they will demand instant admission before we can call our men. In that case you will open the door and they will rush in. At that moment I will escape through the underground passage leading to the *stofa*.

They will no doubt pursue me, but you shall stand behind the door and bolt it behind them. Thus they will be our prisoners."

Soon the monkish pretenders arrived and everything went as Thrond had forecast. The strangers were unwilling to wait and shouted that unless they were admitted at once they would break down the door.

"Impetuous indeed are the monks becoming," answered Thrond. "I will rather open the door than have you break it down." With that he opened the door and, as the intruders entered, he fled through the passage way followed by the "monks." Thereupon Sigurd bolted the door.*

The would-be assassins were now taken out and questioned concerning the object of their errand. On learning their mission, Thrond gave them the same treatment that they had given his workmen and then sent them back to King Harald. Word of the incident spread rapidly and derisively and when King Magnus heard the account he realized at once that King Harald would not long let this affront go unavenged. He therefore personally led several hundred of his men to Ringerike to be on hand to protect his nephew if necessary. With these troops he made camp in a forest near Thrond's house. Thrond was soon informed of the presence of this army, and, thinking it was King Harald and his men, he quickly called a large number of men together and set out to give battle to the supposed enemy. However on approaching King Magnus' position he discovered his error, whereupon King Magnus and his men were invited to Thrond's house.

King Magnus now told Thrond that it was not safe for him to remain in his house and invited him to spend the winter with him. This invitation was accepted by Thrond.

During the winter it was ascertained that it was King Harald's intention to kill Thrond at all costs. When spring came, King

---

* Old settlers say that remains of such an underground passage at the Hönen farm were still visible when they emigrated from Ringerike It is also mentioned by Johan Vibe in *Norges Land og Folk*, Kristiannia, 1895, V, 190-191.

Magnus presented Thrond with a well-manned ship and advised him to seek refuge in Greenland until the situation improved. Thrond accepted the gift and advice, and King Magnus personally accompanied his friend on board the vessel.

Evidently King Harald was kept informed of all these movements, for he was waiting for Thrond behind the first point of land. When Thrond passed it, King Harald rowed out and attacked him. However, in the meantime it had occurred to King Magnus that he had been careless in letting Thrond depart without more protection. He lost no time in manning another vessel and set out in it. When King Harald discovered that King Magnus was coming to the aid of his protegé, he decided that the odds were too great and rowed away. Thereupon Thrond proceeded toward his distant western destination. According to the old saga he reached it safely and remained there for some years.

These words, "he remained there (in Greenland) for some years," are the last that the saga-writer has to tell of Thrond's fate. As he makes no mention of a fatal outcome, the inference may present itself to some readers that Thrond later returned to Norway. There is nothing, however, to support this inference. If Thrond lost his life on the ice of the uninhabitable regions of Labrador or Greenland, as the runic stone of Hönen mentions, it is improbable that the saga writer in Iceland ever heard of it. He would have had little opportunity of learning that the body of the heroic young nobleman was later carried home and there with much ceremony interred in a burial mound. All that the saga writer probably knew was that Thrond spent some years in Greenland, and he states that fact. Nor is Thrond mentioned later in any other document.

There is another objection to such an inference. If Thrond after some years voluntarily returned to Norway, he would be acting contrary to the instincts of self-preservation. His protector, King Magnus, died the same year (1047) that Thrond went to Greenland, and Harald remained the undisputed King of Norway for nineteen years, busily engaged in settling scores with those who had opposed him. Thrond had offended the vindictive King too deeply to have any hope of pardon. Indeed, so great was Harald's hatred of Thrond that he attempted to cross the northern ocean to punish him. And here, in his pursuit of Thrond, we may have the central motive for that strange journey which King Harald made "to investigate the breadth of the northern ocean," and from which he barely escaped with his life as we are told by his contemporary, Adam of Bremen. Not only would King Harald be prompted to make this journey because of his desire for vengeance, but also to do away with a possible rival to the throne. Thrond was of the same ancient royal stock as Harald, and this lineage, added to his personal popularity, made him a potential rival whom the unscrupulous King would spare no pains to remove.

Thus, the known facts of Thrond's life fit the Hönen inscription perfectly. Not only was he a young man of a prominent family in Ringerike, but at the approximate date when the inscription was written we find him in Greenland in close proximity to the regions mentioned in the inscription. Being a prince of the ancient royal stock of Norway, he must have been the most distinguished visitor ever to favor the Greenland colonists. Like other eminent visitors he would be the guest of the Law Speaker at Brattalid, Erik the Red's old homestead and the best estate in Greenland. Here he would hear recited the stories concerning the discovery of Vinland the Good by the former chiefs who had lived in that house. It would be strange, indeed, for a young man of his adventurous courage, energetic initiative and material and spiritual resources not to be drawn by the lure of this strange new land to the West. To a person of his fitness, such a journey must have seemed a pleasant excursion to break the monotony of his enforced idleness. Perhaps the Greenland sagas could have told us much about his visit and adventures, but these old records disappeared with the extinction of the colony in the 14th and 15th centuries.

A Bishop Goes to Vinland

IN VIEW of the wide and favorable publicity that Vinland
received, not only in Greenland, Iceland, Norway and Denmark, but also at the courts and councils of kings and church-
men far away, it seems probable that many others, besides the
two families mentioned, attempted to make permanent settlements there. In comparison with the treeless slopes of Greenland on the edge of a thousand-mile glacier, Vinland with its
mild climate, good soil and vast forests must have seemed a
paradise to the Greenlanders. It is true that we have no record
of these possible pioneers, but this lack may well be explained
by the fact that the Greenland records were lost when its two
settlements were destroyed by the Eskimo. What we know about
the Erikson brothers and Thorfin Karlsevni is entirely through
their connections with important Icelandic families, and their
history was, therefore, preserved in Iceland. But during the
11th and 12th centuries there were thousands of energetic
Greenlanders who were not thus connected, and of them we
know nothing.

It would be strange indeed for a newly discovered land with
such rich resources to remain wholly unsettled by a people
who roamed the seas so freely, and the likelihood that Greenlanders in some numbers had settled in Vinland is further supported by the fact that more than a hundred years after Thorfin's
great enterprise, the Bishop of Greenland, Erik Gnupson, set

sail for Vinland. In six Icelandic annals wherein important events are briefly recorded, we find the statement under the date 1121, in slightly different wording, that Erik, Bishop of Greenland (*"for at leita Vinlands,"*) sailed to Vinland.[16]

This Erik Gnupson was an Icelander who was appointed bishop by King Sigurd in 1112 shortly after the King's return from his great crusade to the Holy Land. In the fall of 1107, when he was seventeen years old, the King set sail from Bergen with sixty large ships, manned by 10,000 crusaders. He arrived safely after many adventures, to the immense relief of King Baldwin of Jerusalem who was expecting an attack by a large army of Turks. Together they defeated the Turks and captured Sidon and other infidel strongholds. The story of King Sigurd's three-year crusade is one of the most diverting and colorful episodes in history.

When King Sigurd was preparing to return to his own country, King Baldwin asked him to choose any reward he wished. After some deliberation, King Sigurd asked for a piece of the cross on which Jesus had been crucified. This was the greatest treasure in Christendom, but the request was granted on condition that King Sigurd should establish the Faith in every way, create new bishoprics and also an archbishopric. The King showed great ardor in fulfilling this promise.

As Sigurd would scarcely select an unknown man from a country as far away as Iceland to become the first Bishop of Greenland, it is quite likely that Erik Gnupson had accompanied the King on his great crusade. If he did indeed accompany Sigurd that fact would again suggest that he was a man of energy and determination—qualities he would well need in dealing with the partly converted Greenlanders.

In any case Father Erik was consecrated Bishop of Greenland a few months after the King's return from the Holy Land and arrived in Greenland some time in 1112. According to Father Ivar Bardson, who was steward of the Greenland bishopric for many years in the 14th century, Bishop Erik had his seat at Sandness in the Western Settlement, where a large church had been built. In 1121 he went to Vinland. He did not return, and nothing more is known about him.

To be a bishop in the Church is to hold a very high and important office, even in such a faraway country as Greenland. It must therefore have been a very compelling reason which made Bishop Erik sail for Vinland. There are only two possible reasons.

One—highly improbable—is that he set out to serve as a missionary to the natives of Vinland. His journey, however, took place long before missionary zeal for the salvation of barbaric nations had been awakened. Many centuries went by after Christianity was introduced into the Scandinavian countries before we hear of any missionaries being sent to the Laps, the Finns or the Eskimo. And if Bishop Erik felt any such impulse, his neighbors, the Eskimo, were already near at hand.

The other incentive could only have been the knowledge that many Christian Norsemen had emigrated to Vinland where they lived without priestly guidance. The conditions of life were not as favorable in the Western Settlement as in the Eastern. It was seldom visited by traders from Norway, and these disadvantages would encourage emigration to the more favorable regions of America. If Bishop Erik had accompanied King Sigurd on his great crusade, he had been a witness of great achievements, and, in emulation of his King, he would not hesitate to make far-reaching decisions. He may, therefore, have been just the right man to concern himself with the religious welfare of the reported people of Vinland. But whatever his character and earlier history, it remains a matter of record that Erik, did sail to Vinland in the course of his bishopric.

In 1891 the church historian, Reverend Luca Jelec gave an address before a distinguished international Catholic Congress wherein he attributes to Bishop Erik the title "Episcopus Groenlandiae regionumque finitimarum" (Bishop of Greenland and the nearby regions). He does not give the source of the title, but it is unthinkable that he would use it without authority before such a learned audience.

Simultaneously, we find John Fiske recording in his book, *Discovery of America,* that Erik Gnupson in 1112 was appointed by Pope Paschal II "Bishop of Greenland and Vinland in partibus infidelium." He, too, neglects to cite the source of the statement, and no source has in fact, been located. Could the authenticity of this title or one of similar meaning be proven, the fact would then be established that there was a Christian colony in Vinland in the beginning of the 12th century. In the meantime many historians in this field have expressed the opinion that colonization attempts in Vinland continued to be made long after Thorfin Karlsevni's time. Besides Jelic and Fiske who have already been quoted, there are many others. About 1600, Claudius Lyschander, Royal Historian of Denmark, wrote that "(Bishop) Erik brought people to Vinland and established the Christian faith there." At the time he wrote this, there were many documents about the western islands available which were destroyed in the great fire of 1728 in Copenhagen.

In 1837 Professor Carl Christian Rafn wrote: "It is probable that many Greenlanders and Icelanders, urged by the desire for good land, emigrated to Vinland and there built themselves homes, although we have no mention of this in Iceland."

Professor A. W. Brögger writes: "It is beyond doubt, that the people of Greenland kept up their connections (with America)."

Professor Richard Hennig writes: "The Bishop (Erik) sailed to Vinland because of its Norse colony, and he felt it his duty to concern himself with their religious needs."[17]

We shall probably never know the location or size of the probable colony or colonies in Vinland; but one thing seems certain: the Bishop must have had definite information about them, as he would never have left Greenland on the mere possibility of finding some settlers there.

In this connection, if only incidentally, it may be mentioned that the first French missionaries to the Micmac Indians in the Gaspé regions found that these Indians had great veneration for the Cross. Dr. John Gilmary Shea relates the following:

> He (Father Christian Le Clercq, who in 1673 became a missionary in Gaspé) found a Micmac tribe, to whom he gives the name of Porte-Croix, because he found among them a remarkable reverence for the Cross, which they regarded as a talisman in all dangers and perils. This veneration he believed to have existed among them before the arrival of the French in their country, as a venerable Indian named Quiondo, whose age was estimated at one hundred and twenty, declared that he had seen the first ship that touched their shores, and that the Indians at Miramichi did not receive the Cross and its use from strangers but from their ancestors. Other Micmac bands which had been converted by missionaries did not adopt this custom, as they would have done had the missionaries introduced it.[18]

Nothing may be positively concluded from Dr. Shea's account, but two Norse finds of the same period as Bishop Erik's visit (12th century) have turned up in the northeastern part of America, although far apart. One is an axe of the 11th century, found about 1880 by a farmer while tilling a small field bordering on Cole Harbor, an indentation on Tor Bay, just west of Cape Canso in Nova Scotia. Mrs. Grover, a granddaughter of the man who found the axe, is still living on the farm.

The axe which was covered with clay and rust was put on a shelf, and no one took much interest in it until 1936. Then a prospector by the name of James P. Nolan saw it. He had a shack near by and was allowed to take the axe home to clean off the rust. At home, he placed the axe in a basin of kerosene to soften the rust. While the axe was still in the basin the shack caught fire and burned to the ground. Later, while, searching in the ashes, Nolan found that the clay and rust on the axe had become loose, revealing a number of mystic marks. Eventually it passed into the possession of the late William B. Goodwin of Hartford, Conn. It has been examined by A. G. Greninger, Professor of Physical Metallurgy at Harvard University, who, in a letter to the writer, dated April 6, 1939, wrote:

> The Goodwin axe is undoubtedly of primitive manufacture; however, from the short study I have made, it would be impossible for me to say whether the manufacturer was alive a hundred or a thousand years ago. Additional study might supply further evidence, and I am awaiting a second visit from Mr. Goodwin before going ahead on this.
> It might be interesting for you to know that the actual metallographic structure of the axe metal is about the only one it could be if the axe actually were about a thousand years old.
>
>   (Signed) Alden B. Greninger.

Aside from the peculiar marks on the blade, the axe is a duplicate of hundreds of similar axes in Norwegian museums from the 11th to the 12th centuries. As it was found on the northeast coast of Nova Scotia, it may have been left by a party of Greenlanders on one their trips to Markland for timber, although it may mark the site of a Norse colony. However, the evidence relating to this find is not completely satisfying.

The other find consists of a sword, a battle axe and parts of a shield which turned up a few miles east of Lake Nipigon, north of Lake Superior (see Fig. 5). These were found by James E. Dodd of Port Arthur, Ontario, a freight conductor on the Canadian National Railway who was also interested in prospecting for minerals and who had filed a claim on some mining land about seven miles east of Lake Nipigon.

On a day in May in the early thirties, he was inspecting his claim for "leads," He saw a dike of granite standing about twelve feet high, down the middle of which was a vertical streak of light-colored quartz. Being somewhat superstitious, he conceived the idea of following this streak downward and dug a hole about three feet deep, when he came to a floor of schist, and the streak of quartzite seemed to make a horizontal turn. In front of the hole which he had dug was a big, half-rotten stump of birch, and to lessen his labor he placed a charge of dynamite under it and blew it up. On shoveling out the loose soil he found the old relics seemingly glued to the schist, because he broke the sword in two in prying it loose. There were also a number of thin, slightly curved, pieces of metal which he did not recognize, but which afterward were thought to be broken pieces of the boss of a shield. The shield itself had evidently been of wood and had rotted away, because only parts of the boss were found along with an old axe. Thinking that these things were worthless Indian relics, he left them on the dump, but later curiosity prompted him to take them to his camp where he dropped them outside his shack.

Mr. Dodd was told that Indian relics had some value, so he took them to his home in Port Arthur and offered his find for sale at a small price, but no one was interested. Then Mr. John Jacobs of the Fish and Game Department of the Province of Ontario, who may have been interested in Indian relics, heard of the find, and called on Dodd. The story he heard was so interesting that he went to the place of the find and himself discovered on the under-lying rock *a picture of the sword in iron rust*. He sent word to Dr. C. T. Currelly, Director of the Royal Ontario Museum of Archeology in Toronto, but apparently the message was never delivered.

Mr. Jacob's visit greatly cheered Mr. Dodd, and he talked with some enthusiasm about his find. But he met with no response among his neighbors. On the contrary, he became the butt of many mild jokes. His wife threw the relics out in the backyard, and Dodd became taciturn. But in 1936 he found a sympathetic listener. It was Dr. E. M. Burwash of the Department of Mines who came to Port Arthur to hold the annual class in mining. He made some investigations and wrote Dr. Currelly that a viking sword had been found near Beardmore, Ontario. This induced the Director to send for Mr. Dodd, and the result was that the Museum bought the find for five hundred dollars in 1936 or 1937.

The Museum authorities planned to write a report on the discovery, but these weapons belonged in a field of research with which they had very little contact, and much correspondence and study were a preliminary necessity. In the meantime no photographs and very little information were sent out. In the fall of 1937 I wrote to Dr. Currelly and asked permission to inspect these finds at the museum. Dr. Currelly immediately granted me this permission because he thought the relics might be part of the equipment of the explorers of 1362 who left the runic stone at Kensington. However, I saw at once that the Beardmore articles were much older, from about the year 1000 or 1100.

In spite of the Museum's caution, fragmentary news of the find leaked out, and, because of its sensational nature, it was mentioned in some newspapers. Then in January, 1938 came a sudden anti-climax. A public lecturer mentioned the find in an address in Winnipeg, and a few days later a railroad pal of Mr. Dodd, named Eli Ragotte, was quoted in a Toronto newspaper interview as saying that Dodd's discovery was a fake—that he, Ragotte, had found the relics in the basement of a house into which Dodd had moved. Quickly the reporters hunted up the owner of the house, a Mr. Hansen, and he said yes, the implements had been left with him by Johan Bloch, an educated young Norwegian immigrant, who had brought them from Norway and left them with Hansen as security for a loan of twenty-five dollars, and Dodd had found the relics there when he moved into the house in 1931. Hansen produced a note signed by Bloch which proved the debt, but it also showed that Hansen's memory was poor, because the note was for forty-five dollars on which ten dollars had been paid. This note seemed conclusive; another historic bubble had burst.

If it had not been for J. W. Curran, editor of the *Daily Star,* Sault Ste. Marie, Ontario, it is probable that nothing more would have been heard of the Beardmore find. He had read my book, *The Kensington Stone,* the subject of which he thought might have some connection with the tradition concerning early white men on Hudson Bay, whom Samuel Champlain in 1610 heard referred to as *Mistigoche,* "the wooden-boat men." He therefore became greatly interested in Dodd's find. In September, 1938 he went to Port Arthur to make inquiries about the find. In company with Dr. George E. Eakins, President of the local historical society, and Judge Alexander McComber, both old residents of the city, he began an investigation which soon assumed extensive proportions.

The first question was: When did Dodd find the relics? Dodd was not sure, but said it was while he lived on Wilson Street. A number of persons were then questioned who had seen the implements shortly after Dodd had found them. They established the fact that the relics were found in the spring of 1930. The next question was: When did Dodd move into Hansen's house. Hansen said it was in 1931, but since his memory was poor it was possible that it was earlier. This was an important question, because if Dodd lived in Hansen's house at the time he found the relics, the probability was that Dodd found the relics there and not on his claim near Lake Nipigon. On being asked, Dodd said he could not remember when he moved. Finally the question was answered by inquiring at the telephone company office. Being a railroad conductor, it was necessary for Dodd to have his telephone moved promptly when he moved from one house to another. The telephone record showed that Dodd did not move to Hansen's house until June 29, 1931. The establishment of this date for the move proved that Dodd's relics were not the same as Hansen's—if the latter had had any.

The committee was curious about this, and Mr. Curran went to see Mr. Carl Sorenson, Royal Norwegian Vice-Consul in the adjoining city of Fort Francis, who was reported to have been a good friend of Johan Bloch. Sorenson said he had known Bloch for fifteen years and he was confident that Bloch had no such relics. This opinion was corroborated by a number of local Norwegian engineers who had also known Bloch for many years. Hansen was asked to name some persons who had seen the relics which Bloch allegedly had left, but he could not name any. He was then asked why he had not claimed the implements until eight years after Dodd said he had dis-covered them at his mine—to which he had no answer. Ap-parently his purpose in making his unsupported claim was to be reimbursed in some way for the small amount owed him by Bloch who had died in Vancouver about 1934.

Mr. Curran then went to Winnipeg to see Eli Ragotte who was reported to have said that it was he and not Dodd who had found the sword. Mr. Ragotte proved to be an old chum of Dodd. He said that some time before 1930, when he was rooming with Dodd, he and the latter were cleaning up the cellar, and while doing so Ragotte saw a rusty iron band. Then, about eight years later, when he saw the report in the Winnipeg about Dodd's discovery of the sword, he thought it was all a silly misunderstanding of the reporter and said that he had found the so-called sword. Upon hearing this, Dr. Currelly re-quested Mr. Ragotte to come to Toronto to inspect the relics. He did so and declared under oath that he had never seen them before. The committee secured eight affidavits clarifying the circumstances of the find.[19] They were chiefly obtained through the agency of A. J. McComber, Senior Judge of the Thunder Bay District of Canada. Altogether, the committee's investiga-tions were so thorough, with results so convincing, that there seems to be no doubt about the authenticity of the find.

This is also the opinion of Dr. Johannes Bröndsted, Professor of Archaeology in the Royal Danish University in Copenhagen, a very cautious scholar. In 1948 he spent four months investigating archaeological finds, supposed to have been left by Norsemen who visited America before the discovery by Columbus. He personally examined the find in the museum in Toronto, inspected the finding place near Lake Nipigon, and spent some time in Port Arthur interviewing many persons who were concerned in the inquiry about the relics found by Mr. Dodd. On November 18, 1948 he held a press conference in the rooms of the American Scandinavian Foundation in New York in which he presented a written report, the opening paragraphs of which read as follows:

> I do not think that a Norse colonization of America in the centuries before Columbus (1000-1500) is impossible at all. There are three main points about the American archaeological material concerning this Norse colonization in pre-Columbian times.
>
> 1. The Viking Find from Lake Nipigon near Port Arthur, now in the Royal Ontario Museum of Archaeology in Toronto: This find, consisting of a sword, an axe, and an alleged shield handle, all of iron, is without doubt genuine. The axe and the sword are certainly real Viking weapons of Norwegian (or Danish) origin, dating from about the year 1000. But the circumstances under which they were found are doubtful, since some local persons claim that these objects were brought to Canada in recent times by a Norwegian settler. Nevertheless, I am inclined to believe that the original story, that the articles found in 1930 by a Canadian prospector were from a grave placed near the foot of a rock, is trustworthy.

But while these weapons are characteristic of the 11th century, the fact does not accurately determine the time when they were left there. There was not much change in the form of the sword or axe until the 13th century, and swords which had been used by great swordsmen were held in high esteem for several generations. Its last owner, therefore, may well have lived in the 12th century.

When we consider what may have brought the owner of these arms to the vicinity of Lake Nipigon, many possibilities present themselves. Most probably he and his companions were on a journey of discovery. The Norse literature of a thousand years ago abounds in illustrations of their active geographical curiosity. The narrative of the curious Ottar handed down to us by King Alfred of England in the 9th century has already been cited as evidence of this geographical curiosity. The same keen interest marked the Norsemen who first saw Iceland, Greenland and America. When Gardar, in about 860, first saw Iceland, his curiosity compelled him to sail completely around it, a voyage of a thousand miles. Likewise Erik Thorwaldson not only explored the habitable fjords in southern Greenland, but sailed far north along the coast and across Davis Strait to Baffin Land. The sagas of Thorwald, Thorhall and Thorfin Karlsevni testify to the same active interest. As America was first thought to be a group of large islands which were named Helluland, Markland and Vinland, it is reasonable to expect that efforts would be made to circumnavigate them. It could not have been long before it was found that Markland and Vinland were parts of a very large land to the south. Helluland, however, being least attractive, would receive least attention. But eventually there would be men who would have been curious about the other side of Helluland. They would push up Hudson Strait and into Hudson Bay.

We know that the early Norsemen penetrated into Hudson Bay because they identified it as Ginnungagap, the dark and fearful gorge through which the waters of the Atlantic ocean and the outer (western) ocean rushed back and forth. *The King's Mirror,* written about 1250, gives the location of Ginnungagap as a recognized fact. It says that beyond Greenland to the north there was no land, nothing but the great and empty ocean, but near Greenland (which would necessarily be to the west) was the strait through which the waters of the Atlantic poured into the outer ocean. Another old record states that "between Vinland and Greenland is Ginnungagap.[20] The Norsemen had good reason to look upon Hudson Strait with its 38½ foot tide as the torrential Ginnungagap.

Having penetrated this dangerous strait, they could hardly do other than assume that Hudson Bay was the unknown outer ocean. They would therefore follow the coast, which runs south for almost a thousand miles. At the head of James Bay they would find big rivers—the Nottawa, the Moose and the Albany. The last has a flow larger than any river in Europe and would certainly be inviting for a trip into the interior of this new continent.

The Albany was an easy river to ascend, being practically free from portages. Its area must have abounded in game, and the possibilities of riches in furs may well have led early explorers onward as it did hundreds of other later pioneers. The James Bay region, according to Radisson, was "the beaver country par excellence." From the southern headwaters of the Albany to Black River, where the find was made, is a short portage.

There, then, unless we are to believe against very substantial evidence that the "finds" were pointlessly forged, disaster overtook them and one of their members died, either in a fight with the natives or by sickness. Inasmuch as his grave lies at the foot of the white vein of quartz which rises like a twelve-foot monument above it, it is probable that he was carried to this conspicuous spot so that his grave could later be easily found. Perhaps he was the commander of this valiant company, and it was expected that his people would plan to bring his remains to Greenland to bury them in consecrated ground, just as Thorstein Erikson tried to do with the body of his brother Thorwald.

But no one came to claim the body of this first explorer of America's interior. The way back to Greenland was long and dangerous, and possibly none of the company returned to tell the tale. But we can still visualize the funeral there on the low ridge clad with solemn spruce trees. Down to the solid rock they dug his grave, then placed him beneath the monument provided by nature. His head was to the west, facing the dawn whence would come the Lord of the Resurrection morning. On his left side his sword was lain, on his right the axe, and over him his shield. Then, perhaps, while his comrades stood bareheaded around the open grave, one of them repeated as much of the litany for the dead as he could remember.

Norse Explorations
in the American Arctic

THE SETTLEMENT of Greenland proceeded so fast that within fifteen years the main part, known as the Eastern Settlement, was filled up, and the immigration overflowed into another colony known as the Western Settlement. As the latter lay more than 200 miles northwest of the parent colony, it was not often visited by men from Norway and Iceland, and we know less about it. The climate there was not as favorable as that of the Eastern Settlement, the farms were smaller and more scattered and much more exposed to the later pilfering of the Eskimo. Danish archaeologists have found, however, that this smaller colony had some well-stocked farms and commodious houses built of stone with paneled interior walls. The number of farms in the Eastern Settlement is said to have been 190, and in the Western less than half that many. As some of these settlers originally had a number of slaves, the total population has been estimated at about three to four thousand.

It is doubtful, however, if the population numbered that many. People in prosperous circumstances seldom leave their old homes and friends and emigrate to a new land. Most of the emigrants were more likely poor people who had few slaves, and as the death rate was heavy in the Middle Ages, their families probably averaged less than four persons. Many of the small houses in distant valleys of the Western Settlement were probably deserted farmsteads which had been rejected for better locations. If we assume that the number of occupied farms in the smaller colony was seventy-five, the population of the Western Settlement would be between 300 and 350; while that of the Eastern Settlement, where the large majority of big farms was, may have numbered about 2000. The Eastern Settlement had twelve churches, and the Western originally had four, but one of these fell into disuse. In the Eastern Settlement was a large and well-built cathedral, of which the foundation still remains.

In one respect the Western Settlement had a better location, for it lay nearer the best fishing and hunting grounds, which were found from Disco Island northward. Here was a greater abundance of walrus, whales, narwhales, seal and reindeer than could be found farther south. In Björn Jonsson's *Annals*[21] we read that all the big farmers in Greenland had ships built to carry on hunting in the far northern waters of Greenland and the islands across Baffin Bay. Besides ordinary equipment, they also brought with them hewn logs, made to fit tightly together, so that they could put up their winter houses quickly.

On the island of Inugsuk, on the west coast of Greenland, near the 73rd parallel a large number of Norse artifacts has been found which indicate that the island was one of their most important hunting stations, and evidently used for a long time. Dr. Therkel Matthiassen excavated a big kitchen-midden here, finding that while its upper layers showed only Eskimo remains; the bottom layers turned up Norse artifacts which included a number of iron knives; pieces of woolen cloth like the cloth found in the cemetery at Herjulfsness; a small wooden tub exactly like old Norwegian tubs; numerous small objects carved from walrus tusks; and remains of a square stone house with a floor of smooth flag-stones.

On the neighboring island of Kingigtorsuak, a thousand feet high and a thousand miles north of the Eastern Settlement, three small cairns were found. The finder was an Eskimo in the employ of Captain W. Graah of the Royal Danish Navy, who in 1823 became the first white man of recent centuries to penetrate that far north. In one of these cairns he found a small flat stone about four inches long containing a neatly engraved runic inscription from the 14th century. Translated, it reads:

> Erling Sigvatsson and Bjarne Thordarson and Endride Oddsson raised these cairns the Saturday before Rogation Day and wrote (here follow six mystic signs which have been a puzzle for more than a hundred years).

The inscription abounds in numerical proportions and cryptic signs and is a very clever contrivance. Professor Magnus Olsen, an eminent Norwegian runologist, has written an exhaustive monograph on the inscription and believes its date is 1333. However, his solution is not complete. As these cairns were built in April, these three men must have spent the preceding winter up there on the 73rd parallel. Not until 500 years later did any other explorer penetrate so far north.

The best hunting grounds appear to have been considerably farther north at a place called Crookedfjord Heath which is described as being "Greenland's end" and "Greenland's last pier" and which seems to have been the region around Etah, north of the 78th parallel. This is the only place on the west coast where there is a sharp turn in the coast line—90 degrees toward the northeast, which could well be called Greenland's end. Here also, according to Björn Jonsson, was found the greatest accumulation of driftwood, trees and other flotsam which the Norsemen thought came from the bays of Markland, but more likely came from Siberia via the East Greenland current which turns north at the south end of Greenland.

Björn Jonsson has preserved for us a report of a voyage made to that far northern outpost probably in 1265. He writes:

> This report was written by Father Haldor in Greenland to Father Arnald who had left Greenland to become the chaplain

of the bodyguard of King Magnus Haakonsson. He said that that summer came men from Crookedfjord Heath who had been farther north than any other. They found no signs of the Skrellings (Eskimo) except at Crookedfjord Heath and therefore concluded that here was the shortest way for them to come, no matter where they came from. . . .

Later (in 1266) the priests of Greenland sent a ship northward to explore the regions north of the most northern area which had hitherto been visited. They sailed out from Crookedfjord Heath until the land disappeared below the horizon. Then came a south wind against them with fog, and they had to run before the wind. They were carried far (north) into the end of the sea, and the land was laid (sank out of sight), the south land and the glaciers. But when daylight came they saw many islands and all kinds of game, both seal and whales and many bears. Toward the south they saw a glacier extending as far as they could see. They found some marks left by the Skrellings, but they could not land because of the many bears. Then they sailed back, three days sailing (about 225 miles), and when they came south of Snowfell they found some signs of the Skrellings. After this they returned to Crookedfjord Heath, one long day's rowing (about 100 miles) on St. James Day.

This voyage was made to carry on the search of the men mentioned in the beginning of the report who reported that they found no signs of the Eskimo except at Crookedfjord Heath. These men concluded that here, at this strait, was "the shortest way for them (the Eskimo) to come, no matter where they came from." Since the Eskimo could not have come by small kayaks across Davis Strait or Baffin Bay which are several hundred miles wide, "the shortest way" must refer to the crossing at Smith Sound which is less than thirty-three miles wide, the land on the other side being visible in clear weather. Furthermore, the clause "no matter where they came from" indicates the possibility of several routes such as Jones Sound, Lancaster Sound or along the coast from the north, all of which meet at Smith Sound. If Crookedfjord Heath was further down the coast, the only *one* possible route for the Eskimo to follow in going to the Norse settlements, would be from the north. The statement that the south wind "came against them" implies that it was the purpose of the Greenlanders to explore Jones Sound or Lancaster Sound immediately to the south of Smith Sound, but that the gale from the south drove them far north into Kane Basin[22] (see Figure 6).

And here, far north near the 80th parallel, we find other evidence of the presence of the early Norsemen. In 1875-76 Sir George Nares led an expedition to Washington Irving Island which lies on latitude 79° 35'. On this island is a mountain top 900 feet high, and here the Captain found two cairns just like the three found on Kingigtorsuak Island. Captain Nares examined them and describes them as follows in his *Voyage to the Polar Sea* (Vol. 1, p. 88):

> On reaching the summit, about 900 feet high, after a laborious scramble up the steep hillside, we found two ancient cairns, far too old to have been erected by Dr. Hayes, the only traveller known to have visited the neighborhood. They were built of conglomerate and rested on a similar base. . . . They contained no record whatever.

On September 3, 1896 Captain Nares again landed on Washington Irving Island. In his second volume, page 162, he writes: "I again examined the two ancient lichen-covered cairns, but could find no record of who had built them. They were probably erected by some enterprising and successful navigator who, if he ever returned home, has not published an account of his discoveries."

Dr. Edward L. Moss who accompanied the expedition has also written a book (*Shores of the Polar Sea*) in which he describes other Norse finds, such as *eider duck nests* (*i.e.* shelters from which eider ducks are hunted) *built in the Norwegian fashion.* He also describes two more cairns found a little farther north:

> On the topmost ledge . . . stood a conical pile of well-packed stones. A second similar one stood a little lower down

to the southward; both plainly the work of a painstaking builder. But who was the builder? Not Eskimo. Structure and site forbade that suggestion. Civilized man had but once visited this shore, and that was when Dr. Hayes, in the spring of 1861, halted his tired dogs on the floes beside the island. He did not climb the bluff, and, besides, such an active sledge traveller would not have loitered to build a pair of cairns except at some crisis of his journey, and then he would have referred to them in his journal.

But the cairns themselves bear witness that they were not the work of any modern builder. Lichens grow but slowly in these regions. Dr. Scott found Sir Edward Parry's cairn untouched by them after thirty-two years. . . . These stones, on the other hand were cemented together by deep patches of orange lichen—the growth of many generations.

With so much evidence of their enterprise and hunting in the distant American arctic, fifteen hundred miles northward, it would be strange indeed if the Norse Greenlanders did not also make occasional visits to the lands to the south. As a matter of fact, we have evidence that they did, but of a different kind. Their presence in the arctic is proven by the Kingigtorsuak inscription, the Inugsuk artifacts, the cairns on Washington Irving Island, their reference to Crookedfjord Heath "very far to the north," and Spitzbergen. Evidence of their southward interest is found, not only in Bishop Erik's journey, but also in the grave near Lake Nipigon, the axe found on the northeast end of Nova Scotia, their trips to Markland (Nova Scotia) for logs and, last but not least in historical importance, their shipments of American furs.

It is clear that all these ships and boats, movable houses, paneled walls, roofs for buildings, coffins, wagons, and a hundred different uses of wood required much timber. In the first years of Greenland's history we read of some timber being brought from Norway, but when Markland was discovered, it was not necessary to go so far for this necessity. The forests of Nova Scotia and Newfoundland were only one-third as far away as were those of Norway. Moreover, there were no harbor duties to pay, and the logs were free for the cutting. No doubt there were frequent voyages to Markland because a community of 3,000 people needs a lot of lumber. But such voyages belonged to the ordinary duties of life and were not mentioned in literature, unless they were marked by some unusual event. Such a special circumstance happened in 1347 when a vessel from Markland bound for Greenland arrived in Iceland without an anchor. This was probably the first vessel from Markland to arrive in Iceland, and it is recorded in several Icelandic annals.

> 1347. There also came a ship from Greenland. It was smaller than the small Icelandic trading vessels. It came into outer Streamfjord [in Iceland]. It had no anchor. There were seventeen men on board, and they had sailed to Markland, but were later driven here by a storm at sea.

This casual notice, as Professor Fischer says, is of importance, not only because it shows that the people of Greenland in the 14th century had not forgotten Markland, but that it was mentioned in Iceland as a well-known country.

On these or other trips to America the Norsemen also did considerable hunting or trading because the shipments from Greenland to Norway included hides of many animals which are not indigenous to Greenland and *must have been caught on the American mainland.* We have this information from Erik Walkendorff, Chancellor of Denmark. In 1510 he was appointed Archbishop of Trondheim, to which archbishopric Greenland belonged. As metropolitan bishop, Walkendorff received all the taxes collected by the bishops of his ecclesiastical domains. Those from Greenland usually were paid *in natura,* accompanied by bills of lading and proper reports. In his time the Greenland diocese was all but a thing of the past, but in the episcopal archives he found old documents relating to Greenland, which told him of many churches in the distant West, and monasteries and priests, once astir with life, but now silent and almost forgotten. They filled him with a keen desire to re-establish communication with this distant diocese where perhaps many Norsemen still lived, although languishing in poverty and without the comforts of the Church. He gathered and collated all the material he could find about Greenland for the purpose of promoting new connections. However these efforts came to nothing when the morose and violent king, Kristian II, suddenly became suspicious of him, and Walkendorff had to flee for his life.

Among the papers prepared by the Archbishop was a list of the exports from Greenland, as shown by the old bills of lading. In this list are enumerated all the various kinds of hides received from Greenland. The Danish zoologist, Dr. Herluf Winge, an expert on northern mammals, has written a monograph on *Greenland Mammals* in which he points out that many varieties mentioned by the Archbishop cannot have lived in Greenland, but must have come from the American mainland. He mentions elk, black bear, beaver, otter, ermine, sable, lynx, glutton, and wolf.[23]

This evidence of much hunting by Norsemen in America, or trading with the Indians, centuries after Vinland was discovered, may help to explain the presence of the eight life-like turkeys which are painted on the wall of a passage in the cathedral of Schleswig, Germany. It was built about 1280, and the wall paintings are supposed to date from the time when the church was erected. But the turkey was not introduced into Europe until 1530, when Spaniards brought some turkeys back from Mexico. As most Germans think that Norse voyages to America ended with Thorfin Karlsevni, many of them think the turkeys in the church are of recent origin. These turkeys are at present the subject of lively debate in Germany. The beauty and dignity of the turkey cock must have won the admiration of the Greenland hunters in America very early, and it seems likely that they would attempt to send live specimens of such a fine bird to Europe, just as they did polar bears and falcons. At present no conclusive argument on the date of the turkey paintings has been presented from either side, but the fact that there were Norse hunters in America in the 12th or 14th centuries cannot be denied.

By means of the ships built with the timber from Markland, the Greenlanders were able to produce so many valuable articles for export that Greenland became an important place of supply —very important for a community of three or four thousand people. Indeed, it became famous all over Europe because of its contributions to the luxuries of life. The tusks of the walrus were an excellent substitute for ivory, and the Greenlanders produced so much of it that elephant tusks were almost pushed off the market. Eiderdown also brought a big price. The Greenland falcons were superior to all others, and were eagerly sought by the rich from Bergen to Bagdad. Finally there were the polar bears; they were considered so desirable as pets that they brought fabulous prices. An interesting illustration of the value of polar bears is the experience of a humble Icelander named Audun of Westfjord. In the first half of the 11th century he conceived the idea of presenting King Sven Estridson with a polar bear. He went to Greenland and purchased a bear, for which he paid all that he possessed. Then he went to Denmark and gave it to the King. The latter was so pleased that he wanted to give Audun a high and profitable office at his court. But Audun had provided provisions for his mother for only three years, and declined the honor. The King then gave him a good ship with a valuable cargo, a big bag of silver, and a heavy gold ring which he took off his own arm. When Audun passed through Norway, the stern King Harald, an enemy of King Sven, was so impressed by his enemy's generosity that instead of confiscating Audun's possessions, he added to them with a gift of a sword with a gold hilt.[23a]

A similar golden experience is related in Ari the Wise' *Landnama,* Book 3, Chapter 3. One of the earliest settlers in Iceland was Ingemund the Old who became owner of a large tract of land in northern Iceland. He captured a female white bear and two cubs, and in 880 he took these to Norway and presented them to the King, Harald the Fairhaired. The King was so pleased that he gave Ingemund a large ship, fully loaded with pine logs.

There were, therefore, many valuable cargos and happy hunters sailing down from the distant arctic. But they did not always return happy. In many old writings we read of the presence of sea robbers in the waters of Greenland. Even as late as 1539 when the Greenland settlements had ceased to exist, Bishop Olaus Magnus gives prominent mention to these pirates in his *Carta Marina*. It has puzzled many what could have called pirates to the humble and distant Greenland.

However, the physical circumstances of Greenland were bound to produce sea robbers. It was a fault of the law. As far as is known, there was no direct death penalty in Greenland. When a man was found guilty of manslaughter, as was not a rare occurrence because of the intermittent family feuds, he was declared an outlaw whom anyone could kill. As it was not sportsmanlike to kill him at the judgment seat, he often had a chance to get away and hide in an obscure spot. If he did not own a ship, it was impossible for him to leave Greenland. Naturally such outcasts of society would band together and prey on the community. Before long they would steal a ship and then lie in wait for a vessel loaded with walrus tusks, pelts, eiderdown and other valuable cargo. If they succeeded in capturing it, they would sail it to some port in Britain or Flanders and exchange the goods for flour, wine and other necessities. *Floamanna Saga* mentions representatives of two different classes of these outlaws. One is Rolf who had sought shelter in a fjord on the southeastern side of Greenland, by whose help Thorgils and his companions were saved. The incident is described below. Rolf evidently was a poor unfortunate who wanted to live and die in peace, and through the influence of Thorgils he was pardoned and restored to the community. The other class is represented by thirty fierce vikings with two ships in a distant harbor of the Western Settlement. Here, they were surprised and killed by Thorgils and thirty men. In the house of the robbers they found much valuable goods and a huge kettle of flour (a great luxury in Greenland) hanging over the fire.

Professor Poul Nörlund, the Danish archaeologist who won deserved fame for his revealing researches in the cemeteries and ruins of the early Norse colonists of Greenland, has advanced the theory that the climate of Greenland was much milder the three first centuries of the present millennium than it is now. This difference, he thinks, made possible the active, profitable and congenial life that is reflected in the writings about those colonists. He believes the climate in the 14th century became much more severe, with the result that the Norse population, deteriorated and gradually perished.

This theory has received new and important support in Rachel L. Carson's "The Sea Around Us." In the chapter "The Global Thermostat," she endorses the theory, originated by Dr. Otto Petterson, that there is a climatic cycle due to great submarine tidal waves nearly 100 feet high. "From astronomical calculations Petterson learned that the tides must have been at their greatest strength during the closing centuries of the Middle Ages. . . . Only about every eighteen centuries do the heavenly bodies assume this particular relation." The last mild period he places at around the year 550; the next apex of warm weather is due to come about the year 2400. "The World's most recent period of maximum tides, and the most rigorus climate, occurred about 1433, its effect being felt, however, for several centuries before and after that year."[24]

Petterson does not explain why a period of excessively high tides would produce a period of rigorus climate, but Carson submits two historical 'proofs' (borrowed from him) to show that the climate of Greenland has greatly deteriorated. They are:

   1. "There is no mention in the sagas that Erik (about 984) was hampered by drift ice in the several years of his exploration of the island."

Negative evidence is almost always worthless. Erik must have met with many difficult problems in his three years of exploration of such a bleak and wild country, but he mentions none of them. He merely says that he reached Greenland and mentions a few places that he visited. It is the most colorless report of any great exploration in history. But only about ten years later another man made the same voyage, and he encountered so much drift ice that it took him four years to reach the southern end of Greenland. See the story of Thorgils below.

2. "The early sagas spoke, too, of the abundant fruit of excellent quality growing in Greenland."

There is no mention of fruit growing in Greenland in any of the sagas, but there is a report written in the second half of the 14th century which mentions it. If this report were true, it would completely demolish the theory that the most rigorous climate occurred in the late Middle Ages, because this report about fruit growing in Greenland was written shortly after 1364. It is from an interview that someone in Bergen had with Ivar Bardson, a priest who had spent more than twenty years in Greenland as steward of the properties of the Church. He returned to Norway in 1364 in company with the survivors of a royal expedition which had spent eight years in America searching for the lost emigrants and supposed apostates from Greenland. We still have Bardson's very clear account of conditions in Greenland in a manuscript of somewhat later date. It closes with the following words:

On the mountains and lower down grow the best of fruits, as big as any apples and good to eat. There also grows the best wheat that exists.

All writers on Greenland agree that this statement about fruit and wheat has nothing to do with Greenland. Presumably Ivar Bardson also mentioned Vinland, where his traveling companions spent several years, and the connecting lines must simply have been lost or had become illegible.

It is possible that the climate of Greenland may have been more severe in the 14th and 15th centuries than it was earlier, but the difference could not have been great. There are many passages in the old sagas dealing with Greenland which prove that the climate was practically the same in the Middle Ages as it is now.

We have good information about the climate of 11th century Greenland in *Floamanna Saga,* which is chiefly a biography of Thorgils Orrabeinfostre, one of the most heroic figures in Iceland's early history. He was a man of wealth and dignity, but in 998 he decided to accept Erik Thorwaldson's invitation to settle in Greenland. They had been intimate friends when they both served as members of the great Earl Haakon's bodyguard about twenty years earlier. Thorgils was accompanied by a couple of dozen men of whom thirteen were his slaves. He also carried a number of cows and a large supply of goods of many kinds. Unfortunately, they had a very bad voyage, being tossed about on the sea for three months, and then the ship was wrecked on the east coast of Greenland. No lives were lost, and most of the goods, including a good boat, were saved. But the winter was a hard one, and eight or ten of the men died.

Finally spring came, and one day Thorgils along with three men climbed up a mountain to see if the ice pack was opening up. When they returned they found that the slaves had murdered Thorgils' wife and run away with the boat and all the provisions and supplies.

Although Thorgils had only his axe and hunting knife, he managed with the help of the others to make a framework of a boat out of pieces of the wreck, and this framework was then covered with hides. In this they made some progress southward. One morning they found that their boat was stolen. They were now in a particlularly bad position, being without any food and with no beach on which to go hunting. But later in the day Thorgils saw a white bear tumbling about on the broken ice. He ran out, killed it with his sword and dragged it ashore.

The next day they found to their surprise that their boat had been returned. Very likely the natives saw Thorgils attack and kill the bear from a distance, and believing he could not be a mortal man but a powerful spirit, they hastened to return the boat the next night.

In this way they struggled along for four years with the greatest difficulty, until they reached the southern end of Greenland. There they found a man named Rolf who had been banished from the settlement because of a crime, living with his family in a hut in the frozen wilderness. He had a small vessel, and with his help they reached the Eastern Settlement. Throughout those four years, summer and winter, the icepack lay impenetrable along the shore, now and then there was some open water near the shore. The description of this heroic journey certainly indicates that the climate was just as severe 950 years ago as it is now.[25]

Another informative narrative about the climate of Greenland in the 12th century is *Einar Sokkeson's Saga*. This saga deals chiefly with a serious conflict that arose shortly after Bishop Arnald, the second bishop in Greenland, reached his diocese. He was consecrated as bishop in 1125 and sailed for Greenland the same year. About the same time a Norwegian trader, named Arinbjörn, also left for Greenland with two ships. On the way a great storm came up which compelled the Bishop to remain in Iceland during the winter. Nothing was heard of Arinbjörn, and it was thought that he was lost at sea.

Four or five years later a Greenland hunter, Sigurd Njalson, was on a hunting voyage with fifteen men one fall in the unsettled region east of the Eastern Settlement of Greenland, near Cape Farwell. They had poor luck, and his men wanted to return home, because the season was getting late, but Sigurd assured them that they would soon have better luck. Very soon after their ship entered a large fjord, they found two vessels at the inner end, one of which was very large and beautiful and was known to have belonged to Arinbjörn. On the shore was a large hut and a tent, and in them they found many dead men. One of the vessels, was a wreck, but the big ship was drawn up on the beach and in good condition. The hunters decided that the men had died of starvation, because the ice pack prevented their ship from leaving the fjord. Njalson and his men sailed the big ship to Gardar in Greenland, the seat of the Bishop, who claimed it for the Church as payment for masses to be sung for the dead men. News of this confiscation reached the heirs of Arinbjörn in Norway, however, and they came to Greenland to claim what was left of his property. As the Bishop would not yield, a very serious quarrel developed resulting in a number of deaths.

These ships presumably carried provisions enough to keep the men alive for a year or two with what they could get by hunting and fishing. But as the field ice kept the fjord closed year after year, the men finally perished.

Inasmuch as a large fjord near the southern tip of Greenland was blocked with ice continuously for at least four consecutive years in the beginning of the 12th century, the indication is certainly that the climate was no milder then than it is at present.

To these evidences from the 11th and 12th centuries, may be added a report from *Speculum Regale* or *King's Mirror,* written about 1250. The author writes:[26]

Some of these (Greenland) icefloes are entirely flat, eight or ten feet thick, and these extend so far from the land that it takes four or more days' travel to reach land over them . . . It is therefore best for those who wish to reach the land (Greenland) to sail southwest and west until they have circled around all this ice, and then to sail toward land. But it has often happened that they have tried to reach the land too early, and then they have been caught in this ice. Some of them have perished, and some managed to extricate themselves, and we have talked with some of them and heard their story. All

who were caught in the ice took their small boats with them
and dragged them over the ice. The ship and all their goods
were lost, and it took them four and five days to reach land.

Captain W. Graah, who in 1829 was the first successful
modern explorer of the coast around the south end of Greenland,
quotes this passage from *Speculum Regale* and says: "Just as
is here described it happened to the Dutch whalers who were
wrecked in 1777, which shows that the ice conditions in the 12th
or 13th centuries when the *Speculum* is supposed to have been
written were the same as in our time."[26a]

The Mass Emigration
to America in 1342

For almost 300 years Greenland was a peaceful and prosperous republic. It produced a number of things which were in
demand in other lands, and trade was brisk and commerce
lively. It had no wars or quarrels with other countries, and its
domestic relations were remarkably quiet. In this it differed
greatly from Iceland, whose record for many centuries is one of
almost constant conflict between rival chiefs. Perhaps the great
and toilsome adventures of the Greenlanders on their far northern hunting trips provided a safe outlet for their excess energy,
and made them peaceful at home. The Icelanders, being an
agricultural people, had no such battles with nature, and seem
to have found their excitement in plotting against their neighbors.

In 1261 the King of Norway finally persuaded the Greenlanders
to accept union with Norway. As they were of Norwegian
origin and had no quarrel with the mother country, this union
was principally a sentimental one, and the terms were few and
of minor importance. They consisted principally of an agreement
that the King of Norway was to be their protector, whose laws
they would accept. In return, the King promised to send two
ships to Greenland each year for trading purposes. Any accept-

able person could ship or receive goods aboard these royal vessels upon obtaining a license, which required him to pay a ten percent tax on the value of the goods when they were delivered.

At first this regulation did not interfere much with the Greenland trade, because there were some men who sailed their own vessels and thus avoided the tax. But in 1294 a royal order was issued prohibiting any sailings to or from Greenland without a license. This was chiefly intended to stop the Hanseatic League, whose aggressive trading practices made life miserable for the governments of Norway and Denmark. From time to time this prohibition was sharpened, and private shipping enterprise became more and more difficult. It was particularly harmful to the Western Settlement. The royal vessel on arriving in Greenland would put in at the Eastern Settlement which was the better and more populous market. The insufficient imports would quickly be bought up, and there would be nothing left for the Western Settlement.

A still greater evil was the increasing irregularity of the sailings of these royal vessels. We find evidence of this irregularity in the long lapses between the death of a bishop and the installation of his successor. Bishop Olaf who died in 1280 was not replaced by his successor, Thord, until 1288. Thord died in 1314 and was immediately replaced by his successor, Bishop Arni. Arni held office until 1349, but so little was known in Norway about Greenland that it was thought he had died in 1325. This false report was corrected only to give way to a new report that he had died in 1328, also an error. Then in 1340 the archbishop of Trondheim was 'reliably' informed that Bishop Arni was dead, and with much ceremony he consecrated Jon Erikson Skalle as bishop of Greenland. The next year, however, a vessel arrived from Greenland and reported that Bishop Arni was still alive. Nothing more was heard about the tenacious Arni until 1364, when a vessel returned from Greenland and reported that he had died in 1349, fifteen years earlier.

In the meantime no vessel from Greenland had arrived in Norway.

This royal monopoly and the irregularity of the sailing of its vessels deprived the people of Greenland of many necessities of life and largely made futile their previously profitable hunting in the Arctic. Such destruction of initiative causes degeneration, and the Greenland colony would perhaps have come to an earlier end, but for the persistence of the Hanseatic League in maintaining a slight hold on the Greenland trade. Even this trade, however, gradually became less profitable and less regular for other reasons.

When self-reliance is thwarted, life loses its charm, and a somber contemplation of the hereafter is apt to take its place. But in the dark days of medieval bewilderment the hereafter was not always a pleasant subject because of the fear of eternal hell-fire which poisoned the lives of our ancestors. The priest comforted the sinner with the assurance that this punishment could be greatly reduced and possible even avoided if the sinner gave his property to the Church, so that many masses could be offered for his soul's salvation. Many a man, accordingly, seized upon this remedy in the hope of easing his eternal soul. But whatever ease his bequest may have won him in the hereafter, it impoverished his dependents, and his sons were reduced to becoming serfs and renters on church property. Ivar Bardson's report, despite its glowing account of Greenland's climate, presents a depressing picture of the economic situation in the Eastern Settlement. He gives a list of all the many fjords with their churches, monasteries and two hundred farms, and he tells us that they nearly all belonged to the cathedral or to a local church or monastery. The descendants of the stalwart pioneers of Erik Thorwaldson and his times had nearly all become tenants of the church. Even the hunting grounds in the uninhabitable region east of the settlement belonged to the cathedral, which exacted a part of whatever fish or game was caught. Greenland had become a land without opportunity!

In 1924 a book was published in Copenhagen entitled *Buried Norsemen at Herjolfsness*. It contains a report of Poul Nörlund's excavations of the graves in the cemetery at that place, where it was found that the dead were dressed in the long voluminous robes and caps with long tails which were in fashion in Europe in the 14th and 15th centuries. Professor Brögger in his *Vinlandsferdene* waxes enthusiastic about the presence of these garments and thinks that they mark the existence of *"an upper class* population." He writes:

> We find here not a humble hunting people's clothing of skin, but the dresses, hose, and hoods of prosperous Europeans. There is something so strangely vivid and rich in this picture that it captures the fancy and compels prolonged reflection. It is not a crippled community that we see here, but a living people with established European connections. At the same time there is something brave and dignified in it which increases the drama of the extinction of the colony and makes it more remarkable and catastrophic.

These are eloquent words, but hardly an accurate description of affairs. Greenland had thousands of sheep, and wool was one article of which there was an abundance. The people of Greenland would learn, both by sight and hearing, from occasional visitors, what styles were in vogue in Europe, and it was possible even for the most humble to copy these articles of clothing without cash expense. As it was the custom to bury the dead in their best attire, we find them now in their home-made robes. It is the *preservation* of these dresses after 500 years that is amazing, not their use in Greenland. Actually, as these discoveries are practically all from the 15th century, they are mementos of a people that were so crippled both physically and economically that their existence came to an end just a few years later. Their physical degeneracy is fully set forth by the anatomist, F. C. C. Hansen in *Meddelelser om Grönland,* volume 67.

But the people of the Western Settlement had another problem which the neighboring community knew nothing about, and that was the encroachments of the Eskimo. These Arctic people play no part in the history of Greenland until the 13th century when the Norsemen began to have some contact with them.

It was inevitable that hostilities would break out between the Norsemen and the Eskimo. No provocation to war is more common and irritating than the struggle of two primitive people for the same hunting grounds. The tensions arising from such competition punctuate the whole history of American Settlement, and are abundantly illustrated in the narratives of the early French missionaries and fur traders in America. The Eskimo would feel particularly resentful because the white men had irons weapons, better adapted for hunting, and ships in which they could come from hundreds of miles away and sail back with their booty. We know nothing about the progressive incidents in this contest for survival, but we can easily imagine them. The Eskimo made no attack in force, because they were not familiar with such tactics, and the problem of providing food for a large war party so far from a home base would be difficult if not impossible. Instead they probably resorted to sniping, the timid man's mode of attack. The Norsemen lived on large scattered farms separated by ridges and marshes, and their cattle often strayed. It would be easy for a small band of Eskimo to kill some of these cattle, to set fire to haystacks far from the farm house, and to ambush any lone men that appeared. This was the way the Sioux war in Minnesota began in 1862, and the scattered farmers found themselves so trapped by the Indians that they were compelled to flee a couple of hundred miles eastward until all Minnesota was depopulated of white men except in the most easterly counties. In all probability the people of the Western Settlement were driven back in the same way, for the day came in 1342 when their settlement lay empty and despoiled. This is told by Father Ivar Bardson, a Norse Greenlander, at that time. Bishop Haakon of Bergen, was an old friend of Bishop Arni of Greenland, and as he had not heard from Arni for many years, he fitted out a vessel at his own expense and in 1341 dispatched Ivar to Greenland with greetings and presents. Ivar reached Greenland in safety and found Arni still alive, but very old and feeble, and at the Bishop's request he remained as steward of the Church properties for many years. In Greenland he learned that the people of the Western Settlement were having trouble with the Eskimo, and the next year, 1342, he was sent to their aid with a company of men. The following is part of the record of his report dealing with this mission: [27]

> . . . There in the West Settlement stands a large church which is called Stensness (Sandness) Church, which church for a time was a cathedral and episcopal see. But now the Skrellings have occupied all the Western Settlement, there are many horses, goats, cows and sheep, all wild, but no people, neither Christian nor heathen. All this was told us by Ivar Bardson Greenlander, who was in charge of the episcopal see at Gardar for many years; he had seen all this, and he was one of those appointed by the Lawspeaker to sail to the Western Settlement against the Skrellings and drive them out. But when they came thither they found no one, neither Christian nor heathen, nothing but some wild sheep and cattle. They took what was needed to feed the men and loaded as many [cows and sheep] as the ships could hold and then sailed home.

There has recently been much discussion as to what became of the people of the eastern Settlement. Some writers have thought that they were exterminated by the Eskimo. But as Ivar Bardson does not mention any signs of bloodshed, this theory is unsupported. Besides, as Nansen says: "Can anyone who knows the Eskimo imagine that they slaughtered the men but not the cattle? These represented food for them, and that is what they would first have turned their attention to."

Nansen and Vilhjalmur Stefansson have a theory that the arrival in the Western Settlement of Ivar Bardson and his company took place just at a time when the Norsemen voluntarily gave up their accustomed mode of life and joined with the Eskimo. They think that the Norsemen eventually recognized

that Greenland was better adapted for hunting than for agriculture, and that they had taken this decisive step and adopted
this supposedly easier mode of life.

While I have great admiration for the achievements of these
two explorers and much respect for their opinions, I cannot agree
with their conclusions in this matter. The Norsemen were no in-
experienced newcomers in Greenland. Ten generations of them
had lived there, and they had learned how to get the most out
of the circumstances in which they lived by the most productive
combination of animal husbandry and the hunting of seal, walrus,
and whale. They would gain nothing by taking up the life of
the Eskimo, and they would lose their native dairy diet and
their large comfortable homes. And what would the Eskimo
think of the intrusion of hundreds of white men into the humble
economy of their life? They would certainly resist such intrusion
with all their power. Nor need such a general pattern of group
conflict preclude the arrival now and then of a white man who
had been declared an outlaw by his own people. He would come
as a supplicant, and the hospitality common among primitive
people could, in such isolated cases, grant him a welcome as
long as he deserved it.

The fact is that there is no evidence whatever that the people
of the Western Settlement were exterminated by the Eskimo or
amalgamated with them. But we do have evidence that their
disappearance was due to emigration, as attested in a 17th
century copy or synopsis made by Bishop Gisle Oddson of an
annalistic record from the 14th century. It reads thus:[28]

> 1342. The inhabitants of Greenland fell voluntarily away
> from the true faith and the Christian religion, and, after having
> given up all good manners and true virtues, turned to the
> people of America *(ad Americae populos se converterunt.).*
> Some say that Greenland lies very near the western lands of
> the world [i.e. America].

This Bishop Gisle Oddson was bishop of Skalholt and had
spent his entire life there, being the son of the former bishop,

Odd Einarson. This episcopal see in the Middle Ages was the principal repository for Icelandic records. In 1630 it was destroyed by fire and all its manuscripts lost. Since Bishop Gisle had the best opportunity of becoming acquainted with these manuscripts, he later (1637) made a synopsis in Latin of some of the more important documents that he could recall. The name, America, of course, was not in the original of 1342. It could only have said "Vinland", or "Markland" or "the western islands." In translating the annal into Latin (the original was written in Norse) the Bishop must also have translated the name.

This copy of the old annal by Bishop Gisle Oddson corroborates and supplements the report by Ivar Bardson, with the exception of the omission of the word *western* (Greenland). It is not strange that the Bishop was able to reproduce it from memory, for it is highly sensational from a clerical point of view: These people had "given up the true faith!" Finally it tells where they had gone, and what year the emigration took place. It is evident that while Ivar's report and the Bishop's annal refer to the same event, the references are so different in detail that they are independent in origin.

Some commentators have pointed to the clause *ad Americae populos se converterunt* as evidence that the emigrants united with the Eskimo. But this imputes to the Bishop an anachronism of speech. As John Fiske says in the introduction to his *Discovery of America*: "In dealing with the discovery of America one must keep steadily before one's mind the quaint notions of ancient geographers." When the Bishop said America, he meant, of course, *continental* America, separated from Greenland by Ginnungagap (see page 101). For more than a hundred years after his time it was still commonly believed that Greenland was an elongation of Europe from the northeast. No one, even now, would think of alluding to the Eskimo of Greenland as people of America.

The fact that when the Bishop spoke of the "people of America" he meant the inhabitants of America and not Greenland is further proven by the sentence that immediately follows his statement: *Some say that Greenland lies very near to the western lands of the world.* It is as if he had said: "They probably had not far to go, because it is said that Greenland lies very near to America." The Norwegian historian P. A. Munch is entirely of the same view. He says: "The attacks of the Eskimo were presumably the cause of what is stated in an account of 1342, viz., that the inhabitants of Greenland fell voluntarily from Christianity and emigrated to other parts of America. . . . This account has all the evidence of truth (*aldeles Trovärdighedens Präg*)."[29]

The question now arises: What people in America did these emigrants plan to unite with? Does it mean the Indians of America, whom the earlier Norsemen called *Skrellings,* with whom they had had considerable trouble? That does not seem likely, for no peace could be expected from such a union. Or does it mean their own people, former Norsemen from the Western Settlement, who had established a colony in America? That must remain an open question, because we have no evidence for or against it. But it is highly possible. It will be recalled that some two hundred years earlier Bishop Erik set out from the Western Settlement in a ship manned by sailors from that district to visit an alleged Norse colony in Vinland (see page 89). If he found it, it is likely that an intermittent connection was maintained. But even if it had ceased, the people of Greenland may have had expectations of uniting with descendants of their own countrymen, which would provide justifiable reason for their emigration. In any case, as the sniping of the Eskimo made life in their old homes too risky, Vinland or Markland would seem a good place of refuge.

This exodus from Greenland of an entire district of people in 1342, to start a new life in America, must have been a bitter and dramatic event. Circumstances, however, offered little choice. The Eastern Settlement was already filled up, and only a few who had relatives there could be accommodated. The others, a few hundred persons, had the choice of remaining where they were to be killed off by the sniping *Skrellings*, or to seek a home in the new land to the southwest where they went for timber. As their vessels were small, they could not take their cattle, but a dozen vessels could take the emigrants and a few milch cows. This limitation of shipping space would explain why Ivar Bardson and his companions found many horses, cows and sheep, but no people. It may even have been the intention of the migrants to return later and get their domestic animals.

What happened to these exiles? We have no definite record of their voyage, but there is some uncertain evidence that some of them at least may have been shipwrecked on the Labrador coast. Cesar de Rochefort gives an account of a voyage of a ship from Flushing, commanded by Nicholas Tunes, who, in 1656, visited the shores of Baffin Land. He describes two distinct types of natives. Of these one kind was tall of stature, well-built, and of fair complexion; the other was the common Eskimo. From the same region, Dr. Franz Boas has recorded a number of striking traditions of a people called Tornit, traditions which seem to suggest that at some remote time a people of a larger physique than the Eskimo lived there.

Many ethnologists and writers have discussed these Tornit or Tunnit people and they all agree that they were representatives of a tall, well-built race of people with light complexions. In 1921, G. M. Gathorne-Hardy made a trip to Labrador to study the remains of the Tunnit. In an address delivered before the London Geographical Society after his return, he said among other things:

> The theory that the Tunnit were merely another Eskimo tribe does not appear satisfactory. All along the Labrador coast, where several different Eskimo tribes existed, the Tunnit are constantly treated by tradition as something not Eskimo, but contrasted with that race.

Sir W. Grenfell in his "Forty Years for Labrador" writes: "The coast line from Ramah to Cape Chidley is just under a

Fig. 1. The area of early Norse explorations in American waters.

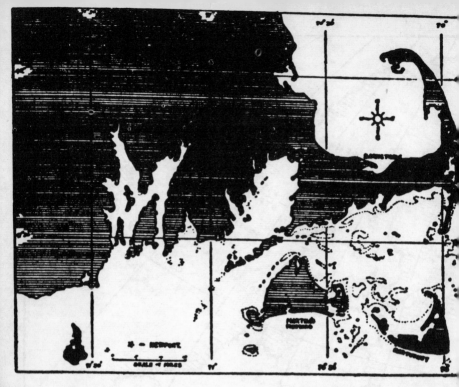

Fig. 2. The Vinland of the Norsem

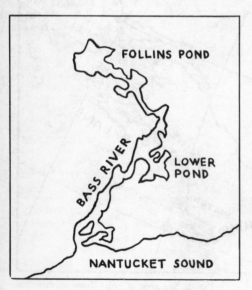

Fig. 3. Site of Leif Erikson's camp.

Fig. 3A. Iceland, as depicted o
Resen's old map.

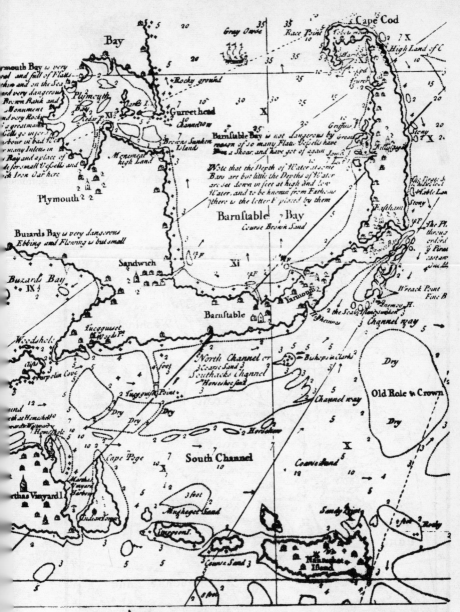

Fig. 4. Chart of Nantucket sound and the coast of Massachusetts from surveys made by Captain Cyprian Southack, under the authority of the British and Colonial governments, shortly before the year 1694. A large island, marked "dry" is shown in the east. The map was published in atlas form with other charts of the Canadian and New England coasts, about 1734, in London.

Fig. 5. Viking weapons found at Lake Nipigon near Beardmor~
northern Ontario.

Fig. 6. Map of Kane Basin.

Fig. 7. The Kensington Stone.

Fig. 8. Part of the inscription on the Kensington Stone, showing its corroded condition.

ᛒ:ᚢᚢᛏᛏᚱ:ᛁᛁ:ᚠᚠ:ᛏᛁᚱᚱᚤᛏᛏ:ᛒᛁ:

8 göter ok 22 norrmen på

:ᛁᛒᚦᚷᚢᛏᛌᚢᛏ ᚠᚷᚱᚦ:ᚠᚱᛁ:

oppagelsefarp fro

ᚤᛁᛏᛌᚷᛏᚦ:ᛁᚠ:ᚤᛏᚢᛏ:ᚤᛁ:

winlanp of west wi

✳ᚷᚦᛏ:ᛌᚷᚤᛏᚱ:ᚤᛏᚦ:ᚠ:ᚢᛏᚠᚷᚱ:ᛏᛏ:

hape läger wep 2 skjar en

ᚦᚷᚤᚢ:ᚱᛁᚢᛏ:ᛏᛁᚱᚱ:ᚠᚱᛁ:ᚦᛏᛏᛁ:ᚢᛏᛏᛏ:

pags rise norr fro peno sten

ᚤᛁ:ᚤᚷᚱ:ᛁᛁ:ᚠᛁᚢᛏᛏ:ᛏᛏ:ᚦᚷᚤ✳:ᚷᛒᛏᛁᚱ

wi war ok fiske en pagh äptir

ᚤᛁ:ᛁᛁᚤ:✳ᛏᚤ:ᚠᚷᛏ:ᛩ:ᚤᚷᛏ:ᚱᚢᚦᛏ:

wi kom hem fan 10 man röpe

ᚷᚠ:ᛌᛌᛁᚦ:ᛁᚢ:ᚦᛏᚦ:AVM·

uf blop og pep AVM

ᚠᚱᚷᛏᛌᚢᛏ:ᚷᚠ:ᛁᛌᛌᚤ:

fräelse af illy

✳ᚷᚱ:ᛩ:ᚤᚷᛏᚢ:ᚤᛏ:✳ᚷᚤᛏᛏ:ᚷᛏ:ᚢᛏ:

har 10 mans we hawet at se

ᚷᛒᛏᛁᚱ:ᚤᛁᚱᛏ:ᚢᚤᛁᛒ:ᛌᛪ:ᚦᚷᚤ✳:ᚱᛁᚢᛏ:

äptir wore skip 14 pagh rise

ᚠᚱᛁᚤ:ᚦᛏᛏᛁ:ᚢ✳:ᚷ✳ᚱ:ᛌᚠᚠᚠ:

främ peno öh ahr 1362

Fig. 9. Transliteration of the Kensington inscription.

Fig. 10. Government surveyor's plat made in 1866. In the center a hill is marked with a crescent. This is where the Kensington Stone was found. Adjoining this is a slough designated by a crooked line marked "dry."

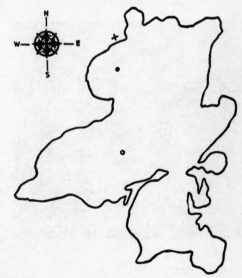

11. Outline sketch of Cormorant Lake.
e cross shows location of mooring stone
l camp site.

Fig. 12. Mooring hole, 7¾ inches deep, found on the beach directly in front
Peter Nelson's house, six miles south of Lake Park, Minn. Mr. Nelson has liv
on this spot more than eighty years. His father homesteaded this land about 18

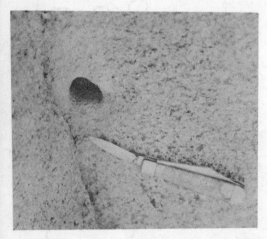

Fig. 12A. The mooring stone on "the island
where the Kensington Stone was found.

Fig. 13A. The Cormorant Lake fire-steel.

Fig. 13B. The CLIMAX fire-steel, found five miles north of Climax, Minn.

Fig. 13C. The Cormorant Lake axe. much reduced in size.

14A. The Wells, Minnesota ≥rd.

Fig. 14B. The Estenson halberd

Fig. 14C. The Alexandria, Minnesota halberd.

[137]

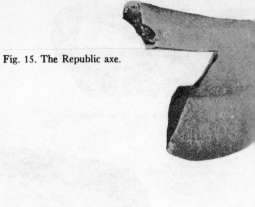

Fig. 15. The Republic axe.

Fig. 16. Other 14th-century implements found in western Minnesota.

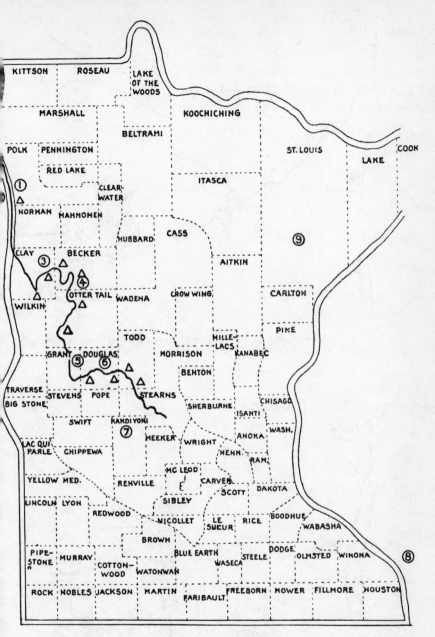

Fig. 17. Outline map of Minnesota showing counties and route of travel as marked by mooring stones (triangles) and medieval artifacts (circles).

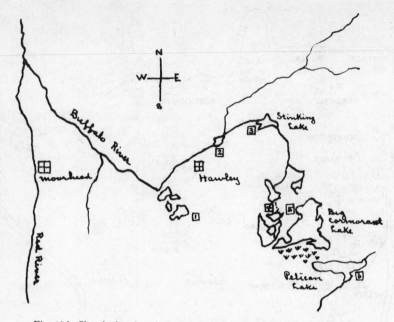

Fig. 17A. Sketch showing the location of the six mooring stones in the upper group. Scale 1″ to 12 miles.

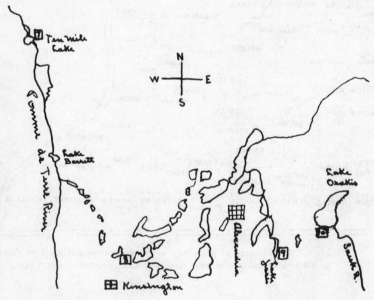

Fig. 17B. Sketch showing the locations of the four mooring stones in the lower group. Scale 1″ to 8 miles.

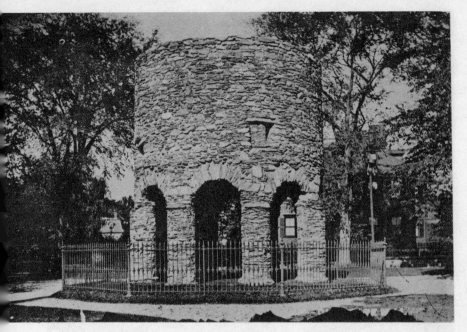

Fig. 18. The Tower in Newport.

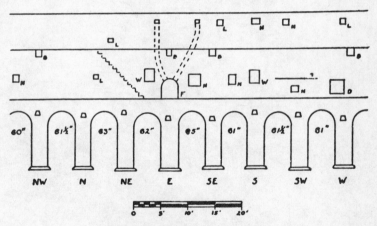

Fig. 19. Developed interior elevation of the Tower.

B—Beam holes (4) for supporting upper floor
N—Square recesses (6) serving as shelves
W—Windows (2)
L—Small loop holes for defence (4)
G—Groove in wall
F—Fireplace
D—Doorway entered from outside building

Fig. 20. The Altar groove and recess.

Fig. 21. The lavatorium of the Abbey St. Bavo, built in the 12th century

Fig. 22. Remains of Varnhem Abbey in West Gothland, Sweder
In the center is seen the base of an octagonal lavabo.

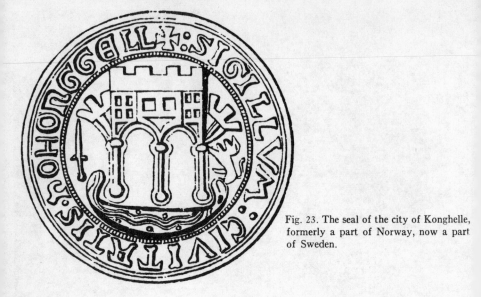

Fig. 23. The seal of the city of Konghelle, formerly a part of Norway, now a part of Sweden.

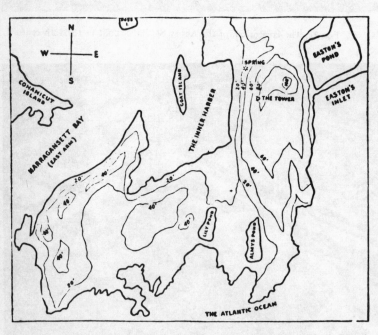

Fig. 24. Outline sketch of the lower end of Rhode Island.

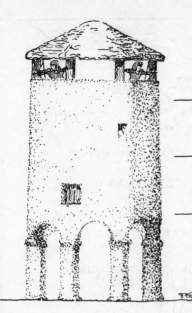

Fig. 25. Probable appearance of the Tower when built. Drawing by Stanley B. Parker.

Fig. 26. Base of the east column of Newport Tower showing disturbed condition of stone work. Photo by W. S. Goodwin Jr.

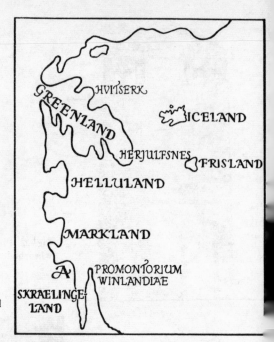

Fig. 27. Stefansson's map of Greenland and parts of America, 1570.

Fig. 28. Resen's-copy of 160? of an ancient map of Green- land and parts of America.

[146]

FRETUM
DAVIS

Grønlands Ob
DESERTA GR

GRONLAN
DIA

CIRCULUS

Gyn
nunga
Gap

GRONLANDIA
OCCIDENTALIS
Westur bygd

GRONLANDIA ORIENTALIS

FRIS
LAND

OCEA

Fig. 29. Thorlacius map
Greenland, 1668.

[147]

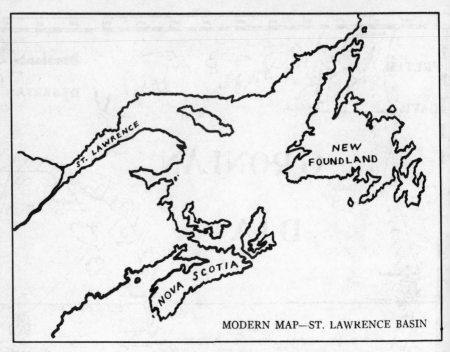

MODERN MAP—ST. LAWRENCE BASIN

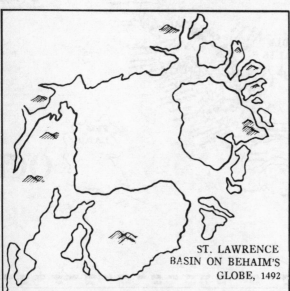

ST. LAWRENCE
BASIN ON BEHAIM'S
GLOBE, 1492

Fig. 30. The Gulf of St. Law:
as shown on Behaim's glob
1492 compared with modern

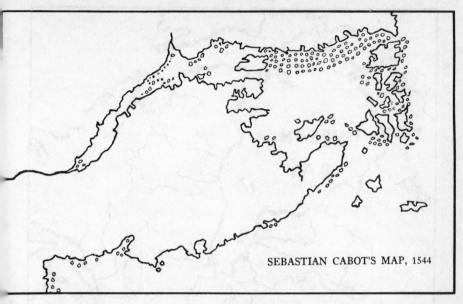

SEBASTIAN CABOT'S MAP, 1544

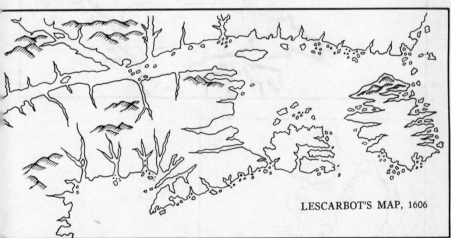

LESCARBOT'S MAP, 1606

Fig. 31. Two 16th Century maps of the Gulf of St. Lawrence.

HUDSON

BAY

ST. LAWRENCE

MARE GLACIALE (SCULUS)

FRETUM TRIUM

Fig. 32. Tracing of a part of the Gemma Frisius globe of 1537 showing Hudson Bay compared with a modern map of the same.

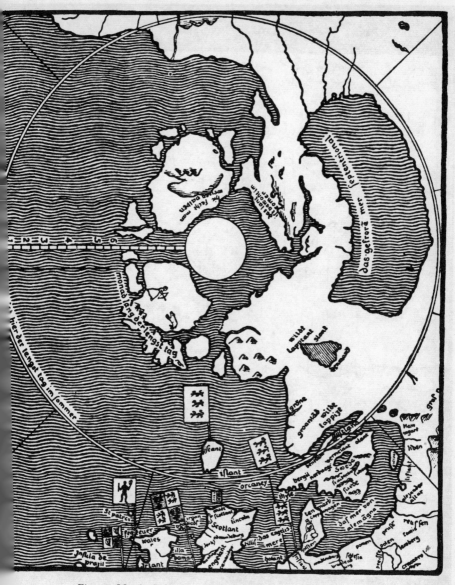

Fig. 33. Martin Behaim's globe of 1492, the northern part, including the Gulf of St. Lawrence—the *Gulfo* Quadrato.

[152]

hundred miles and on it live a few scattered Eskimo hunters. It has been claimed that a large race of Eskimo called *Tunit*, to whom the present race were slaves, used to be on this section of the coast. At Nakvak there are remains of old stone houses suggesting the possibility of truth in this."

Mr. L. E. F. English, Curator of the Newfoundland Museum in St. John's, in a letter of January 12, 1954, reports that a medieval Greenland sword was found not far from Hopedale, Labrador. "The sword," he writes, is 22″ in length and has a circular pommel and cross guard. The handle and hilt are of whalebone." The sword is now in the museum in St. John's.

It seems that these Tunit were not able to establish permanent villages on the Labrador or Baffinland coast, but were driven farther and farther north and west. Vilhjalmur Stefansson found a group of them on the shore of Coronation Gulf and spent a couple of months with them. He describes them at length as a very pleasing people. In the tribe of 200 people he found fifteen or more who were marked reversions to the original type. Professor Wm. Hovgaard in commenting on Stefansson says:[30]

> The widespread nature of the European characteristics among these tribes seem to show that the mixture took place at a very remote period . . . Since no intercourse between Eskimo and Europeans seems to have appeared in post-Columbian times . . . the only, or at least the most plausible explanation of the facts recorded by Stefansson seems to be that the Blond Eskimo are related to the Norse Greenlanders.

A Royal Expedition Sails to America in 1355

*I*T WAS mentioned in a preceding chapter that the seventeen Greenlanders who had been to Markland (Nova Scotia) in 1347 arrived in Iceland. These men, no doubt, had heard about the exodus of the Western Settlement in 1342, which must have been a much discussed subject in Greenland. It was therefore a most important item of news for them to relate on their arrival in Iceland. This news resulted in conferences with Jon Guthormson, one of the leading chiefs of Iceland. He was at that time in both public and royal disfavor. Sensing the political value of being the bearer of important tidings, he provided these Greenlanders with quarters for the winter, and the next spring he conducted them to the King in Norway to whom they reported that the Western Settlement had been laid waste.

This was no doubt grievous news to the king because he held the Greenland colonies in high esteem. The year before he had written his will, in which he left a sum, equal to about eight thousand dollars to the Greenland cathedral. But when the news of the apostasy and emigration of the people in the Western Settlement reached him, he was just starting out with a big army to compel the Russians to accept the Roman Catholic faith. King Magnus Erikson was an ardent, well-meaning monarch, but simple-minded and intolerant, who could not abide heresy, and his main endeavor in life was to compel the Greek Orthodox Catholics in Russia to accept the Church of Rome. In this campaign he was partly successful, captured a big fortress, and compelled hundreds of Russians, on the threat of death, to be baptized. Then he left a large garrison in charge of the fortress and returned with the army to Sweden. The Russians reassembled, and after a siege of six months they re-captured the fortress and put the garrison to death with much atrocity.

The king had no intention of dropping his crusade because of this defeat. But simultaneously with the news of it came the report from the western part of Norway that a pestilence had broken out, which threatened to exterminate the entire population. This was the terrible Black Death which in the middle of the 14th century spread over all Europe and Asia and laid many millon victims in their graves. The loss of life was not so great in Norway and Sweden as in other countries, owing to the more scattered condition of the population, but, even there, fully twenty-five percent of the population perished in the two years 1349 and 1350.

This terrible catastrophe did not stop but only delayed the king's attempts to convert the Russians. He sent a delegation to Pope Clement VI, asking him to declare a "holy war" against Russia, and without waiting for an answer set out with an-other army in 1351. This campaign was more disastrous than the former, and when he returned to Sweden the next year he had lost many men and all his financial resources.

On his return, however, he was met with good news. The Pope had hearkened to his request and ordered that a holy crusade be preached in Germany and Poland as well as in the Scandinavian countries. He also offered King Magnus the loan of half the tithe money (collected in Sweden and Norway) for 1351, and promised him the use of half of all the tithes collected during the four following years.

Full of cheer and the determination to plant the Roman cross in Russia, King Magnus now awaited the collection of the tithes. By 1353 abundant funds were coming in, and the king prepared for another campaign. But now the report was heard that the plague had spread such death in Russia that it would be suicidal to go there. Terrified by the memory of their own sickening experience, the people refused any inducement to take part in the proposed crusade.

The king was therefore obliged to give up his great mission against the Russians. However, he had the funds provided through the cooperation of the Pope, and was thus reminded of his obligations toward Greenland. His people there were falling away from Christianity. Seeing he could not go east, he would go west and there restore his subjects to the Church. We have a late copy of a letter issued by him in 1354, in which he provides for an extraordinary expedition to Greenland. At its head is placed Sir Paul Knutson, formerly Lawspeaker of Gulathing.[31] The following is a translation of the letter.

Magnus, by the grace of God, King of Norway, Sweden and Skaane, sends to all men who see or hear this letter [his wishes for their] good health and happiness.

We desire to make known to you that you [Paul Knutson] are to select the men who shall go in the Knorr [the royal trading vessel] . . . from among my bodyguard and also from the retainers of other men whom you may wish to take on the voyage, and that Paul Knutson the commandant shall have full authority to select such men whom he thinks are best qualified to accompany him, whether as officers or men. We ask that you accept this our command with a right good will for the cause, inasmuch as we do it for the honor of God and for our predecessors, who in Greenland established Christianity and have maintained it until this time, and *we will not let it perish in our days.* Know this for truth, that whoever defies this our command shall meet with our serious displeasure and receive full punishment.

Executed in Bergen, Monday after Simon and Judah's day in the six and xxx year of our rule (1354). By Orm Östenson, our regent, sealed.[32]

This is a forceful letter. The king emphasizes that the purpose of the expedition was not a commercial enterprise, but a holy mission to re-establish Christianity in Greenland. He also warns that whoever refuses to serve in this effort would meet with his serious displeasure.

The same determination to succeed is seen in the selection of the personnel. The king appointed Sir Paul Knutson as commandant, one of the leading men of his time, and a member of the Royal Council. He was previously the business manager of the Queen Dowager's large possessions in Sweden and Norway, a highly responsible office. Later he was Judge of Gulathing, the largest judicial district in Norway. This was the man chosen to lead this expedition into unknown parts of the world.

The rank and file of the men was also exceptionally good. While the commandant was given a free hand in selecting those who were best fitted to accompany him, he was instructed to choose some of the men from the King's Bodyguard, made up of the most promising young men of the kingdom, who served the King as his personal guards, messengers, and councillors. To become a member of the king's retinue required not only good birth, bodily fitness, and superior skill in arms, but also much tact, courtesy, and good sense. Appointment to the King's Bodyguard was the first major step toward knighthood, and all members of the bodyguard were considered to belong to the nobility.

The king was a descendant of the Folkunga family, the most powerful in West Gothland, Sweden, and his bodyguard was made up largely of young men from his own province. This favoritism was one of the chief causes of the rebellion a year or two later which deposed him as King of Sweden. Only West Gothland remained faithful to him, thanks to his bodyguard.

We have no report on the results of this expedition, and some critics have therefore assumed that it never took place. But such an assumption shows a failure to understand the religious fervor of the times. A king who was so worried about the eternal welfare of the people of another nation that he spent large sums of money to teach them the "true" faith— such a zealot would surely not be indifferent to the fact that his own people were relapsing into idolatry. He would do what he could to save his subjects and countrymen from hell-fire if he had the means and the time to do so. His emphatic letter to Sir Paul Knutson shows that he was profoundly disturbed about the matter.

Moreover, documentary evidence that the expedition took place can be found in Bishop Olaus Magnus' work, *Historia de gentibus septentrionalibus,* in a passage that is evidently an echo of the Paul Knutson expedition. The bishop writes:

> (In Greenland) live a kind of pirates who make use of skin boats . . . in which they attack merchant vessels, seeking to sink them by piercing their hulls from below instead of attacking them from above. In the year 1505 I personally saw two of these skin boats above the western portal within the cathedral dedicated to the sainted Halvard where they were put on the wall for general exhibition. It is stated that King Haakon captured them when he with his battle fleet passed the coast of Greenland just as they (the natives) prepared to sink his vessel in the sea . . . [33]

This passage is highly significant. It was, of course, an error when the cicerone of the cathedral told the future bishop that King Haakon had personally commanded this expedition. The years of his reign, 1355-1380, were filled with wars and intrigues, first with the Hanseatic League and then with King Albrecht in his vain attempts to secure his legitimate right to the throne of Sweden. Professor Munch's very complete biography shows that King Haakon did not once leave the Scandinavian countries. Divested of this embellishment, the information conveyed is that a royal naval expedition operated in Greenland waters during King Haakon's reign; that it was not of a commercial nature, but sailed in war vessels, and that it had unfriendly relations with the Eskimo. What else could be so described but the Paul Knutson expedition? It took place in King Haakon's time,[34] it was a royal expedition sent to Greenland, and it was not of a commercial nature. It was easy for oral tradition to dramatize this expedition for the redemption of the Greenland apostates into a royal battle fleet with the king himself in command.

But why did the Bishop of Oslo give these Eskimo kayaks a place of honor within the great cathedral? In those days there was no scientific interest in the customs of barbaric peoples, and a cathedral would be the last place for the exhibition of the crude craftsmanship of savages. But there was a religious reason which perfectly justified the presence of these skin boats on the wall of the cathedral. St. Halvard was the patron saint of Oslo, and he had been canonized, among other merits, for having given his life in attempting to save a person in great distress. His church was therefore the proper place to preserve these kayaks which, being the only mementos of the Paul Knutson expedition, symbolized the self-sacrifice of these men who had lost their lives in their crusade to save the apostate Greenlanders from eternal damnation. The very fact that they were allowed to occupy a place of honor in the Cathedral of Oslo and to remain there for generation after generation, until in fact the Protestant Reformation swept away all reminders of Catholicism, must emphasize how highly they were revered as mementos of a great religious enterprise.

According to Professor Storm, this expedition did not return from its western voyage until 1363 or more likely 1364, when the news finally reached Norway that Bishop Arni of Greenland was dead.[35] In 1365 a new bishop was appointed.

As this expedition was gone for eight or nine years, the question arises: Where did it go? No doubt it first went to Greenland to get what information there was about the apostate emigrants.

Here Paul Knutson would quickly learn that there was only one direction in which to look for these departed Greenlanders.

They could not have gone northward because the land in that direction was unfit for their mode of life; moreover, they wanted to get away from their enemies, not approach them. But only a few years previous, Hauk Erlendsson, a neighbor and predecessor of Paul Knutson as incumbent in the office of Gulathing's Lawspeaker, had compiled and transcribed a new edition of the saga that bears his name, *Hauksbook,* in which he tells about Vinland, the favorite region in America for all the early Norse explorers. Most likely, these new emigrants from Greenland would also sail to Vinland the Good, where some of their people had gone with Bishop Erik a couple of centuries earlier. Paul Knutson, whose business it was to be informed about the western lands to which he was going, very likely had read this book and knew as much about Vinland as was told therein. As to his finding Vinland, that would not be difficult. In Greenland he would hire a pilot from among the many men who had sailed to Markland, and Vinland was said to be only a couple of days sailing beyond, towards the southwest. On arriving there it would have been reasonable to select as good a harbor as possible, because he would have had to take into consideration the possibility of a long search for the people he was seeking, which would have necessitated a fortified headquarters with good land adjacent where food could be grown for the men of the expedition. The location of this harbor will be discussed later.

The Oldest
Native Document
of American History

IT HAS BEEN mentioned that the two Eskimo skin boats were given a conspicuous place on the wall of the cathedral in Oslo, where they remained for almost 200 years as a memorial of the great royal missionary enterprise of 1355-1364. Whatever report came back with them has now been lost in the mist of time, but there for hundreds of years stood the skin boats, the only surviving evidence of King Magnus's expedition.

Then, in the nineteenth century, a pioneer on the Minnesota frontier made a discovery which bridged a gap of more than 500 years and brings us back to Sir Paul Knutson and the young men of the King's Bodyguard who so courageously sailed away to save the souls of their countrymen in Greenland in 1355.

This discovery was the Kensington Stone, the oldest native document of American history.

There is a small village named Kensington in the southwestern corner of Douglas County in the west-central part of Minnesota. To the north and east lies the great lake park region of Minnesota, to the west and south stretches the endless prairie.

Up to 1867 this area had not yet been invaded by white men, but in that year the first settlers began to appear—a few poor but hardy pioneers who tackled the wilderness, several days' journey beyond the nearest railroad point. It was second-rate farm land with many moraines and swamps, and in consequence the settlement grew slowly. The land on which the stone was found was not tilled nor settled until 1891, at which time a man named Olof Ohman took possession of it.

Since the character and qualifications of Ohman have come up for discussion in a number of investigations of the Kensington Stone, a few biographical details will be pertinent here.

Olof Ohman was born in 1859 in Helsingland in the far north of the inhabited area of Sweden. He came to America in 1881 and worked at whatever labor was available among the early pioneers of Douglas County, Minnesota. The going wage was then one dollar a day, and even by industrious saving it was not until 1891 that Ohman was able to make a part payment on the tract of land near Kensington, Minnesota. He set to work at once to grub the trees.

Ohman was a large and powerful man. To remove tree and stump in a single operation, he dug a trench around the entire tree, cut the horizontal roots, and then, using the tree itself for leverage, pulled out the vertical roots. In November of 1898 he felled an aspen with a ten-inch trunk and found clutched in the two main vertical roots a flat stone almost three feet long on which were chiseled hundreds of marks that were obviously some sort of alphabet. (See Figure 7.) It was obvious that the stone had been in that spot for at least as long as the tree above it, for the roots had grown to the contours of the stone and were flat on the side that clutched it.

The news of Ohman's discovery spread, and many curious neighbors came to inspect the inscription, but though the carved letters were very neat, no one could so much as identify the language. Ohman himself, though curious, had had only nine months of schooling in his life, and though he could sign his name, he had to ask for help when it was necessary to write a letter. He turned therefore to J. P. Hedberg, local dealer in real estate, insurance, and steamship tickets. There is preserved a photostat of a letter written by Hedberg to the editor of the *Svenska Amerikanska Posten*, a weekly Swedish newspaper published in Minneapolis. The letter reads as follows:

Kensington, Minn. Jan. 1, 1899

Swan J. Turnblad
Minneapolis

I enclose you a copy of an inscription on a stone found about 2 miles from Kensington by a O. Ohman he found it under a tree when Grubbing. he wanted I should go out and look at it and I told him to haul it in when he came (not thinking much of it) and he did so, and this is an exsest copy of it the first part is of the flat side of the stone the other was on flat edge. I thought I would send it to you as you perhaps have means to find out what it is—it appears to be old Greek letters. pleas let me hear from you and oblige.

Yours truly

J. P. HEDBERG

The editor did not know the language of the inscription nor could he find anyone who did. After two months of inquiry he printed Hedberg's letter and the copy of the inscription in the issue of February 28, 1899.

Shortly after Hedberg sent his letter, Mr. S. A. Sieverts, manager of the bank in Kensington, sent either a copy of the inscription or the stone itself to Professor O. J. Breda, head of the Department of Scandinavian Languages at the University of Minnesota.[35a]

Unfortunately, Professor Breda knew very little about runes, and although he struggled with the inscription for two months, he was unable to translate all of it. There were fourteen words which baffled him, including the date and all other numerals. However, he made out the word *Vinland*. That was the name that Leif Erikson had given to a certain part of America, and

Breda therefore concluded that the inscription purported to tell something about Leif Erikson's discovery. But as that discovery occurred about the year 1000, when the language was entirely different from the language on the stone, he decided that the inscription was spurious. He sent a report on the inscription with his conclusions to the University of Oslo, and there they were accepted without question. The story was used, publicly and privately, as a sample of "the irresponsible trickery that characterizes the American people." This scoffing attitude was in part a result of jealous resentment because of the great emigration to America in the closing decades of the 19th century. During the seven years from 1886 to 1892 about 300,000 of Norway's and Sweden's young men and women had been persuaded to leave for the United States. This was a tremendous drain of manpower from countries with such small populations. The upper classes, therefore, had reason to feel unfriendly toward America, and the newspapers missed no opportunity to print stories about the depravity "characteristic" of America with the hope of checking the emigration. The report came back from Oslo swiftly and sternly: the Kensington inscription was a silly, meaningless forgery.

This verdict left the people of Kensington and vicinity in great confusion. They did not question the verdict of the judges. If the great scholars in the home country said the inscription was a forgery, then, of course, it must be so. But a bothersome question persisted in their minds: How could a forgery be committed without a forger? The settlement was only thirty-one years old, and the disposition, aptitude, and education of every man was well known. There were none who had the knowledge, skill and time to sit for days carving ancient inscriptions on rocks which could bring them no profit. Privately the antecedents of every man were inquired into and checked, but to no avail. Then someone mentioned Sven Fogelblad, a kindly old minister who had lost his license to preach because of his fondness for liquor. He did not live in the settlement;

in fact, he had no home, but tramped about from settlement to settlement and was always welcome because he brought people up to date on births and burials in other places. He was very lazy and had no mechanical skill, but could do a fair job repairing a leaky pan and helping the children with the catechism. For a while he was suspected because many believed that as Fogelblad had studied theology, he must be informed about all kinds of mystic arts. Others, however, doubted this line of reasoning and finally a self-appointed committee called on Reverend Nordström, the pastor of Hoffman, a community about ten miles west of Kensington. He told them that runology was not taught in the theological seminaries, thus upsetting the theory of Fogelblad's philological training as a natural consequence of his ministry.

There was in any case the question of opportunity. The stone was found in plain view of Nils Flaten's house, and as it was too heavy to be carried, the inscription must have been chiselled on the spot where it was found. But any such "forger" would certainly have been seen by Flaten who had lived there since 1884. And what could have been the motive for such a laborious forgery? Completely mystified, Olof Ohman hauled home his stone and dumped it down by the granary door, fortunately with the inscribed face down. For nine years it lay there dishonored and forgotten, its message apparently as dead as last year's leaves.

At the time the stone was found and rejected, I was a student at the University of Wisconsin, absorbed in the writing of my Master's thesis on The Age and Home of the Elder Edda. I, therefore, knew nothing about the Kensington Stone. But nine years later I accidentally came in contact with it. At that time I was writing a history of the Norwegian settlements in America. In order to get material for this work, it was necessary to visit all these settlements and get the facts from the old pioneers. One of the last settlements I visited was Kensington, a very small Scandinavian community. As I went from house to house inquiring about past experiences, almost the only thing I heard was the story of this runic stone. As I had studied runes and Old Norse in the university and knew a little about these things, my curiosity was aroused, and I went to see Mr. Ohman. He showed me the stone and told me that certain scholars in Norway or Sweden said it was a forgery. As I had read the works of several of them and held them in highest esteem, I did not doubt their verdict. But this neatly engraved stone was a work of art, and I thought it would be an interesting souvenir of my history-hunting years. Ohman did not care for the stone, and the result of my visit was that he gave it to me.

The book which I was writing demanded my immediate attention, and some months passed before I could begin the study of my "souvenir." The inscription was not difficult to decipher (see Figure 7). The following is my translation made at the time; the words in the parentheses are not in the inscription:

> (We are) 8 Goths (Swedes) and 22 Norwegians on (an) exploration journey from Vinland round about the west. We had camp by (a lake with) 2 Skerries one day's journey north from this stone. We were (out) and fished one day. After we came home (we) found ten of our men red with blood and dead. AVM (Ave Virgo Maria) save (us) from evil.
> (We) have ten men by the sea to look after our ships 14 days-journeys from this island. (In the) year (of our Lord) 1362.[36]

I then consulted the old newspapers to learn why it had been condemned. To my surprise I found that Breda's rejection was based on the fact that the inscription was not written in Old Norse, the language of Leif Erikson. But the inscription had nothing to do with Leif Erikson and his time. The date is 1362, and by that time the language of eastern Norway and Sweden had changed into a speech not much different from that of the present, just as England's Anglo-Saxon by Chaucer's time had changed to a speech much like the present. While the matter of the date did not prove the authenticity of the inscription, it did show that it had been condemned on false evidence, which, in turn, suggested the possibility of other errors. I was also much impressed by the circumstances of the stone *in situ,* which seemed to eliminate the possibility that the inscription was made in recent times. I wrote a couple of articles about these things which came to the attention of the Minnesota Historical Society, and it appointed a committee to investigate the matter.

This commitee had a very capable personnel. Professor N. H. Winchell and Dr. Warren Upham were nationally famous geologists; E. C. Mitchell was an antiquarian, O. D. Wheeler was a lawyer, and F. J. Schaefer was rector of a Catholic institution of learning. Upon request I sent the stone to St. Paul, and it lay in the office of the Secretary of the committee for more than a year. It was weighed and measured and reported to be 36 inches long, 15 inches wide, five and a half inches thick, and weighed 230 pounds. It was ascertained that the stone when found by Olof Ohman lay with its face down. While the stone remained in the office of the Society, it was examined microscopically for evidence of the age of the inscribed characters, not only by members of the committee, but also by many visiting scientists. After much study in every possible direction, the committee in April, 1910 rendered a unanimous favorable opinion on the authenticity of the inscription.[37]

At the same time there was another committee at work, appointed by The Norwegian Society of Minneapolis. This committee was headed by Dr. Knut Hoegh, a prominent surgeon of that city. He made several trips to Kensington and other places for the purpose of obtaining statements and affidavits from persons who had inspected the stone and the stump of the tree immediately after it was dug up. Affidavits from a number of persons were thus obtained. Although working independently, this committee came to the same conclusion as the other.[38]

Many scholars, however, refused to accept these findings. They based their objection on the fact that the inscription had been rejected by several experts when it was first found, and concluded, therefore, that it must have been forgery. They forgot, or did not know, that that early rejection was clearly based on false premises. The result has been a long controversy on questionable runes and linguistics.

It seems to me that these irregularities are good evidence of 14th century authorship. A forger would naturally try to make his inscription as free as possible from linguistic and runological fault. To that end, he would pattern it after textbook usage. Certainly he would not present different spellings for the same word.

On the other hand, a man of the Middle Ages, working under tension would naturally make many errors. Spelling and grammatical usage had not become standardized in the 1300's, but varied from district to district; the writer's education may well have been sketchy; and he was far removed in time and space from either previous writing experience or models to refer to.

Even today the letters of passably educated persons present frequent blunders in grammar, spelling and sometimes even in formation of characters. Yet they are the work of men who read and write daily. It would seem that those who cavil at such irregularities in the inscription lack a realistic conception of human nature.

The linguistic aspects of the inscription have been very thoroughly examined and accepted in three detailed studies by Professor William Thalbitzer, Professor S. N. Hagen and myself.[39] Thalbitzer's dissertation was translated and re-published by the Smithsonian Institution. The reader will find a survey of the most recent arguments in Appendix A and B of the present volume.

It would greatly simplify the solution of the question concerning the authenticity of the inscription if the critics would lay aside their philological calipers for a while and take a good look at the circumstances surrounding the finding of the stone. They would then find three independent facts so clear and convincing as to leave no doubt about the age of the inscription. These three proofs are:

1. The age of the tree above the stone.

2. The reference to "this island."

3. The weathering of the inscription.

THE AGE OF THE TREE

Dr. Knut Hoegh of Minneapolis made a thorough inquiry concerning the size of the tree and correlated his findings with the age of similar trees in the vicinity which were cut down and their annual rings of growth counted. This study indicated that the tree was about seventy years old. These figures were checked by comparison with the statistics presented in two pamphlets published by the Federal Forestry Bureau, one dealing with aspens in Maine, the other with aspens in Utah.[40] Based on the counting of annual rings of growth of thousands of trees, the figures showed that an average tree with a diameter of eight inches breast high (the size of the tree above the stone), if grown in Maine with an annual rainfall of 41 inches, would be about 42 years old. If grown in Utah with a rainfall of 12 inches, it would be 96 years old. If grown in western Minnesota with a rainfall of 26 inches, which in rainfall is midway between that of Utah and Maine, it would be 69 years old. These findings agree very well with the affidavits obtained by Dr. Hoegh and show that the inscribed stone was in its finding place at least twenty years before the first settlers came to Minnesota and almost forty years before any Scandinavian came to Douglas County where the stone was found.

THE REFERENCE TO "THIS ISLAND"

The inscription refers to the finding place of the stone as an island ("14 days journeys from this island"). No one would think of calling this elevation an island now, because it is merely a slight rise on a rolling prairie. Nor was it an island when the first settlers came. Figure 10 is a photostatic copy of the original plat of the township made by the government surveyor on the spot in 1866, the year before the first settlers came. This plat shows every elevation, lake, swamp and watercourse, and the topography is precisely the same as it is now. Even the small swamp to the northeast of the finding place of the stone in section 14 is shown and marked "dry," and the steep part of the knoll where the stone was found is marked with a sign something like a crescent. To change any part of this area into an island would require some tilting of the surface of the land. Is there any probability that any such disturbance of the topography has taken place?

Yes. It is a well-known fact that the greater northern part of the continent has been subject to many upheavals in the aftermath of the glacial invasion. When the last glacier spread a blanket of ice, many thousand feet thick, over Canada and the northern states of our country, this tremendous weight depressed the surface of the earth hundreds of feet according to the thickness of the glacial ice. Later, when the ice melted, the surface sprang back again in a series of upheavals in adjusting to the enormous decrease in pressure upon it. In most places little is known of the height of these successive upheavals, but in northwestern Minnesota we have very specific information because of the fact that the broad Red River Valley was once a great glacial lake. The valley extends from the continental divide at Brown's Valley, Minnesota, and slopes northward about 400 miles to Lake Winnipeg. When the southern part of the glacier melted, the valley became a great lake because the outlet to the north remained closed for a long period. This former lake left thirty-one broad and high beaches which mark the boundaries of the lake at successive periods.

These lines of beaches are not horizontal as would be expected, but have an upward tilt to the north averaging a little more than a foot per mile. Thus, we find the great Herman beach, which marks the highest altitude of the glacial lake, is 1055 feet above the sea at Lake Traverse, the southern outlet of the lake, and 1182 feet at Maple Lake, 120 miles farther north in a straight line. These measurements prove that the earth's crust at a much later time was subjected to a series of uplifts which raised it 127 feet in this distance.[41]

According to Dr. Upham, each of these 31 successive beaches is the result of a new upheaval because they are not truly parallel with each other but follow slightly different angles of incline. There are also some irregularities in the altitude of the beaches which indicate minor local disturbances.

These many upheavals and other disturbances must have taken many thousand years as they successively built up very wide and high beaches (300 to 400 feet wide and 15 to 20 feet high) and also vast deltas covering thousands of square miles. The latest may therefore well have taken place within the last 500 years. In fact, Prof. L. E. Martin,[42] Prof. F. T. Thwaites, and Dr. Warren Upham all say that these upheavals and tiltings are going on at the present time. As the Kensington Stone was found only 15 miles east of the great Herman beach, it is probable that the oscillations of the nearby surface closely followed the pattern recorded by the beaches. Because of these disturbances, Prof. N. H. Winchell, State Geologist of Minnesota writes:

I am convinced from the geological conditions and the physical changes which the region has experienced, probably during the last 500 years, that the stone contains a genuine record of a Scandinavian exploration into Minnesota, and must be accepted as such for the date named.[43]

THE WEATHERING OF THE INSCRIPTION

The inscription covers the larger half of a slab of graywacke. This is a very hard stone which weathers slowly, but many geologists have called attention to the fact that the inscribed characters in this area show a weathering which is just as marked as the uninscribed area of the stone. A sample of these expressions is Dr. Upham's statement. He says.[44]

> When we compare the excellent preservation of the glacial scratches shown on the back of the stone, which were made several thousand years ago, with the mellow, time-worn appearance of the face of the inscription, the conclusion is inevitable that this inscription must have been carved many hundred years ago.

In the lower left corner of the inscribed area is seen a lighter colored surface (see Figure 8). This is a layer of calcite. This softer stone has been so corroded by rain, after the inscription was made, as to remove a sizable layer of its surface. In fact, it is so worn down that some of the characters here have been obliterated and can only be read by help of the context. In most photographs they show up more plainly because the runes have usually been traced over with a pencil to make them readable.

In view of the fact that the stone when found lay with its inscribed face down, and was so well-covered with soil that an eight-inch tree grew upon it, how did it obtain its weathered, corroded appearance? Certainly not when it lay buried in the ground. The Geological Survey of the Department of the Interior writes me that:

> The weathering of stones is mainly chemical and takes place only at the surface of the ground. The stones may, therefore, be perfectly fresh or unaltered until they are exposed for a time at the surface to the corrosive action of rainfall containing acids absorbed from the atmosphere and surface soils.[45]

A good illustration of this process is given in note 45. This weathered appearance therefore proves that the stone, after it was inscribed, stood upright exposed to the elements for a long time. Eventually it fell down, and it must have remained in that position for a considerable period to give time for it to become covered with soil. These two long periods must therefore be added to the age of the tree.

Had the stone been carved at its place of discovery? Even eliminating the strong evidence of the inscription's reference to "this island," there can be no doubt on the basis of these findings that the stone lay underground for the sixty-nine years represented by the age of the tree. Thus, we know as surely as evidence can point out that it was there in 1829, decades before the first white settlers arrived. Moreover, some time would have been required for soil to cover the stone. On this evidence alone it must certainly have been in its finding place at the start of the 19th Century.

The evidence is unmistakeable, moreover, that the stone had stood upright long enough to undergo substantial weathering. Dr. Upham cites this weathering as conclusive evidence that the stone had been carved "many hundred years ago."

Geologists who have examined the stone's weathering have been impressed from the first by its evidences of great age. Two months after the stone was first found Professor George O. Curme of Northwestern University had it in his office for two weeks and subjected the inscription to repeated microscopic examination. Although he deferred to Professor Breda's insistence that the inscription was not written in old Icelandic and was therefore a forgery, his estimate of the age of the inscription leaves no doubt of his own findings:

> The letters of the inscription were evidently carved with a sharp instrument, for they are clear and distinct in outline. But the fact that the upper edge of the incised line is rough and rounded as a result of the disintegration of the stone, while the bottom of the incisions is sharp and clear shows plainly that many years must have elapsed since the inscription was cut.

> In other words, the external appearance of the Kensington rune stone, so far from speaking against it, is such that the inscription may well be 600 years old.[45a]

THE HUNT FOR A FORGER

Despite the accumulation of physical evidence, the first doubts cast by faulty reasoning on the authenticity of the Kensington Stone continued to color the attitude of scholars and it was, accordingly, with doubt and even with definite disbelief that the committees appointed to investigate the Stone began their work.

This was also the early attitude of the members of the committee appointed by the Minnesota Historical Society. Professor N. H. Winchell, for instance, told me a couple of years later that he welcomed his appointment to this task, because he at that time had no faith in the authenticity of the inscription and looked forward to exposing me as a promoter of a hoax. Someone must have made the inscription, but who could that someone be? A pioneer settlement on the frontier in the heart of America seemed a most unlikely place to find a runic inscription; but someone had been there who felt so expert in runic lore that he buoyantly chiseled the next to the longest of all known runic inscriptions. It was therefore natural that the committee would first investigate Olof Ohman who found the stone.

Because of lack of other possible suspects, Ohman became the target of all investigators from 1898 to the present time. It has become an either-or problem; either the inscription was made by Ohman or it is authentic. As Karl M. Nielsen, an eminent philologist of Copenhagen, said in 1950: "If the inscription was made in the 19th century, then the author can be none other than Ohman."

It has been shown above that the position of the stone when found, in full view of Nils Flaten and his family, besides the age of the tree under which it was found, the mention of the finding place as an island, and the age-old patina of the inscription, all separately prove that Ohman could have had nothing to do with the chiselling of the inscription. But, to make the record complete, the conclusions of the investigators are here added. Professor Winchell, the Secretary of the Historical Society, visited Ohman and the people in the vicinity three times. He wrote a long and detailed report on Ohman and closed with these words:

> The honesty and candor of Mr. Ohman become evident to anyone who converses with him. Not one of all who have interviewed him, whether believers or non-believers in the authenticity of the inscription, has seen any reason to question his veracity.[46]

Dr. Knut Hoegh, the chairman of the committee appointed by The Norwegian Society of Minneapolis, also made several visits to Ohman and others. His report concludes as follows:

> There is no possibility that Ohman can have made the inscription. He is an intelligent but uneducated farmer who according to his own statement had had only a few months' schooling in all his life. He appears to be very dependable; his personality would make him an excellent witness in a court of law. He cannot with any probability be supposed to have carved the runes and planted the stone.[46]

Winchell also interviewed the local pastor who had confirmed all the sons of Ohman. "He said he had known Ohman for twenty years and he was convinced that Ohman was utterly incapable of making the inscription."

THE TECHNIQUE OF THE RUNE-CARVER

An unexpected expert testimony was added to the record recently when Mr. Jay Edgerton of the *Minneapolis Star* interviewed the well-known Minnesota sculptor, John K. Daniels. Mr. Daniels, it developed had made a careful study of the carving technique used in making the inscription. The following is a verbatim copy of Mr. Edgerton's report of the interview:

> A sculptor, trained to work in stone, familiar with the chisel and what it does to surfaces, sees things the untrained eye

misses. Daniels believes these things bear on the authenticity or spuriousness of the Kensington Stone.

The rune stone (Mr. Daniels explains) is fascinating to a man who works in stone because of the highly individual characteristics of its carver—or carvers. There may have been two of them. If the stone is the work of one man, then certainly he was ambidextrous. He could work with equal facility with both his left and right hands.

Daniels explains that the chiseling on the stone is what a sculptor would describe as "one stroke" work. It was done with a hammer and chisel mostly working from right to left—although towards the end of the inscription the strokes are from left to right. He says that the inscription was put on quickly with sure deft strokes by a person thoroughly familiar with carving runes. The whole job may have taken about two hours.

The carver of the rune stone, in Daniel's opinion, was interested only in getting his message on the stone as quickly as possible. And the sculpted evidence is unmistakable that the job was done in a hurry. Such swift work bespeaks the accomplished artist and is quite inconceivable in the hands of a rustic laborer or farmer like Olof Ohman or any of his neighbors.[47]

Mooring Stones
and Camp Sites

A MOORING STONE is a large boulder or part of a rock formation on the shore of a lake or fjord, in which is chiseled a hole,
several inches deep, for the purpose of holding a ringbolt. It
thus serves as a pier for mooring a boat. In Norway and Sweden,
where there are many fishermen, and where the water is often
deep right up to the shore, making it difficult to build piers,
there are hundreds of them. They are also common on the
rocky shores of inland lakes in these countries.

In the city of Wilmington, Delaware, where the Swedes settled in 1638 and built a fort, a vein of rock emerges on the
bank of Christina River, and here may still be seen about a
dozen of these mooring rings or their broken remains. In or
near Gloucester, Massachusetts, where there were many Norwegian fishermen, there are also mooring holes or rings left
by them.

In the interior part of America, no mooring stones are known
to have existed, except in Minnesota, where ten have been
found. They are not scattered about over the State, but are
found along a crooked waterway from Hawley in the northwestern part of Minnesota to Sauk Centre in the central part.
They are all found on the shore of a lake or former lake, and

their pattern is the same in all. The holes are a little less than an inch in diameter, but not quite round, and from four to seven inches deep. The axis of each hole inclines slightly toward the lake, and the old settlers in each vicinity report that these chiselled holes were there when they came. Dr. J. Bröndsted in Copenhagen inspected some of these mooring holes and was impressed by the evidence of their age. He writes: "The Minnesota mooring holes seem to indicate the presence of pre-Columbian Nordic people." [48]

I have traveled over the route and inspected these ancient holes many times, and it is plain that they mark a passable waterway across a large part of the State. Figures 17A and 17B are sketch maps showing the location of all the ten mooring stones, as precisely as is possible on such small maps. It is clear that these mooring holes were made by a party of men who traveled across the State in a large boat. They could not have been early furtraders because the latter used Indian canoes, which required no special mooring—they were light enough to be picked up and carried up on the shore. Likewise, the pioneers used only flat-bottomed punts which were easily pulled up on land.

Who were these men who left these ten mooring holes as mementos that they camped on the shore of these lakes for at least ten days? They must have constituted a fairly large party since they used a boat so big that it required this kind of mooring. The only large party of men reported to have visited this area before immigration began was the Kensington Rune Stone party. They were presumably familiar with this characteristic Norse method of mooring a boat, and as they were twenty in number and probably carried considerable freight, they needed this kind of mooring. Upon consulting several ship captains, I learned that this would require a boat about 27 feet long, weighing about 1500 pounds. It is, of course, possible that two boats were used.

Furthermore, as the Kensington inscription says that they came from the north, they must have traveled right through this region. In fact, two of these mooring stones are located on the two spots mentioned in the inscription. It mentions "the island" where they left the inscribed stone, and here we find a mooring stone. It also mentions a lake marked with two skerries about 75 miles north of "the island." This is Cormorant Lake, the only lake in western Minnesota which is thus marked. Here also is a mooring stone.

Finally, these mooring stones are all in the same area where most of the medieval Norse implements have been found, as is told in the next chapter. Let us now see to what extent, if any, these mooring stones agree with the route which these explorers would necessarily have followed to reach Cormorant Lake and the finding place of the Kensington stone.

The inscription says that thirty Swedes and Norwegians set out from Vinland (on the Atlantic coast). Nothing is said about how they reached Minnesota, but it must have been by way of Hudson Bay. There are two things that prove this. One is their statement that they came to "the island" from the north. The other is the fact that only from Hudson Bay is there a waterway leading into northwestern Minnesota. They could not have come by way of the Great Lakes, because the inscription says that they left ten men in charge of their vessels by "the ocean," that is, the salt sea. We do not positively know why the party divided at Hudson Bay, but it is not unlikely that these adventurous young men were curious to see what the interior of this new continent looked like. Shortly before they left Norway, news had come from Venice of the great discoveries made by Marco Polo in the Celestial Kingdom of the great Khan, beyond the vast deserts. These selected members of the King's Bodyguard may have been keen to learn if something similar was to be seen in this new land. However, it was possible that the great river before them (the Nelson) came from a high table-land like Norway, where progress by boat would be impossible. It would seem reasonable that ten men were left in charge of their sailing vessels as a safety measure, with instructions to remain until a certain date, after which they were to sail.

It is also possible that they may have thought that an overland journey would be shorter than the long sea voyage by which they had come. The bleak ramparts of Hudson Strait, Labrador and Newfoundland certainly offered them nothing to make them wish to make a second visit.

The waterway from Hudson Bay via the Nelson River and Red River to northwestern Minnesota is fairly direct. The lower part of the Nelson is wide and placid. The upper part is difficult, but not difficult enough to have prevented the early Hudson's Bay Company men from pushing through, and the Norsemen of 1362 could probably also manage it. On reaching Lake Winnipeg, they had a straight course southward for 300 miles. As it would be necessary to spend several nights in harbors along the east coast, it is likely that several mooring holes may be found along the shore; but a thorough search has not yet been made. At the south end of the lake is the mouth of Red River which also has a straight north and south channel for about 300 miles.

After several weeks of this continuous course southward, it is likely that the explorers would become restless, because their destination (Vinland) lay mainly eastward. They would therefore look for a promising branch leading east or southeast. The most promising tributary from the east is Buffalo River. It drains about a thousand square miles of land and joins the Red River about twelve miles north of Moorhead, Minnesota. Moreover, its course, as far as the explorers could see across the flat prairie, was due southeast. Finally this is the *only* waterway that leads to Cormorant Lake, the lake with the two skerries.

After rowing their heavy boat against the current for two days, the explorers would find that the river channel made a turn of ninety degrees and continued in a northeasterly direction. This was not so good. But toward the southeast they saw a string of lakes (perhaps one big lake at that time) extending as far as they could see. It might well have been too promising an opening to be neglected, for a very short portage could bring them to the lake. But on proceeding six or seven miles they came to the end and were confronted both east and south by a horizon of gently rising firm land. Was there an opening somewhere? The answer called for many hours of work by the scouts. Meanwhile the daily need of food had to be supplied, and a camp was made for the night.

Here, on the south shore of this lake is mooring stone number 1 (see Figure 17A).

This mooring stone lies just behind the farm buildings of the late O. N. Bjorndahl in section 12, Skree township, about seven miles straight south from Hawley. It was reported by Mr. Bjorndahl in 1931. He was not among the earliest settlers who came in the late 1870's, but being an intelligent man, he inquired of them if they knew anything about this stone. He found it was well known, because stones are very rare on the bed of former Lake Agassiz, and was told by several men that the deep hole in it had been noted by them, because the fishing was very good in this lake and it was frequently visited. Even without this testimony, Bjorndahl was convinced that the hole could not have been chiseled as late as 1875, because its patina showed a long period of exposure.

As the explorers found themselves in a dead end, the only thing they could do was to return to the river the way they had come and see if its channel found a way around the high land to the east. They rowed up the river about ten miles and came to a small lake. Here, on the south side, lies mooring stone number 2. It lies about sixteen miles from the first, which distance suggests one day of travel, because more than half of the distance was against the current. Reverend S. G. Hauge, who has been pastor of the local congregation for more than fifty years and lives close by, writes:

> The stone is very large, the part above the ground weighing perhaps two ton. The hole which is eight inches deep and somewhat triangular in form is weathered so smooth as to seem like glass inside. Bjorndahl, who had measurements with him, found that in its diameter and position it was just the same as the hole in his own stone and in the stone at Cormorant Lake. It is now about twenty feet above the river level. It is not difficult to believe that the water may have been that high, as it has been almost that high since I came here. It is a most remarkable discovery for it is plain to everyone that the hole was not bored or drilled since white man settled in this region.[49]

From this mooring stone to the next is only three miles, which seems too short for a day's journey. But it was probably the hardest day of the entire trip. The main river turned off in a northerly direction just above the little lake, and the travelers chose to follow the smaller stream which led eastward. It is and was a small stream, filled with boulders and very rapid. It must have been a back-breaking job to drag the heavy boat against the current, but with twenty husky young men it was accomplished. At the west end of Stinking Lake, from which this branch issues, lies mooring stone number 3.

Although I have spent a part of every summer for many years in searching for mooring stones, I have found only two. The other eight have been reported to me by local residents and summer resorters. One of the two I found is this stone at Stinking Lake. I felt confident that the explorers after their mighty struggle with the boat in that stony creek would need a rest upon reaching the lake, but I found no one who had seen any mooring stone. I walked clear around this lake, but saw only its myriad of dead and dying little frogs which are probably the cause of its evil name.

After a careful inspection of the shore, I found that the lake level at one time was about four feet higher than at present. In that case the mooring stone was probably not lying on the beach, but was protruding from the surface of the very steep, almost perpendicular, hillside. In the course of time erosion would liberate the stone, and it would slide down, possibly into the lake. This theory proved correct for I found the stone after some search, almost completely immersed in the slimy bog which has now taken the place of the lake, close to its outlet. It is a very proper specimen of an ancient mooring stone. It is five feet long, thirty inches wide, and of unknown thickness. The mooring hole is 7½" deep, and its interior is as smoothly weathered as any of the others.

With the river's help, the explorers had gotten up to the plateau which is 300 feet above the Red River valley prairie. At the east end of the lake they continued up the same watercourse which for the greater distance led through a string of lakes, south-southeast from their last camp site. Finally they came to a low ridge separating the Buffalo River basin from the Pelican. Here they made a portage to Nelson Lake about 1000 feet away. The distance from the Stinking Lake site is about sixteen miles. As the portage would take a half day, this is a fair day's run. On the north shore of Nelson Lake is mooring stone number 4. Fig. 12 shows a photograph of it.

This stone lies directly in front of the house of Peter Nelson whose father was one of the first homesteaders in this region early in the 1870's. Peter Nelson says that neither he nor his father bored this hole, and that no one else had bored any holes on his property. The hole is 7½" deep.

From Nelson Lake (or Tub Lake as it is also called) there is a dry run a half mile long to West Cormorant Lake. This run is now high above the lake level, but Mr. Nelson says that in his youth he often speared pickerel in it. West Cormorant is a large shallow lake with many islands, but its reputation for fish is poor. At the south end is a low reef which formerly was under water. Here connection is made with Big Cormorant Lake, the biggest and deepest of all the lakes the travelers would have seen in Minnesota, and containing two skerries (naked rocky islands) just like hundreds of skerries they had seen in the homeland. In the northwestern corner they found some large boulders well suited to serve as pier for the boat. Here is mooring stone number 5, seven inches deep (see Figure 11). The weathered condition of this hole was noted by a party of men in 1879 before any settlers had taken land around the lake.

It is possible that several days were spent at this campsite because the Kensington inscription, after describing the location, says: "We were out and fished *one day.*" Possibly their food supply had greatly dwindled since they left their campsite number 1 four days earlier. This lack of food is indicated by the fact that no less than ten men went out to fish. But while they were far out, perhaps behind a promontary, the ten men in the camp were attacked by the Indians and all were killed.

The land around Big Cormorant is not desirable for farming as it is mostly low and swampy on the south, east and north sides, and has big stony hills on the west side. It therefore had few if any settlers until in the 1880's. But this mooring stone was seen in the spring of 1870 before there was a single settler in all Becker County. Below is a copy of a letter by Mr. E. O. Estenson, a highly respected citizen of Crookston, Minnesota, who was a member of the group mentioned. He is now 95 years old, but still vigorous in mind and body.

Crookston, Minn., Nov. 1, 1945.

In the spring of 1870, my father and some other men set out from Hartland, near Albert Lea, Minnesota, to look for land in the northern part of the State. I was permitted to go along. I was then ten and a half years old. We had a team of horses and a covered wagon.

After traveling several hundred miles, we came to Cormorant Lake in Becker County, Minn. We were now well beyond the last settlers. The entire Red River Valley and surrounding parts were empty of white men, except for a few Indian forts

and Hudson Bay trading posts. We camped on the west side
of this lake, near its northern end. Here we caught some fish.
We had no boat, but there were some big rocks there, and
the water was deep enough so we could fish from the shore.
We cleaned our fish on these rocks and noticed a neatly drilled
hole in one of them. We were puzzled to find this drilled hole,
but thought that the Indians had somehow made it. We then
turned northwest and followed the Red River for about sixty
miles until we came to a spot, later known as Frog Point, about
five miles northwest of the present village of Climax in Polk
County. Here we found very good land and settled, but we
first continued north into Canada.

On our return to Hartland, we stopped again and fished at
Cormorant Lake. It was very easy to locate the rocks because
a small, naked, rocky island lay a few hundred feet off shore.
While my father was cleaning the fish, I was poking in the
crevice between two big rocks and found a small fire-steel.
The next year, 1871, we moved up and became permanent
settlers, the first white settlers in Polk County.

E. O. ESTENSON.

This hole is seven inches deep, its inner surface showing an
ancient weathered appearance.

Cormorant Lake has no inlet but has had two outlets. Now
there are none, because the water level has dropped perhaps
fifteen feet in the last thirty years. The rocks on which the men
stood while fishing in 1870 are now 150 feet from the lake
and high above it. The skerries which were perfect skerries in
1919, when I first saw them, are now the outer end of two
wooded peninsulas.

There is no telling which of these two outlets was used in
1362, but both of them lead to Pelican Lake where we find the
next mooring stone. The shorter route is southward by means
of a creek which comes out in the form of a big spring, just
a few rods south of the big lake. The creek meanders down
through a large swamp to Pelican Lake, three miles south.

Pelican Lake is fed by a river and at its outlet is a dam,
so that the high water level of ancient times is mantained.

Near the outlet of the lake, on the southeast side, is mooring stone number 6, a short day's run from the campsite on Cormorant Lake. This stone was reported to me by Shelley Hanna, a graduate student at the University of North Dakota, majoring in archaeology, who said that his brother, Marshall Hanna, and John A. Staples, an instructor in the University, found it while searching the shore of Pelican Lake for mooring stones. I have a written statement from Mr. Staples confirming his part in the discovery of the stone. It was found where a small rocky point projects into the lake. The stone lies near the end of this curving point, on the inside of it. It is four feet long, a little more than three feet wide, and the hole is five inches deep, smoothly polished on the inside.

As this area on the southeast side of Pelican Lake consists of stony moraines and small swamps, it is still a wilderness of eight or nine square miles save for a few tourist cabins of recent date. Shelley Hanna feels sure that the hole was drilled before the coming of the tourists, and he noted the weathered condition of the interior of the hole. A farmer in the vicinity remembers seeing the hole more than thirty years ago, before there were any tourist cabins in the vicinity.

The following is part of the report on this stone, made by Otto Zeck, an archaeologist of Detroit Lakes, Minnesota:

> The whole hook-shaped point is composed of stones of all sizes. The lake shore, both north and south, is very stony. There is no road of any kind into this location. I had to walk a half mile through the woods from a small farm to the east. The only possible way to haul out building stone would be by boat—which would require a steam-driven barge—or by sled in winter. Early in the winter the ice would not be thick enough, and after the first snow storm from the northwest this area would be drifted very deep with snow, especially where the stone lies, on the inside of the hook.

Here we have all the six mooring stones in the first group, *one day's journey between each,* depending upon the circumstances encountered such as going upstream or downstream, portages etc.

Upon leaving Pelican Lake, the explorers had an easy time because they were now able to float down stream for fifty miles. However, at the end of that distance they came to a sudden stop, because the river made an abrupt turn to the west. From a hill nearby, they could follow it westward with their eyes until it joined Red River, thirty miles away.

As they found only solid land to the south, they were obliged to turn east. Here they found a string of lakes, some of them connected, until they reached Swan Lake, five miles away. In view of the laborious journey from the big bend to this lake, it is probable that they camped here where fishing would be better than in the small lakes they had passed, but I have not yet had any opportunity to inspect it.

At Swan Lake they came to another watercourse, the Pomme de Terre River, which flowed southward. Ten miles south of Swan Lake they came to a large lake, called Ten Mile Lake. Here is found the seventh mooring stone on the northeast side of the lower part of the lake. The hole is now in a horizontal position on a vertical plane of the stone. This deplacement appears to be due to the fact that at one time the stone evidently lay higher up and had fallen some distance, as it now lies at the base of a perpendicular bank of clay about twenty feet high. The arguments in favor of the theory that it is a mooring stone from ancient days are: (1) The explorers must have passed through this lake as it is the only waterway leading from Pelican Lake to the camp near Kensington. (2) Its location corresponds with that of other mooring stones in that it lies at the base of a very steep bank with fairly deep water outside. (3) The hole has a very smooth patina characteristic of great age. (4) It could not have been chiselled by any one intending to blast it for building stone because the spot is inaccessible to any vehicle. There is, moreover, an abundance of good stone needing no blasting along the more easily accessible beach.

Against this theory is the fact that the hole is only three inches deep while other mooring holes have a depth of from five to eight inches. This difference may perhaps be due to the possibility that the explorers decided the location was bad. It is on the most conspicuous spot on the whole lake and can be seen from afar. As the catastrophe at the lake with two skerries had taken place only three or four days before this, it is likely that the men were somewhat nervous about the possibility of another attack and therefore deemed it imprudent to place their camp in such a conspicuous spot, and moved to a less conspicuous spot.

There is no waterway by which the travelers could leave the Pomme de Terre and turn east until a spot is reached about three miles south of Barrett Lake. Here is a string of lakes (possibly at one time a single lake) leading southeastward for ten miles until the former island is reached where the runic stone was found. Here is mooring stone number 8.

As the inscription says this spot was an island where they camped and carved the inscription, this, of all places, required a mooring stone. But on two different occasions I carefully inspected the lower hillside of the former island without finding any. Then the thought occurred to me that if the boat was moored near the spot where the inscribed stone was found, it would be on a very steep hillside. Such a steep slope would be subject to much erosion, and eventually the stone, over-balanced by frost, would roll down like many other stones now at the bottom of the hill. If this mooring stone in hurtling down the hillside struck another stone, it might well have broken, and parts of it may have bounced farther out over the lower-land.

With this thought in mind, a third search was made, and this time it was successful. A few feet from the base of the hill, on top of which the rune stone was excavated, lies a large pile

of stones made up of boulders of all sizes and shapes which
have tumbled down from the hillside and were later piled up
by the owner of the land. In this pile is a very large boulder
which at some time must have met with a severe collision, because a large "chip" has been knocked off its rounded surface.
This accident appears to have happened several hundred years
ago because the fractured surface shows just as much weathering
as the uninjured part of the boulder. In the very obtuse angle
left by this detached part is a chiseled hole about one inch
deep and three-quarters of an inch in diameter. The inside of
this hole has also been made perfectly smooth by weathering.
If this angular cavity was filled by a segment of stone which
approximately conformed to the rounded contour of the boulder,
and if a hole was chiseled through this segment in line with
the inch-deep hole that now is there, the hole would be from
six to eight inches deep and would in every way correspond
to the mooring holes described above. See Fig. 12A.

Upon leaving the island, the explorers found easy going in
the right direction because a string of beautiful, closely connected lakes runs northeastward, almost surrounding the city
of Alexandria. The uppermost in altitude is Lake Jessie, four
miles southeast of Alexandria. Here on the east side, at the
bottom of a steep hillside, is the ninth mooring stone, just about
a day's travel by boat from the "island." The hole, 7½" deep,
is about twenty inches above the level of the lake, which could
never have been more than a few inches higher than it is now,
because there is free drainage to the lower lakes. Like the others,
its inside is smoothly polished. This stone was found by Professor
R. B. Harvey of the University of Minnesota.

Ten miles east of Lake Jessie is Lake Osakis, a very large
lake. The area between these two lakes is mostly flat, poorly
drained land which may have been a lake bottom. On the south
side of Lake Osakis, a couple of miles east of the village
of the same name, is a big boulder which appears to have been
intended as a mooring stone. But the hole is only one inch

deep. It does not seem likely that this hole was made by a pioneer in search of building stones, because it is inaccessible as it lies at the foot of a twelve-foot perpendicular cut in the bank. Furthermore, there is an abundance of stones of all sizes in the neighborhood. Moreover, the spot is right in front of, and on the land of an old settler, Adolph Anderson, whose father homesteaded the land. Mr. Anderson is positive that no one chiseled that hole while he or his father lived there. This stone was found by my son Harold.

A more probable theory is that it is an abortive mooring hole. The explorers may have arrived there in the afternoon and intended at first to spend the night there. Then it was discovered that only a mile to the east was the outlet of the lake, whence issued a river (Sauk River), carrying a large volume of water. Being delighted with the prospect of easy and speedy progress downstream in a favorable direction, it was decided to float down the river some miles.

No mooring stones have been found east or south of Lake Osakis, nor is it likely that any will be found, because the Sauk River flows southeast until it joins the Mississippi, and no mooring stones would have been needed. The Sauk, if that became their course, is a small river and they could have moored on it simply by making fast to one or two trees on the bank. And if they continued down the Mississippi they would have found plenty of backwashes with overhanging trees to which to make fast.

Perhaps someone will say that these travelers were lucky in finding this waterway across the State. But they were not lucky, because there are three other possible routes, two of which would be shorter and less laborious. For instance, they could have continued up the Red River to Lake Traverse. There they could have made easy connection with the Minnesota River which holds a straight course southeastward with very few obstacles. This route would have saved one third of the distance to the Mississippi. But they had no maps and could only find their way a short distance at a time. Their progress was hampered as well as helped by their big boat, and their route was dictated by the physiography of the region.

There are two other ancient campsites on the same route, not marked by mooring stones. One is marked by a firesteel found in a layer of charcoal and ashes on the bank of a former channel of Red River in Polk County. The following letter from the finder of this campsite describes the circumstances clearly:

Climax, Minn., June 8, 1914.

I have your letter concerning the firesteel which I found. I settled here in June, 1871, and we were the first to take land around here.

A short time after I settled here I was boring holes (for fence posts) with a six-inch posthole auger. When I got about two feet down I heard something scrape against the auger and I pulled it up, thinking I had struck a stone. The dirt clung to the auger, and I examined it looking for the stone and found the little fire-steel. It was much rusted, and there was also some charcoal and ashes. It must have been there a long time, because the place where this hole was bored was on a dry elevation.

OLE JEVNING.

Firesteels were introduced early among the Indians, and specimens may be seen in some museums. But it was found that the firesteels brought in by the fur traders were markedly different from the one found by Ole Jevning. I wrote to the directors of a dozen museums rich in Indian artifacts, but none had seen a firesteel like it (see Figure 13B).

In 1928 I made an extensive trip through Europe for a comparative study of this firesteel and other finds. Only in the Scandinavian museums were there any such firesteels, and in the University Museum in Oslo the Minnesota firesteel was immediately recognized as a Norse implement of the Viking age. The museum kindly gave me the following statement identifying the firesteel:

Upon request I will state that the firesteel which carries the same (identification) mark in its entire form, with the spiral ends, is of exactly the same type as the firesteels which have been found in Norwegian graves from the Viking age in great numbers.

Oslo, September 18, 1928.
EIVIND S. ENGELSTAD

There can be no doubt that this implement was left in its finding place hundreds of years ago, because it would take centuries for the dust of the prairie to cover the ashes of the camp fire and the steel two feet deep. Before the prairie was plowed, there was very little dust, but as the firesteel was found just inside of the timber that lines the former channel of the river, what little dust there was would settle there as the forest would check the wind. L. J. Young, Professor of Silviculture at the University of Michigan in a letter dated January 14, 1943, gives the following information of the precipitation of wind-borne dust particles when opposed by a forest:

When wind approaches a belt of trees, the velocity begins to decrease gradually to within about 100 feet of the windward edge of the belt. By the time the belt is reached, velocity is reduced to about 80%. At a distance of 50 feet or more inside of the belt, the velocity is reduced to about 2% and remains at about that level until the lee of the belt is reached.

The river did not flow near the site of this camp in 1871, but had dug a new channel more than a half mile west of it. As the travelers would camp close to their boat in the river, this shift also indicates a great age because a forest, centuries old, now lies between the river and the camp site.

The twelfth camp site is at an inlet of Sauk Lake about twenty miles down the river from Lake Osakis. Here we find the structural remains of what appears to have been a Christian altar.

These explorers and their priest no doubt celebrated the Mass at frequent intervals, so it is not strange if they did so at this campsite. But here they appear to have taken special pains to make the rite as impressive as possible. It happened that they found here a huge crescent-shaped rock twenty-seven feet long. The peculiar shape of this rock must have reminded them vividly of the chancel in their beloved churches across the sea. With youthful ardor they appear to have added a few details to make this concave rock seem like a real church, because we find near the right end of the crescent two short chiseled horizontal holes twelve inches apart, apparently intended to receive two brackets to carry a waist-high table top, that is, an altar table. About sixteen feet away at the other 'horn' are two other holes apparently designed to hold supports for the canopy which is a necessary part of a medieval altar.

Another reason for such an altar would have been the date of their arrival at Lake Osakis. The Feast of the Assumption of the Blessed Virgin comes on August 15th and, if the travelers left Hudson Bay about June 1st, they may well have arrived at the big rock by mid-August. It may also be that their forest festival was an expression of gratitude that their worst difficulties had been overcome. For many weeks they had labored to find a waterway leading eastward toward their headquarters in Vinland. Now, at last, they had found a river which seemed to favor them. They were devout men, and nothing would be more natural than that they give praise.

As this huge rock lies in a region of inferior farming land and was not settled until in the eighties, it was possible to find a number of the very earliest settlers who testified that the holes in this rock were present and showed much weathering when they came.[51]

These twelve camp sites show that at some time in the distant past a party of men traveling in a big boat passed along this marked route. That, in itself, does not prove the authenticity of the inscription. But the fact that such a mooring technic is characteristic of Norwegian and Swedish usage, and the presence of Norse medieval implements along the

trail, indicate that the men who left the mooring stones were
Norwegians and Swedes. As we have the inscription on the
Kensington Stone which mentions the camp sites at Cormorant
Lake and at the finding place of the stone, and as it is extremely improbable that a second expedition duplicated this
great journey, the only reasonable conclusion is that these
travelers were the men mentioned on the Kensington Stone.
Every successive camp site and mooring stone is in fact, if not
in words, a sign stating that Norsemen passed this way in 1362.

Fourteenth Century

Implements Found

in Minnesota

THE PUBLICITY which the Kensington Stone received during the half century of discussion concerning its merits, produced a large number of letters from various parts of America, in which the writers told of old finds they had made or heard of. Most of these finds proved to be Indian artifacts, such as Indian copper implements, silver crosses presented to Indian chiefs, and Indian axes. But among them were also iron implements of antique form, which proved to be of Scandinavian origin of the late Middle Ages, that is, from 1200–1500. A dozen weapons and implements of medieval type and purpose have been found in northwestern Minnesota.

A frequent reaction to these discoveries is that their presence there was due to the many Scandinavians in northwestern Minnesota, some of whom supposedly had brought these relics from their homeland.

This explanation, however, does not suffice. North Dakota has the largest percentage of Scandinavians of any state in the Union, but only one medieval artifact has been found there, and that was right on the borderline of Minnesota. Northern

Illinois and Kansas have large settlements of Swedes, but no old Swedish arms have been found in these states. The densest concentration of Scandinavians in rural areas is found in a belt along both sides of the boundary line between Iowa and Minnesota, extending into Wisconsin, where there are several counties north and south of the city of La Crosse which are predominantly Scandinavian. In this very thickly settled Scandinavian area, where there are many times more Scandinavians than in northwest Minnesota, only one ancient weapon has been found.

The fact is that the national origin of the people of northwestern Minnesota has nothing to do with the presence of these ancient relics, because most of them have been found under circumstances which eliminate the possibility that they were brought in by the early pioneers. Mention has already been made of the firesteel found near Climax, Minnesota. As it was found by the first settler in unplowed soil, two feet deep in a layer of charcoal and ashes, the birthplace of the people in the vicinity had nothing to do with its presence. It is unquestionable proof of the presence of white men in that vicinity several hundred years ago.

Two other firesteels of the same type have been found. The small one (see Figure 13A) was found in a crevice of the rocks at Cormorant Lake in 1870 by the first party of white men known to have visited this spot (see page 185 above). In the university museum in Oslo may be seen several precise duplications in size and ornamentation from the Middle Ages. The other, known as the Detroit Lakes firesteel, was found about twenty-five miles northeast of Detroit Lakes, Minnesota, in a region not yet settled by white people. Nothing definite is known about its discovery, but as it is of the same type with spiralled ends, it was probably left by the same party of men. As these small firesteels were easily lost in the process of making fire, it is likely that more will turn up.

In addition to these firesteels, several axes, halberds, a spear and a sword have been found. These have been inspected by Dr. J. Bröndsted, Director of the National Museum in Copenhagen, who recognized all but one as authentic medieval implements. The most interesting of these finds are some small ceremonial halberds, of which at least three have been found. The first was found in 1871 by Mr. E. O. Estenson of Crookston, Minnesota, who has already been mentioned as having found a firesteel at Cormorant Lake. Mr. Estenson, eighty-six years old when I interviewed him, made the find when he was eleven. The following is his own report of the find (see Figure 14B):

Crookston, Minn, Oct. 25, 1945.

The axe that you bought of Dr. Grassick was found by me in 1871 on the Dakota side of the Red River, opposite Frog Point where my father took a homestead the year before. The river-bank was eroding, and I saw the handle of the axe sticking out about two feet below the grassy surface of the top of the bank. It was in the same battered condition, with a mineralized handle and broken blade, as it is now.

E. O. Estenson.

The second halberd was found about three miles north of Alexandria, Minnesota (see Figure 14C). The following is a report about its finding as made to me by a former owner:

Tucson, Arizona, Sept. 23, 1938.

We have had a summer home at Lake Darling near Alexandria for the last twenty years, and about fifteen years ago I was given a rusty iron battle axe which had been found by a neighbor, Mrs. C. I. Mansur of St. Louis, Mo. whose summer home is on a point of land jutting into Lake Darling called Brown's Point. This neighbor was having her driveway changed, and in cutting down some trees, the axe was found about three feet under the ground entangled in the roots of a very large oak. . . .

Esther Henderson (Abbot).

It was at first thought that these two implements were relics of the fur trade. Dr. Grassick in Grand Forks, who was somewhat of an antiquarian, even believed he could name the trading post where it had been purchased. He pointed out that there used to be a Hudson Bay post at the place where the 'axe' was found. This information terminated any interest that professors at nearby North Dakota University may have had in the find.

On carefully checking, however, it was found that the Hudson Bay Company had built a trading post at this place some time in the summer of 1871. But whether or not the implement was found a few days before or after the post was built cannot matter. It must be assumed that if the company dealt in weapons of this kind, they would be new and not old junk. Upon inquiry, Mr. Clifford P. Wilson, curator of the company's museum in Winnipeg, wrote me he was quite sure that the implements did not come from any Hudson Bay Post. Nor were there any such implements in the company's museum.

As the Hudson Bay Company has carried on a very extensive trade with the Indians of the north for almost 300 years, from which they have an abundance of souvenirs in their museum, this fact raised a serious doubt about the theory that the implements were Indian trade axes. For further information and discussion, I sent the axe to the curators of five of the museums having the largest collections of Indian artifacts in the northern states, Milwaukee, Madison, St. Paul, Ann Arbor, and Toronto. Their answers were all to the effect that this implement was not a relic of the fur trade. Mr. Charles E. Brown of the Wisconsin Historical Society Museum wrote: "No such implement is listed in any of the fur trade invoices that I have seen. In its expensive construction it is unlike all other trade articles. Moreover the slender handle makes it worthless as an axe for Indian use. It looks to me like an ancient Norse weapon."

The circumstances of these two halberds *in situ* were such that they must have been in their finding places a long time before the coming of the first settlers. Mr. Estenson says in his letter above that his implement was found "two feet below the grassy surface of the top of the (eroded) bank." It must have taken hundreds of years for the winds of the prairie to build up two feet of soil above it. Great age is also indicated by the microscopic and spectrographic analysis to which their metal has been subjected, the results of such testing having definitely demonstrated their metallurgy is not of a modern kind.

Another and emphatic evidence against the theory of importation by early settlers is the fact that this type of halberd is so rare that I have been unable to locate a single specimen in any of the Scandinavian museums. The likelihood that settlers may have come to America with so rare an item in their baggage, and that having once arrived here they immediately buried it at least two feet underground is too fantastic for serious consideration.

In reviewing the history of the halberd, we find that the English and French halberds of the 14th and 15th centuries were of a somewhat quadrilateral shape.[55] The Norse halberds, on the other hand, had a more harmonious outline. Sommerfelt and Knudsen describe it as follows:

> The Norse halberd . . . of the 14th and 15th centuries had a long handle of wood which ended in a spear-head, and below this was an axe blade in the shape of a half moon. Opposite this was a pointed axe hammer.[56]

This is a good description of the Minnesota halberds even to the mention of the pointed axe hammer. They are also thus identified by Dr. Grieg, formerly of the University Museum in Oslo. In Archbishop Olaus Magnus' great work of 1555, there are many illustrations of halberds used before his time, and their appearance is much the same as that of the Minnesota halberds.[57]

There is, however, one peculiarity about these halberds. The halberds of the Middle Ages were stout effective weapons of warfare, but the Minnesota halberds are very small and light, the blade weighing only about a pound. As they plainly were too light for warfare, they must in all probability have been made for ceremonial usage. The halberd has always been the favorite ceremonial weapon. It is so used at present by the Swiss Guard at the Vatican, and it was used in the same way in former times. The *Century Dictionary* defines the word *Halberdier* thus:

> A soldier of the bodyguard of a sovereign or high official. . . . The halberd was commonly borne by such attendants rather as an official badge than for actual service.

We may therefore assume that, just as the Lictors of Rome carried the Fasces as an emblem of Consular authority on their errands to distant officials, so the members of King Magnus' bodyguard, who were his official representatives, carried some ceremonial weapon as a sign of royal authority. These artistically shaped ceremonial halberds with their graceful curves, their surfaces shining like polished silver, would have made an ideal symbol. As the King's mandate to Paul Knutson, the commander, states explicitly that the expedition was to consist in part of members of the King's bodyguard, the evidence once more accumulates in a way not to be lightly disregarded that these ornamental halberds found in northwestern Minnesota were indeed ornaments of King Magnus' bodyguard.

By accident the question of the authenticity of these halberds was confused (though only on the surface) by the fact that this emblem of royal authority in the 14th century was 600 years later chosen to serve as a challenging symbol in a 'cut-throat' tobacco advertising campaign. The American Tobacco Company, annoyed by competition, decided about 1890 to wage a "battle axe" campaign for supremacy. The idea, it seems, was suggested by the discovery of one of these ceremonial halberds which was mistaken for a battle axe, whereupon a Battle Axe Plug was put on the market.Thousands of near-facsimile axes were made, hinged to a cutting-board to cut the plugs, and distributed to retail merchants. Each plug was also provided with the battle axe trademark. Later many of these tobacco cutters were converted into light axes by cutting off the hinged lever. These tobacco-cutting axes, of which there are still many in existence, are so closely similar to the Frog Point and Alexandria halberds that many think the latter were also tobacco cutters. But while they are externally similar, their chemical structures are totally dissimilar. I asked Professor R. A. Ragatz, Chairman of the Department of Chemical Engineering, University of Wisconsin, to analyze the metal of one of the tobacco cutters. The following is his reply:

Madison, Wis., February 22, 1945.

This letter pertains to the tobacco cutter patterned after a medieval halberd. I cut a small piece out of the frame (not the cutting blade) of the halberd part of the tobacco cutter, and made the following findings.

The metal is a rather poor quality of gray cast iron, showing the following micro-constituents: graphite plates, ferrite, pearlite, steadite. The structure is totally different from that shown by the frames of the two genuine halberds you sent me last fall. The frames of the two genuine halberds were made of malleable cast iron, and consisted of globular graphite and ferrite.

From my examination I can state positively that the two halberds sent me last fall were not of the same origin as the tobacco cutter recently submitted.

R. A. Ragatz

In the previous chapter, mention is made of a party of land seekers who in 1870 camped on the shore of Cormorant Lake in Becker County. They were the first white men known to have visited Becker County. They had no boat, but cut some poles and were able to fish while standing on large boulders at the water's edge. While fishing they made a number of interesting discoveries.

They found that one of the boulders on which they were standing had a seven-inch hole in it, about one inch in diameter —a true mooring hole (see Figure 12). They also found a small medieval firesteel in a crevice between the rocks (see Figure 13A). Finally, while engrossed in their fishing, they discovered an old-fashioned axe-head lying at the bottom of the clear water (see Figure 13C).

When I was given this axe, I doubted that it was Norse, because I had seen none like it. I, therefore, made no mention of it. But in 1950, when I visited various Scandinavian museums to check this as well as other finds, I came upon several exact duplicates of this axe, and it was identified by all the specialists whom I consulted as being a true 14th or 15th century axe.

These three finds, incidentally, mark the spot where the ten men were killed.

THE REPUBLIC AXE

Another axe of indisputable age came to light a few years later outside of Minnesota. According to Morgan H. Stafford of Boston, Massachusetts, who obtained this axe shortly after it came to light, it was found in 1878 by a prospector in a wilderness near the present village of Republic in the northern peninsula of Michigan. He stooped down to take a drink from a stream. There he saw an axe, but upon lifting it up above the water, the handle seemed to dissolve in his hand (see Figure 15).

Professor J. Bröndsted, who spent some weeks in America in 1948 for the purpose of investigating reported pre-Columbus Norse finds, thinks this is a Finnish axe. He was told that the Finns in Republic had similar axes which were used for squaring timbers. He therefore thinks it was a 19th century product.[58]

It is easy to be misled by a similarity. It is not Finnish but Norse because I saw an *exact duplicate* in the Lillehammer museum in Norway. Moreover, it is a weapon and not a broad-axe as is shown by the fact that the outer end of the helve is protected by an iron 'sleeve,' five inches long, to prevent the head of the axe from being shorn off by the opponent's axe.

If this were all we knew about this find, I would not claim that that this implement is evidence of the early presence of Norsemen in America. But the circumstances of the find put the matter in quite a different light. I borrowed the axe and sent it to Professor Darrah of Harvard, who is a recognized authority on vegetable microstructure. The following is his report:

May 15, 1937.

The wood in the handle of the axe found near Republic, Michigan is of subarctic spruce and might well have come from Norway or northern Canada, but not from as far south as the Great Lakes. It is significant that spruce is not strong or durable, and one can justifiably infer that spruce was used because other woods were scarce. The wood as now preserved in the axehead is dense, mineralized and obviously decomposed. As to the reported fact that the protruding handle was decomposed to a paste-like substance, it is my opinion that this indicates a submergence in water for several hundred years.

This set of conditions makes recent age out of the question.

W. C. Darrah
Research Curator of Paleobotany
Botanical Museum of Harvard University.

This analysis by an expert produced three proofs that this implement was not a Finnish axe of the present time. First, is Darrah's report on the great age of the handle—the "paste-like" condition of the handle indicating "a submergence in water for several hundred years." Secondly, the dense mineralized condition of the wood in the axehead which also indicates great age. Third, his statement that it is of subarctic spruce, not grown as far south as the Great Lakes. We must therefore visualize the owner of the axe as being so far north that the only available material for a handle was subarctic spruce. This brings us up to the vicinity of Hudson Bay. Later the axe was brought down to the region south of the international boundary. This happened several hundred years ago, as indicated by the pulpy condition of the handle and the mineralized condition of the wood in the axe-head. We have positive evidence of only one such journey from the subarctic region southward, and that is the one made by the company of eight Goths and twenty-two Norsemen who came from Hudson Bay southward in 1362 and reported their plight on the Kensington Stone.

It now remains to ascertain if there is any coincidence between the route of the explorers, as marked by mooring stones, and the distribution of the old implements reported above. The trail of a band of travelers is usually marked by various articles which are left behind or lost on the way. Perishable articles will, of course, soon disappear, but an iron weapon will remain in the grass or timber until carried away. It is likely that some of the articles would be picked up and carried away by Indians, but, as every archaeologist knows, the greatest concentration of artifacts is nearest to the point or line of distribution. If there is any connection between the Norse implements and the mooring stones, it is reasonable to expect that the finds would be centered along the route traced above.

Of the thirteen medieval implements which have been found in the United States under circumstances which exclude the possibility that they were brought in by 19th century immigrants, nine have been found within twenty-five miles of the route marked by the mooring stones. Five of these nine—the Climax firesteel, the Climax halberd, the Cormorant Lake firesteel, the Cormorant Lake axe, and the Alexandria halberd —have been found right on the waterway marked by the mooring stones. The sixth, the Lake Lakota boat hook, was found about a mile from this waterway. The seventh, the Brandon axe, was found about ten miles north of the finding place of the Stone. The eighth, the Erdal axe, was found five miles east of Pomme de Terre River, down which the explorers must have passed if we assume that the mooring stones do mark a route. The ninth, the large "beard-axe," was found twenty-two miles southwest of the course down the Sauk River, in northern Kandiyohi County, Minnesota. The remaining four (see Figure 16) were found farther away, but still in the same general area of the continent. Almost certainly a number of implements would have been taken by the Indians at Cormorant Lake where ten of the white men were killed and these implements would then have been scattered by the Indians in their travels. The account in the saga of Thorfin Karlsevni describing how an Indian threw away a captured axe when it failed to cut stone (p. 73) is evidence of the fact that the Indians would take loot and also of the fact that they would not necessarily prize it, that they might indeed throw it away capriciously. There is a very high probability that the four scattered implements, undoubtedly medieval Norse, were among the prizes taken by the Indians at the Cormorant Lake massacre. Figure 17 is an outline map of Minnesota showing the location of the mooring stones and the finding places of the medieval implements. Figures 17A and 17B are larger scale sketch maps showing the same locations in greater detail. No late medieval weapons have been reported from any other area in America except two adze-like implements found deep in the ground near Prince Albert, Saskatchewan, Canada. Professor Bröndsted informs me that they are medieval and that similar specimens are on exhibition in the royal Museum in Copenhagen. These may perhaps have been lost by the same explorers while ascending the Nelson River or while skirting Lake Winnipeg, or they too may have been scattered by the Indians.

It is on these facts that the case for the Norse penetration of Minnesota in the 14th century must rest. There is the authenticated fact that an expedition sailed from Norway at a time that exactly fits the evidence and with a commission that might reasonably bring a search party to these parts. To this evidence of reasonable likelihood, must then be added the conclusive evidence of the Kensington Stone that a party of Norwegians and Swedes did reach these parts in 1362, that they left a boatguard of ten men on the shore of Hudson's Bay while twenty of them pushed inland as far as Lake Cormorant, near the present Kensington, at which site ten of them were killed by Indians.

The Stone Tower
in Newport

COMPARED WITH the history of other countries, that of America north of the Rio Grande is an open book. There are few unexplored periods or places in American history, and almost every village and county has its early history well-documented if not formulated. There is a fairly open trail that leads back to the first pioneers in almost every community.

In view of this condition of our past history, it is historically fascinating to turn to a building in beautiful Newport, Rhode Island, the origin of which is still a mystery to almost everyone. It is a round stone tower, built of field stones, standing on eight round columns with circular arches between. It is medieval in appearance with small, deeply splayed window openings and a number of small loopholes. The roof is gone and also the two floors, but otherwise it is pretty much as the builders left it (see Figure 18).

The Tower is about twenty-five feet in diameter and about the same height (Figure 19 showing developed interior elevations will help the reader in following this description). It has two stories above the columns, the lower being about twelve and a half feet above the base of the columns, the other about seven feet above the first. The upper story has no windows, but three small loopholes evidently intended for defense rather than for illumination. The lower story has four large aumbries or cupboards but only two small windows, one on the south, the other on the east side. The impression in the mortar shows that the window frames were made of approximately four inch by four inch timbers. There is a larger opening on the west side which former commentators also called a window. But, as it is only eight inches above the former floor, it could not have been a window but the doorway and must have been reached by a ladder, just as we find similar doorways in fortified buildings of the Middle Ages. Directly above this doorway, at the top of the building, is a small loophole through which a rope could be passed for pulling up such a ladder.

This doorway in all its detail is most interesting because it has no parallel in any building from colonial times. One must go back to the Middle Ages to find anything similar. It is deeply splayed, but has no door frame. On the inside, the doorway is about four feet high and three feet wide, surmounted by a segmental arch. But this arch extends only half way through the thickness of the wall. The opening on the outside is a full foot lower in height, and the entrance was further hindered by a threshold almost a foot high. This doorway is precisely like the doorways found high up on the walls of the fortified churches of Sweden dating from about the 13th century (see Hugo Frölen, *Nordens Befästa Rundkyrkor,* Stockholm, 1911). They could be entered only by crawling, and a defender on the inside could dispose of intruders as fast as they came.

Opposite this doorway is a primitive fireplace with an *arched* opening which is also strongly medieval in character. It has *two* small flues which run up within the body of the wall and open to the outside about six feet apart, a foot below the top of the building.

There are two other strange features in the first story. One is a groove in the wall about seven feet long. The groove has an increasing depth toward its ends, up to eight inches, which may indicate that it was for the reception of a slab or table top which could not be trimmed, perhaps a slab of slate (see Figure 20). But this was not an ordinary table for it is from forty to forty-two inches above the floor, depending on the original thickness of the flooring below. The height of a common table is thirty inches. I shall return to this groove later.

The other puzzle is the thickness of the first floor construction. Immediately above the top of each column is a large cavity, evidently intended to receive the ends of the four heavy timbers that carried the floor above. The average height of the *bottom* of these beam holes above the base of the columns, as measured by architect Thomas Marvell, is eight feet and ten inches. But all commentators are agreed that the *top* of the floor was at the height of the hearth of the fireplace which is twelve feet and five inches. This makes a thickness of forty-three inches for the floor construction! The thickness of the second floor construction is only sixteen inches. Why should the lower floor be more than two feet thicker? It must have been an urgent need, that allowed it to take up so much valuable vertical space.

The only possible answer is that the construction was meant to make the floor absolutely fireproof. This fireproofing could have been achieved by laying a two-foot covering of clay or concrete on top of the beams and covering the under side of the latter with a layer of mortar. Frölen (*Nordens Befästa Rund-kyrkor*) states that all the fortified churches of Sweden had such fireproof ceilings under the first floor. Frölen also mentions that eighteen of the twenty-one round churches in the Scandinavian countries had their entrance high up on the south-west side. The Newport Tower had its entrance on the south-west side and some fifteen feet above the ground.

Every detail in the planning of the Tower is medieval in character, a fact which has been noted by all scholars who have given the Tower careful study among them Rafn, Enlart, Allen, Means, Pohl, and Bröndsted. The latter after making a careful examination of the Tower in 1948, stated in a Press interview: "If this tower were in Europe, it would be unquestionably accepted as of 13th or 14th century Scandinavian origin."

When Peter Easton built the first windmill in the vicinity of Newport in 1663, he was handsomely rewarded by the town. It gave him a tract of land a mile long on the east water front. This place, still known as Easton's beach, is a popular amusement area. One would therefore think that the Tower in "its stone-built dignity and architectural subtlety," so superior to any dwelling or church in the colony, would also have received some recognition, whether built as windmill or fortification, if built shortly afterward; but the record is silent. The only tradition we have of the Tower is the one recorded by the historian, Benson John Lossing. In 1848 he was the guest of Governor William C. Gibbs, whose family for a half century owned the land on which the Tower stands, and who lived just across the street from it. Lossing concludes his description of the Tower with the following words:

> Of its existence prior to the English emigration there is now (1848) but little doubt; and it is asserted that the Indians, of whom Mr. Coddington and other early settlers solicited information concerning the structure, had no traditions respecting its origin.[59]

There is, in fact, documentary evidence to show that the Tower was standing before the first English colonists settled at Newport in 1639. Attached to a petition applying for a tract of land in the American colonies, signed by Sir Edwin Plowden and addressed to King Charles I in 1630, there is a list of "commodities" (conveniences, produce, merchandise), which the desired land possessed, and which the petitioners planned to make available for the mother country. Among these commodities is specifically mentioned *"a round stone tower* capable of housing thirty men." The petition makes it clear that this stone tower was not meant to house the garrison of the proposed colony, but was a valuable existing convenience for trading with the Indians to promote "intelligence with the savages." The writer of the petition takes a broad view of the necessity of creating good relations with the Indians and thus outlines his policy:

> Security and profit may be increased if orderly intercourse
> be established with the savages of Virginia on the south, New
> England on the north, and the Dutch plantation sixty miles
> on the west.

The headquarters of the colony were planned to be located near the east end of Long Island, and as Newport is fifty miles to the northeast, it might be objected that this stone tower was too far away to be considered a commodity or advantage of the proposed colony. But the writer of the petition did not think so, because in section ten he lists other distant commodities. He says: "For dryde coad and trayned oyles is also sixty miles to the northwards a Bancke where there is also good places to dry it." Mr. Frederick J. Pohl was in England in 1954 and verified the correct reading of the petition as printed.

It may be objected that this round stone tower was not necessarily in existence when the petition was presented, but was planned to be built. But in such case it would not be listed as a commodity. This word refers only to existing advantages. As further proof we see that while the headquarters of the colony were necessarily planned to be built, they are not listed among the commodities. Another proof of the existence of the tower is that the writer has a definite idea of its location. It is not near the proposed headquarters, but a long distance away so that a "well defended pinnace" is needed for the voyage.[60]

This petition was granted July 24, 1632, seven years before the first white settlers came to Newport, and four years before Roger Williams, the first settler in the state of Rhode Island, came to Providence.[61]

There is other evidence supporting the conclusion that this tower was in existence before Rhode Island was settled. We have the report of William Wood who came to Boston in 1629.

During his stay here, he visited a large number of pioneer towns in Massachusetts and took notes on their location and resources. He compiled these notes in a small book called *New England's Prospects,* published in London in 1634. The book also contains a map of Massachusetts and Rhode Island, which, while rudely drawn, is better than any other of the same region which appeared for many years afterward. Each town settled by the English is named, and its proper location is shown by a certain sign (_+_). The names of the principal Indian chiefs are also marked on the map in the area of their dominion.

As this map was published in 1634, five years before the first white settlers came to Newport, one would not expect to find any English names on that site. But there is one. On the east side of Narragansett Bay, near its mouth, we find a town or settlement marked by the usual sign and called *Old Plymouth.* It is exactly in the position now occupied by Newport.

The name of Plymouth occurs twice on Wood's map. Plymouth on Cape Cod Bay is shown in its proper place, but is called New Plymouth. This is not a mistake by Wood, because it is so called in the patent from the Council for New England in 1629. Wood was presumably informed of the fact that New Plymouth was the oldest settlement in Massachusetts. One can only conclude that he must have seen or heard that building remains at the mouth of Narragansett Bay indicated a greater age, and therefore called the site *Old Plymouth.* At best, however, one can only guess at Wood's reasons for settling on this name. What is established beyond any guessing by Wood's map is the fact that he found reason for believing that there was a town at the mouth of Narragansett Bay before any English towns had been established anywhere in the area, and that whatever he found or heard led him to locate it exactly at the site of the Tower.

An interesting report of remains of earlier white occupation at this site was also made by Giovanni Verrazano, 110 years earlier. (See Chapter xxii.)

The Purpose of the Tower

*T*HERE HAVE been many theories about the origin of the Tower. The following is a list of them, each of which had its supporters:

1. It was built by Benedict Arnold as a windmill in 1675-1677.

2. It was an English watch tower built about 1640.

3. It was the inner rotunda of a Scandinavian fortified church in the Middle Ages.

4. It was a baptistery.

5. It was a pirate's nest.

6. It was an ancient heathen temple built in the remote past.

The three last theories, formerly held in high esteem, are now almost forgotten.

1. THE WINDMILL THEORY

The Tower is commonly called "the old stone mill" because Benedict Arnold, who owned the land on which it stands, mentions it in his will dated December 24, 1677 as "my stone-built windmill." However, it is nowhere mentioned that he built it. His statement is therefore merely one of ownership and gives no clue to the origin of the Tower.

This Benedict Arnold (not the traitor famous in American history) was born near Ilchester in Somerset, England on December 15, 1615. On May 1, 1635 the Arnold family emigrated to America and settled near Providence. In 1651, Benedict moved to Newport, where he acquired much land by trading with the Indians. In 1663, Peter Easton erected a windmill near Newport. This windmill served the little settlement for twelve years and then blew down August 23, 1675. As the Newport Tower is first mentioned February 28, 1677, the supporters of this theory believe that the Tower was erected in the eighteen-month period between these two dates.

Most recent writers[62] agree that the Tower cannot have been planned as a windmill by Benedict Arnold or any other colonists. There are a number of important reasons for this belief:

1. The Tower could not have been built in 1675 or 1676 because that was the period of King Philip's War, a time of the greatest anguish for all the settlers in Massachusetts and Rhode Island. It was a war to the death, with many thousand Indians appearing suddenly, here and there, spreading death and terror. More than a dozen towns in Rhode Island and Massachusetts were destroyed, including Providence, and every house but one between the latter and Stonington, Connecticut, a distance of forty-five miles, was burned. Twelve hundred scattered homes were destroyed and 600 white settlers were killed. With every able-bodied man out fighting the savages, agriculture became impossible, and the old men and women had a desperate time to find food and fuel. The Tower contains more than 5,000 cubic feet of stone, sand and lime, which at 200 pounds per cubic foot amount to more than one million pounds of material. When the war finally came to an end after a great battle fifteen miles west of Newport in the fall of 1676, the overworked and underfed people were subjected to a great

plague and many more died. To think that Arnold, who at that time was sick and feeble (he died the following year), and his harassed neighbors in such a time of terror and misery would spend their time in building a big and fanciful structure of stone a half mile outside the village is preposterous.

2. Before the recent invention of the American steel windmill, there were two types of windmills in use. One was the post-mill which was in use several centuries before the colonists settled in America and continued to be in use up to a hundred years ago. It got its name from the fact that the mill was pivoted on a vertical post, which made it possible to turn the structure with the attached wings into the wind. The other was the tower mill which was attached to the ground but had a revolving top or hood to which the vanes were attached. The Newport Tower is supposed to have been of this second sort by all proponents of the windmill theory.

However, R. T. Hopkins, author of "Old Windmills of England," who is considered an authority on windmills, says that tower mills only began to be built in England in the time of Queen Ann (1702-1714). If this is true, then of course, the Newport Tower was not planned as a windmill. This late introduction of the tower type is also supported by the fact that the Dutch who were leaders in windmill construction apparently did not erect any tower windmills on Manhattan Island during the first century of their occupation. In the New York Public Library are many prints from the 17th century showing pictures of New Amsterdam. While the post-mills are frequently seen in these prints, the tower mills do not appear until the next century.

3. Another proof, and a decisive one, that the Tower was not planned as a windmill is that its top or hood *could* not be rotated. A revolving top requires a true circular track, but the top of the Tower is not a true circle: it is oval, and there is a difference in the diameter of as much as thirteen inches. While

the builders made a perfect job of laying out their construction on the ground on a true circle, they evidently were not interested in making the top truly circular, although that would not have been difficult.

4. Still more anomalous, when the Tower is viewed as a windmill, is the presence of the eight round columns and arches. A gristmill is a strictly utilitarian construction, and what would be the need of columns and arches in a pioneer windmill? Flour cannot be ground in the open because the wind which makes the wheels go around would also scatter the flour. Nowhere in the world is there another windmill like this one.[63] From a miller's point of view, the entire lower half of the Tower is not only a waste of labor and material, but a most undesirable construction because it would impose upon his customers the heavy burden of carrying their bags of grain up an additional twelve feet.

2. THE WATCH TOWER THEORY

Professor J. Bröndsted of Copenhagen made a local study of the Newport Tower, and wrote a very good and well-illustrated commentary on it.[64] In this he rejects the windmill theory, but suggests, conditionally, that the Tower may have been built as a watch tower about 1640. It is probable that the pioneers needed a watch tower, but an adequate one would require only a small caboose on an elevated platform—not a stone structure containing a million pounds of stone and mortar in the medieval manner.

In considering the purpose and origin of the Tower, it is important to bear in mind the extremely limited circumstances of the first settlers. We do not have as much detailed information about the conditions at Newport as we have about those at New Amsterdam and Plymouth, but they must have been much the same. These pioneers were all very poor and confronted by the huge task of taming the wilderness; starvation was a constant threat for many years. The Dutch on Manhattan Island made the best progress, but they were still so poor that it took many years before they were able to finish their humble little church. The settlers at Plymouth would have perished the first year but for the help of the Indians; as it was, half of them did die that year. In Newport the prospect of making a living by farming was even less favorable than in the other two colonies because of the excessively rocky soil. There are still many stone fences around Newport as mementos of those back-breaking years. In 1640 the Newport settlement was only a year old, and nothing could have been further from the thoughts of these pioneers than to build a huge stone structure with columns and arches to be used as a lookout.

Another palpable objection to this pioneer's watchtower theory is that there are only two small windows in the whole building. These are in the first story; in the upper story there are only three tiny loopholes, almost as well designed to obstruct observation as they are to assist it.

While the Tower was not planned as a watch tower, it was at one time discussed as being suitable for this purpose, but was rejected. There is preserved in the library of the Newport Historical Society the original minutes of a town meeting held in July, 1756.[65] The local watch tower in the village had reached a stage beyond repair, and someone suggested that a new "look out" be built "upon John Banister's stone mill." A committee was appointed to see if the owner of the old tower was willing to have this done. He was agreeable to the idea and said "the Town could build a look out house on his mill" and keep it there as long as desired; he also promised to give "a ten-foot way to it." The compensation asked was "ten peppercorns per year"—a purely nominal consideration. Upon further debate, however, it was decided to build a new watch tower on the previous site.

This record is more or less incidental to the present discussion but it might plausibly be taken to indicate that the old stone tower in 1756 had no roof. Since it is not likely that the owner would have permitted the wrecking of it, to make possible the erection of a small house on top of the wall, for such a nominal compensation as ten peppercorns. Nor is it likely that the tower had any floors at that time, for if it had, it would not have been necessary to build a whole house—a roof with a watch station providing a better view than that offered by the three loopholes would have sufficed. It therefore seems that the tower in 1756 was just about as it is now—a hollow rotunda without roof or floors.

The fact that the tower in 1756 was without money value is significant. It was only eighty years after the time when Arnold is said to have built it, and as the tower shows evidence of having been very well constructed, such quick decay is surprising. This impression is emphasized by the known frugality of the early English settlers who took good care to maintain their buildings in good condition. Its general state of disrepair, therefore, would certainly indicate that the tower was built a long time before the colonists came.

3. THE SCANDINAVIAN CHURCH THEORY

But if we assume that the Tower was built long before the English colonists came to Rhode Island, the situation becomes quite different. The only conceivable pre-colonial builders could be the Norsemen. Any such party of explorers who chose to establish a headquarters there in pre-colonial times would realize that they were largely at the mercy of a strange and savage people. It is reasonable that for greater safety they would build a stone building that could not burn or be knocked over. The fact that it was built on eight columns must indicate that they planned eventually to build a church, but they would have soon realized that the eight open arches were the weak points of their defense. It would not be safe to have a ceiling of wood with a trap door, either with or without a stairway,

because such a wooden construction could be destroyed by fire
from below, and the occupants would perish. It was therefore
necessary to make the floor above the arches impregnable, by
following the example of the round-church builders in Sweden
who constructed similar thick concrete floors covered with clay.

There is such a close and detailed resemblance between the
round fortified churches of Sweden and the Newport Tower,
that Dr. Frölen, the leading authority on fortified churches in
Sweden, writes: "The Newport Tower has undoubtedly been
the inner rotunda of a carefully built round church."[66] The
italics are his.

It is not likely that the builders of the Tower were pleased
with this thick floor construction which closed off about two
feet of the upper part of the arches. But it was a temporary
necessity. Presumably, they were so enthusiastic about the beauty
and fertility of this new land that they expected to return and
take possession of it as a royal colony. Then, when order was
established, they would remove the offensive floor and substitute a domed ceiling, build a surrounding ambulatory, and
erect a chancel on the east side where the altar would be placed.

The secret of the origin and purpose of the Tower must be
found in its columns and arches. Generally speaking, the shape
and style of any house or edifice constructed by man is not
accidental, but the product of conscious imitation, subject to
such limitations or improvements as the circumstances permit
or make necessary. In other words, when the builders saw fit
to use columns and arches in their tower, it must in the natural
course of things have been because they were imitating one or
more buildings they had seen and wanted to duplicate, at least
in part. In order to find the purpose of the building we must
therefore find the prototypes of the Tower.

Some years ago I read a description of the Benedictine Abbey
of St. Bavo (Bavons) in Ghent, Belgium. In it was a picture of
a part of the abbey showing a small building much like the
Newport Tower. In 1950 I went to Ghent and found that this

building was even a closer parallel than I had thought (see Figure 21). It dates from the 12th century and is a two-story octagonal building of about the same diameter and height as the Tower in Newport, and stands on eight columns with circular arches between. Its position is within the cloister garth in front of the monastery buildings and separated from them by the cloister walk which surrounds the quadrangle. The lower part within the columns was known as the lavatory, where the monks washed their hands before and after eating. The room above was a chapel, known as the sanctuary, where the holy relics and treasures of the abbey were kept. There was originally no stairway in the building, and access to the upper room was only by way of the second story of the dormitory, through a small door with a threshold about eight inches high.

In Sweden there are, or rather were, a number of these cloister sanctuaries on eight columns. In the little village of Varnhem, where the great plain of West Gothland is bounded on the east by the high, timbered ridges of Billingen, stands a grand and beautiful church which was built about 1260. This church and adjacent abbey belonged to the Cistercian order which was an offshoot of the Benedictine and had many monasteries in Sweden and Norway.

While the church is still in good condition, the abbey is in ruins. But the State Archaeologist has here created a most picturesque and informative ruin-park, in which the entire ground plan of the abbey is revealed by the remains of the original walls and columns which stand at a height of two to six feet. Among these remains are also the remains of an octagonal "lavabo" of the same horizontal measurements as the octagon in Ghent. (See Figure 22.) Like the latter, it also stands alone within the cloister garth, separated from the living quarters of the monks by the cloister walk. Remains of the eight columns are still standing, but only to a height of two or three feet above the foundation. According to Axel Forssen, the architect in charge of the preservation project, remains of an arched ceiling have been found, also ornamental faucets, showing that the building was supplied with running water. When the debris of former destruction was removed, pieces of glass were found, indicating that the upper story of the octagon had glass windows.[67]

On the western edge of West Gothland, about a half hour's drive north of the city of Gothenberg, was a similar sanctuary. It has long since disappeared, but its general appearance is preserved in the seal of the city of Konghelle which was located here. When King Sigurd the Crusader returned to his own country with a large fragment of the Holy Cross, he built up Konghelle and made it the finest city in Norway. He also placed in its church the precious holy cross which he had made from a piece of the wood of the original. But the glory of the city was of short duration. In 1135, a few years after King Sigurd's death, a great horde of Wends from Poland came in 250 vessels and attacked the city. There was at the time only a small garrison present, and after several weeks of fighting the Wends were victorious, but with a loss of most of their men. They burned the city, but the head priest was allowed, after some apparently miraculous intervention, to remove the Holy Cross and other treasures from the church before it was burned.

The city castle was not rebuilt, but an Augustine monastery was built on its ruins. In its octagonal sanctuary built on eight columns, the Holy Cross was kept. About 1300, King Erik Magnusson renewed the privileges of the city and gave it a seal. This seal shows an image, somewhat embellished, of the sanctuary, where the Holy Cross was kept, as a fitting symbol of the city's past greatness (see Figure 23).

The remains of another Cistercian monastery with a similar octagonal lavatory and sanctuary may still be seen in the county of Louth near Drogheda in eastern Ireland. It was founded in 1142 through the effort of Bishop Malachy of Down, later canonized as Saint Malachy, who after visiting Clairvaux became so impressed with Bishop Bernard's work that he introduced the Cistercian order to Ireland. Mellifont was the first of a large number of Cistercian abbeys in Ireland. According to Thompson, this lavatory is "the only surviving example in the British Isles." An illustration in Thompson revealed five columns and four connecting arches still (1931) standing.

It is evident from the close correspondence of the structural plan of the Newport Tower with that of the four lavatory-sanctuaries described above, that the edifice which the builders of the Newport Tower had in mind was not a windmill, but a cloister appendage which was familiar to them. Very likely the priest who drew the plan had been an inmate of a Swedish Cistercian monastery.

As shown above, the Newport Tower is practically identical in type and size with the cloister sanctuaries. These in turn have their archetypes in the octagonal baptisteries built during the first millennium after Christ, many of which may still be seen. As baptism was the first requirement for salvation, these buildings were eight-sided because the number eight symbolized salvation. Architecturally, these baptisteries became the parent of another type of ecclesiastical structure, the round stone churches in northern Europe. These were nearly all built in the 12th and 13th centuries and are a direct result of the great Crusades. There were not only many crusaders who went to the Holy Land, but also many penitents who in atonement for their sins made a pilgrimage to Rome and the Holy Sepulchre. In Italy they saw some of these round churches, and many of these pilgrims built similar houses of worship on their return home. It is estimated that more than 200 round stone churches were erected north of the Alps as a result of the Crusades. In England there are fourteen, of which four are still in use. In Sweden and Denmark there are twenty-seven, many of which are still in use. They are nearly all built on a rotunda of columns, eight or less in number, with a surrounding lean-to or ambulatory. The largest of these round churches with an inner nave encompassed by eight columns was the Church of St. Olaf in Tunsberg,

Norway. Only the foundation and parts of the pillars now remain.

The best example of this type which has survived in its original shape (but with some additions) is the Church of the Holy Sepulchre in Cambridge, England. It was built about 1125, a round stone building on eight columns, and surrounded by an ambulatory. In its floor plan it is identical with La Rotunda in Brescia, San Tomaso in Bergamo, both in Italy, and St. Olaf's Church in Tunsberg, Norway. The two in Italy were built in the seventh and eleventh centuries, the Norwegian in the twelfth.

Dr. F. J. Allen, Secretary of the Cambridge (England) Antiquarian Society, has pointed out that the Newport Tower, in form and dimensions, is "remarkably similar" to the Cambridge Church.[68] Below are his horizontal measurements of the Cambridge Church (not including the ambulatory) and my measurements of the Newport Tower:

	Cambridge	Tower
External diameter	26' 6"	24' 8½"
Internal diameter	19' 6"	18' 5½"
Mean diameter	23'	21' 7"
Diameter of columns	3' 6"	3' 1½"

In many countries, but especially in Sweden, these round churches underwent another interesting evolution. Owing to political conflicts in the Middle Ages, it became necessary to have community centers of defense, and in rural districts where there were no castles, the local church often became the community fortress. The combination meeting house, fort, and jail built in Plymouth, Massachusetts in 1622 shows how American colonists prepared for defense in the same way. In the Scandinavian countries there were about 150 fortified churches, some of which proved their fitness to withstand hostile attacks for months at a time.

This need for defense made necessary a number of altera-
tions in the old octagonal church plan. The outer wall of the
ambulatory or surrounding lean-to was found to be too low for
defense, and this was raised to the full height of the building.
Instead of a cupola or dome, one or two upper stories were built
above the pillars for the habitation and protection of the occupants. The windows in these were very small and sharply
splayed, many loopholes were made to enable the defenders to
use their bows without exposing themselves, and fireplaces and
cupboards were installed. Most important of all was the provision for making the building fireproof. The floor above the
columns was made of a thick layer of concrete and clay, and
the narrow entrance was in the upper story, fifteen feet from
the ground. In West Gothland, Sweden, some of these mediaeval
round fortified churches may still be seen.

All these arrangements are duplicated in the Newport Tower.
Since past experience had revealed the weakness of a low ambulatory, this was not built, although it may have been planned
for the future, as is indicated by the offsets on the outside of
the building.[69] We find the same small splayed medieval windows as in the Swedish churches, with heavy four inch by four
inch frames, and the door fifteen feet above the ground.

Of particular interest is the floor construction above the
columns which is very massive. It has been supposed by many
commentators that this construction was planned as a permanent
floor, but this is impossible. Recently, The Preservation Society
of Newport County hired a competent architect to make careful measurements of various parts of the Tower. He found that
the beamholes at the top of the columns in which the timbers
rested that carried the floor were at an average height of
8' 10" above the average height of the bases of the columns,
while the upper surface of the floor was 12' 5" above the bases.
This makes a thickness of 3' 7" for the floor. In contrast the
upper floor was only 16", including the timbers that carried it.
As no sane miller would think of using up almost four feet of

his limited space in constructing a floor, this fact should
permanently dispose of the windmill theory.

There remains to be considered a mass of additional evidence
in support of the Scandinavian Church theory, but the case
will be clearer if we pause first for a more detailed analysis
of the measurements of the tower.

The Measurements
of the Tower

*I*N ADDITION to the testimony of these early visitors who saw the Tower several years before the first settlers came to Rhode Island, we have decisive evidence in the Tower itself that it could not have been built by English people. This evidence is found in the fact that the Tower was constructed to units of linear measure which are foreign to England and America. The following is a brief report on this examination.

When I began my study of the Tower, I thought it best to make as complete measurements as possible. I was assisted by three friends,[70] and we obtained the horizontal measurements given in the following table:

Interior diameter	18' 5½"
Mean diameter	21' 7"
Over-all diameter	24' 8½"
Diameter of columns	3' 1½"

These figures struck me at once as freakish. It is not reasonable that the men who designed a building with artistic columns and arches would use such fractional measurements in laying out the ground plan of the building. An error of an inch or two might be possible, but an error of more than eight inches in a distance of less than twenty-five feet is incredible. In comparison we have the exact measurements of the Church of the Holy Sepulchre in Cambridge, England, the dimensions of which are a little larger than those of the Tower; see page 223 above. Fearing that we had made some blunders, I wrote to Mr. Benson and asked him to get an assistant and to make new measurements. He did so with the help of William S. Godfrey, Jr., an archaeologist who was then (1948) making excavations beneath the Tower. The following are their measurements:

Interior diameter	18′ 5″
Mean diameter	21′ 7″
Over-all diameter	24′ 9″
Diameter of columns	3′ 2″

As will be seen, they are the same as the former measurements with the fractional inches omitted.

Since these measurements were thoroughly checked, the question arose: Could it be that the builders used a different foot measure from that now in use? Down through the Middle Ages there were and still are many different foot units. After applying a number of former units of measure in vain, I found that the above figures are all divisible into whole numbers of feet by 12.35 inches, leaving a margin of no more than a fraction of an inch in each operation. When this unit is used as a divisor, the measurements of the Tower are resolved as follows:

Interior diameter	18 feet
Mean diameter	21 feet
Over-all diameter	24 feet
Diameter of columns	3 feet

What is this unit of 12.35 inches? It is the length of an ancient foot measure, which in Denmark was known as *den sjaellandske fod*. It was also in use in the lower Rhine region. When the Hanseatic League became dominant, this unit became the standard foot measure in the Rhineland, Prussia, Denmark, Norway, and other parts where the League controlled trade. Its length expressed metrically is 0.3139 meters. The English foot is and was equal to 0.30479 meters, and it was in standard usage 150 years before the English colonists settled on Rhode Island.

According to the International Encyclopedia, "a yard of Henry VII, dated 1490, and one of Elizabeth, 1588, are undoubtedly the oldest British standards of length, and they differ only about one-hundredth of an inch from the present Imperial British yard."

Professor J. Bröndsted, in his comprehensive discussion of the Newport Tower, recognized the importance of finding an antiquated unit of measurement in the dimensions of the Tower. But he doubted the reliability of the measurements because they had not been done by a "scientifically trained architect." I therefore suggested to The Preservation Society of Newport County that a qualified architect be engaged to make new measurements. The suggestion was accepted, and on March 1, 1952, the Tower was measured again by Architect Thomas Marvell, Fall River, Massachusetts, who was accompanied by Richard Kinnicut, Little Compton, Rhode Island, another architect. They were assisted by Herbert Smales and William King Covell, both of Newport.

Mr. Marvell made careful measurements using two tapes for the distances and determining the angles by means of a transit. The following are his measurements of the interior diameter between opposite columns:

1–5	18′ 3⅞″
2–6	18′ 4¼″
3–7	18′ 4¾″
4–8	18′ 3⅛″

The average of these diameters is 18′ 4″. This is within one inch of the measurements made by Benson and Godfrey, and is about as close as may be expected from the measurements of two different parties.

The diameters of the columns are as follows:

#1.	3′ 1″	#5.	3′ 1⅜″
2.	3′ 1¼″	6.	3′ 1½″
3.	3′ 0¾″	7.	3′ 1⅞″
4.	3′ 1⅞″	8.	3′ 2⅝″

The average of these column diameters is 3′ 1½″. In order to get the overall diameter, it is therefore necessary to add to the interior diameter, 18′ 4″, the diameters of two columns which is 6′ 3″. The sum of these measurements is 24′ 7″. When this total is divided by the old unit, 12.35″, the quotient is 23.88′ which is 23′ 10⅔″, a figure within a trifle more than an inch of 24 feet by the ancient unit.

Thus, it was shown above that the interior diameters are about two inches shorter (one inch at each end) than they should be to agree perfectly with measurements made by the old unit. This variation may be accounted for in part by the fact that the center of most of the columns are about one inch inside the true circle that runs through all of them. Mr. Marvell clarified this positioning by placing a tracing paper over the plat showing the actual position of the columns and then superimposing a theoretical circle of the right diameter. This circle showed that the center of one column was exactly on the circle while the others were about an inch inside the circle. This careful positioning gives the key to the builders' plan. As such a close correspondence to a true circle could not be accidental, it shows that the builders planned the dimensions precisely. Mr. Marvell writes: "The measurements of the Tower have been a surprise that they were laid out as carefully as they were; even in modern buildings of this size and type it is not unusual to find distances varying from one to two inches."

This circle was presumably first marked on the ground and the position of each column was marked on it. Any slight deviation from this line would be merely accidental and would not alter the original plan of the building. The diameter of the circle therefore reveals the length of the unit employed. This diameter is 21' 7⅓". This number divided by 12.35 gives us a figure within hundredths of an inch of twenty-one feet.[71]

In the Middle Ages and long afterward there was a high regard for the luck and potency of certain numbers. Some of them were considered sacred. Most important was the number three which represented the Trinity. In the measurements of the Tower, this number occurs repeatedly as a factor. Measured by the Norse foot, the columns are three feet in diameter; the inside diameter of the building is 3 x 6 feet; the mean diameter is 3 x 7 feet; and the overall diameter is 3 x 8 feet. The outside boundary of the building was reached by a radius of twelve feet, and twelve represented the Apostles who carried the gospel in every direction. This particular combination of devoutness and numerology is one more evidence of medieval practices which, were it not already well established that the Tower was pre-colonial, would in itself go far toward proving that point. Certainly such concern with numerology might well have smacked of witchcraft to the devout Protestant settlers of the seventeenth century. This same veneration for holy numbers is expressed in the very choice of an octagonal base supported by eight pillars. The number eight, as noted, represented salvation. Baptism was an absolute necessity to salvation, and baptismal fonts were octagonal in shape. So also were the great baptisteries or bishops' churches.

Whereas Mr. Marvel found the dimensions of the Tower surprisingly precise, he also found a serious defect in the alignment of the bases under the columns. They differ in elevation as much as five inches. The same is also true of the imposts of the pillars.[72] It is evident from these discrepancies that the builders had no proper leveling implement. This lack is especially significant in view of the fact that the early colonists had no trouble in getting their foundations truly horizontal. A level, practically the same as our spirit level, had been in common use in England for centuries before Rhode Island was settled.

It is mentioned in Chaucer and Langland's *Piers Plowman,* and there are thirteenth century illustrations of it. As the build- ers of the Tower evidently did not have any level, the lack is a further indication that the Tower was built by a party of transient visitors who were not supplied with all the tools needed in making a permanent settlement.

These four circumstances exclude the possibility that the Tower was of colonial or even of English origin: (1) the "rownd stone towre" mentioned in Sir Edmund Plowden's petition of 1630; (2) Wood's map of 1634 marking an earlier settlement at the site of Newport; (3) the non-English unit of measure- ment; and (4) the fact that the builders of the tower had no leveling instrument.

ARCHAEOLOGICAL DIGGINGS

Thus far no evidence has been found to show that the Tower was built by the English colonists of the 17th century, whereas there is strong evidence against this possibility. Recently, how- ever, under the supervision of William S. Godfrey, Jr., an archaeologist, excavations have been made in the ground beneath and immediately around the Tower and Godfrey's report tells of finding several colonial artifacts in these diggings. Godfrey concludes that the Tower was built by Governor Benedict Arnold or by his contemporaries.

If the soil beneath the Tower had remained undisturbed since the Tower was built, the position of these finds would have been important evidence. The fact is, however, that the site has been dug up many times. We have the report of Governor Gibbs, the one-time owner of the Tower, that some time before 1848 he dug down to the bottom of the foundation. Furthermore, Mr. Godfrey in his report says that he found at least five previous excavations. There is no telling how many more have been made, because Mr. Godfrey says that it was not always possible to tell if the soil had been disturbed. In the report to The Preservation Society of Newport County, delivered September 24, 1948, he wrote:

> . . . We found at least five previous excavations, and their relationship is of great importance to the present central problem. The earliest of these pits, the hardest to identify, and the only one of major importance is the *annular* trench which was dug to receive the bases of the eight columns. Unlike the other excavations (made by treasure hunters) which were re-filled with material other than that which was removed, this original trench was filled with the same yellow clay which had been dug out, and this clay blended with the natural clay of the area.

Another difficulty is that he did not find conditions at the construction level such as he had reason to expect. In the same report he writes:

> The next problem was to establish the construction level. . . . This would contain reject and waste material from the building, which in this case would be plaster lumps and chips of stone. . . . Re-examining the stratigraphy which I previously briefly enumerated, we see two layers of plaster fragments: one very thin, below a layer of charred material, one relatively thick above it. Since we know that this cannot be the construction level, but is a level of destruction, plaster which has since fallen from the tower . . . this leaves the small layer of plaster under the charred layer for consideration. If the construction level is in existence still, this must be it, and there are several questionable items about this layer. . . . In other words, our second definite method of dating the structure has become doubtful because of its complexity.

There are three things about his reports which show confusion in the process of the excavation and nullify the conclusion which Godfrey finally reaches.

1. After having mentioned the builders' excavation of the large circular construction trench, seven feet wide, which was to receive the foundations of the eight columns, he says: "It must have been necessary to fill in the construction trench be-

fore the above-ground building was done. . . . Apparently
this refilling was done before the foundations were capped with
mortar." In this he is no doubt correct, because it would have
been difficult to proceed with the work of building the columns
until the excavated soil was removed by refilling. Likewise, it
was necessary to level off with soil the rough stones in the
trench outside the position of the columns. Only then would
the mortar be mixed so as to have it fresh for the masonry
work.

However, in a letter to me dated January 22, 1949, Godfrey
wrote:

> The limits of the trench were exceedingly hard to define:
> we could only be sure of its extent to any degree of certainty
> because of finds of fragments of plaster which had been in-
> cluded in the material with which the trench was refilled.

This raises the question: how did the plaster fragments get
down to the bottom of the trench when this was filled in with
dirt *before* the masonry work was begun? These plaster fragments were so plentiful that Godfrey found them in immediate
association with all the finds he unearthed.

To this there is only one answer: this filling of soil must have
been re-excavated or turned over very thoroughly after the
masonry work was completed so as to permit the plaster fragments to drop down to the lowest levels. Only the assumption
of such re-excavation could explain why there was so little
evidence of the presence of the construction level; the plaster
which had accumulated at the construction level had been
scattered by new digging. As it is not likely that the builders
re-excavated the trench, the reasonable conclusion must be
that treasure hunters had been at work, and that the pipe
stems and rusty nails which Godfrey presents as evidence of
colonial construction were left by these seekers.

2. The heel-mark. In *Archaeology*, 1950, page 85, Mr.
Godfrey tells with much relish of the discovery of a heel-mark

in the bottom of trench D. "Here under the refilled material of the trench we uncovered a definite trace of a square-heeled boot. Crusoe was no more astounded." This was immediately above a deep pickaxe mark which had been filled and tamped down with the heel.

But whether the Tower was built in the 14th or the 17th century, a heel mark was nothing to be astounded over. Boots with square heels were in use in the days of Edward II (1284–1327). Sandals with square heels were used in ancient Pompeii. What is astonishing is the deep pickaxe mark in the floor of the trench. Why should any of the builders dig *below* the trench? It was no 'careless pick-stroke' as Godfrey describes it, but a ponderous swing which sent the pickaxe "ten inches deep" into tough, resilient yellow clay. Evidently the giant must also have used a special broad pickaxe, because Godfrey says the gash in the clay was two inches wide! Common pickaxes are only three-quarters of an inch wide. And how did it happen that this thrust into the subsoil should reveal not only the heel mark, but also a piece of pipe stem, a rusty nail, a fragment of the bowl of a pipe, a small piece of glass and several fragments of plaster? What were all these things doing *beneath* the bottom of the trench?

The answer is, of course, that Godfrey had not yet reached undisturbed soil. The treasure hunters had dug down deeper than he, and in so doing had left their souveniers, including the heel print.

3. Godfrey's chief discovery was a piece of clay pipe which he found under the center of one of the columns. He says that the plaster facing of the buried part of the column had largely disintegrated, leaving an opening eighteen inches long, "hardly wide enough to admit my arm." In a later article he says this opening was almost a foot wide.

Fortunately, Godfrey has given us a photograph of the base of this column and the big cavity under the column where he found the fragment. According to him, we see the construction of the column just as it was when the builders left it (see Figure 26). But it is plain that the lower stones do not lie in their original position. It is recognized by all that the men who built the Tower were exceptionally careful masons. The Tower has stood for hundreds of years, and there is not the slightest crack in it. Such stability could only be accomplished by placing each stone carefully and firmly.

But the photograph tells another story. The bottom stones of the pillar do not fit at all, and no mason would be guilty of such poor work. Godfrey says the mortar had "disintegrated," and he was thus able to stick his hand into the very center of the columns. But lime mortar does not disintergrate when it is protected from the elements. The 'disintegration' in this case was probably caused by the crowbar of some treasure hunter, who, having failed to find the treasure in the loose soil, conceived the idea that it was hidden in the base of a pier. No better illustration of later treasure hunting could be produced than this battered base, the crushed mortar, and the tunnel a foot wide reaching into the very center of the column base.

In excavating an area so completely uprooted and disemboweled as was the ground beneath the Tower, it is not safe to make any important conclusions about the age of any small find. Due consideration must also be given to other evidence of the age of the Tower such as the historical background, its architectural period, its ecclesiastical characteristics, its provisions for defense, its linear unit, and its lack of leveling instruments and tools for trimming stone.

Mr. Godfrey mentions the absence of Norse finds as negative evidence of a Norse origin of the Tower. But all these repeated diggings by treasure hunters surely imply that certain strange finds had been made, enough at least to give currency to the belief that the Tower was probably an old time pirate's headquarters.

With these details in mind, we may now return to the theory that the Tower was a fortified church of the Middle Ages.

THE SCANDINAVIAN CHURCH THEORY (*continued*)

There is much evidence that the Tower was planned as the inner rotunda of a fortified church. One irreducible piece of internal evidence is the presence of an altar and an altar cavity (see Figure 20). Its position is shown in Figure 19 near the right end, which shows the developed interior elevation of the Tower. The altar table has long since been demolished, but the groove in the wall, about seven feet long, into which it fitted, may still be seen. I discovered this groove in 1941, but the following spring, when Philip Ainsworth Means' fine book on the Newport Tower came out, I found that I was not the first to notice it. He mentions that John Howland Rowe "discovered it in 1938. . . . Rowe suggests that it was designed to receive one edge of a wall table of some kind." But this suggestion does not suffice, as will be shown below.

The first step in determining the significance of this groove is to find its relation to other parts of the room, its height above the floor, and other possible indices. The position of the former floor is fortunately not a controversial matter. All writers who have discussed it agree that the floor was on about the same level as the hearth of the fireplace. Careful measurements show that the top of the groove is about forty-one inches above this level, depending on the thickness of the floor covering. The supposition that the groove was for the support of an ordinary table top must therefore be rejected, because table tops are from twenty-eight to thirty inches high, while the top of this groove is about twelve inches higher. Its height would be approximately at the shoulder of a person sitting beside it.

The suggestion has been made that it was intended as a high desk. But was there so much bookkeeping that a special desk was needed? It has been shown above that the Tower was not planned as a gristmill, but as a habitation with a fireplace and cupboards. Being a habitation, it would undoubtedly have a table and benches. Since it was the temporary home of a group of explorers, a special desk for bookkeeping is unthinkable. What little writing they may have done could more easily be accomplished on their table.

Another objection to the theory that this slab was a desk or table is its position with reference to light. If there were a table, certainly it would be put by a window, both to get good light, and to see what was going on outside. Just a few feet to the left of this groove is the south window, through which there was a grand view out over the ocean—an ideal place for a table. But instead we find this "table" placed against a blank wall. There are two such wall spaces, not broken up by a door, window, cupboard or fireplace. One is on the north side, but this wall space is largely taken up by the stairway to the upper floor. The other is the quarter section between the door on the west and the window on the south, and it is here that the "table" groove is located.

There is another peculiarity connected with this "table-top." Under the middle of it is a recess seventeen inches square and seven inches deep, neatly surfaced with plaster. This seems like an awkward place to store things. One would expect to find the shelf *above* the table, where its contents could be seen and easily reached.

As a person would have to use this table in a standing position, it might be thought that it was a work bench. But again we are confronted with too much height and the absence of good light which is indispensable for a work bench. The recess or shelf, moreover, is in the wrong place for storing tools.

These conditions exclude all tabular structures but one—an altar. The regulation altar of the Catholic Church is long and narrow. It is from forty to forty-two inches high. It is usually placed before an opaque background, in order that nothing of a mundane nature may distract the attention of the worshipper. Furthermore, Mass must be celebrated by candle light. All of these conditions are fulfilled by the slab that we assume was fixed in the groove. But there are more. The *Catholic Encyclo-*

paedia devotes a dozen pages to the construction and furnishings of an altar. Among other things, it demands an altar cavity—"a small square chamber in the body of the altar in which are placed the relics of one or two canonized saints." Where is this placed?

The altar cavity in a fixed altar is either at the front or back of the altar, *"midway between its table and the foot."* As an altar cavity for the reception of sacred relics, the position of the strange recess found in the Newport Tower is precisely right. Its very limited use also explains its very shallow depth.

We find the same kind of altar with a similar recess for sacred relics below it in several medieval round churches in Sweden. Frölen describes one which may still be seen in the Agnestad Church in West Gothland. There, as in the Newport Tower, the altar was structurally a part of the wall behind it. There is a similar altar and cavity in the Hamar Cathedral, Norway, built about 1300, and in the church at Varnhem in West Gothland, built about 1265.

The early Catholic missionaries in the Great Lakes region had no means or men to put up stone churches, but placed their altars in their bark cabins. It is not required that altars in such improvised places of worship be placed in the east end. The place for the altar in the Newport Tower was also improvised, since it may be assumed that the builders meant to place the altar at some later time, in an apse to the east of the nave, as was the custom in the Middle Ages. As will be shown later, the builders of the Newport Tower were also members of a missionary expedition which, because of its purpose, included one or more priests. To such a group of men an altar in their headquarters would not be fantastic, but a most highly prized source of comfort and encouragement. The silver chalice and the monstrance containing the sacred host, the shining candlesticks, the missal and breviary, and the crucifix suspended on the wall above, would all speak to them of the purpose, power

and sustaining blessing of the Mother Church, whose loyal sons
they were.

The presence of this altar is of great importance in determining the age of the Tower. As has been shown, it is built
according to the ritualistic usage of the Catholic Church, which
means that its builders were Catholics. But there were no
Catholics among the colonial settlers of Newport. In 1680 the
Privy Council of England sent a list of questions to Governor
Peleg Sanborn at Newport, concerning all aspects of the colony.
In answer to the question concerning the religious views of the
colonists, the Governor replied, " . . . *as for Papists we know of
none amongst us.*"[73]

The Identity of the Men
Who Built the Tower

IT MUST have been a colossal task to build the Newport Tower
without the aid of beasts of burden. Five thousand cubic feet
of soil had to be excavated and later refilled. A lime kiln was
necessary, and the construction of the building requiring more
than a million pounds of stone, sand and lime. The builders
must, therefore, have had plenty of time at their disposal. The
type of building also indicates that this was no hasty job, because
it takes longer to build cylindrical columns and circular arches
than to build a rectangular house.

Who were these men who quietly toiled here on the hill at
Newport, centuries before the English colonists settled in America? Only a half dozen even remote possibilities suggest themselves. Were they explorers, or traders, or shipwrecked sailors?
Or were they missionaries, or a relief expedition searching for
lost countrymen? The first three possibilities we can reject at
once because transient visitors do not build stone churches.
There remains the possibility that they were missionaries, as
attested to by the very fact of erecting a church, and that they
had an ordained priest with them, as evidenced by the presence
of the altar. Finally, there is a possibility that they were a
relief expedition whose headquarters were here at Narragansett

Bay, while a search was being made, far and wide, for the men they were seeking. There are therefore only a limited number of possible explanations for their long stay here and their building of a church—they were a missionary expedition, or a relief expedition, or both in one.

The royal expedition of 1355-1364, of which the Kensington Stone is a memorial, was precisely ordered as a combined missionary and relief expedition. And on the Kensington Stone it is recorded that these men came from Vinland, a clear implication that the headquarters of the expedition was there. Vinland was the old name of the eastern part of the south shore of New England. Paul Knutson, the Commander, was commissioned to restore Christianity in Greenland, which meant that he was to find its emigrant apostates and bring them back into the Church. The expedition departed on its mission in 1355, and presumably spent the summer of 1356 in Greenland, making inquiries concerning the emigrants. Some time in 1357 the expedition may have reached Vinland, which would seem to them the likeliest place to which the Greenlanders would emigrate because of its renown. Upon arriving there, a fortified base was necessary, and the commander would send out searching parties, north and south, scanning the shore line for signs of the lost people. Eventually, the commander would be convinced that the lost Norsemen were not in these parts, and the thought of abandoning the mission would have occured to him. But to yield to such a thought would be to incur the stigma of incompetence. Then, too, it may have occurred to some members of the expedition that they were searching for the lost emigrants in the wrong place. These Greenlanders whom they were seeking were accustomed to a sub-arctic climate, and their mode of life was based on such an environment. When they emigrated, perhaps they would follow the same climatic parallel to which they were accustomed.

We may therefore assume that the question of climatic environment would also come up. And it seems likely that, when it did, the commander would dispatch a vessel or two north-ward, manned by hardy and capable men, with instructions to search the sub-arctic shores of this new land as far as possible, perhaps also to sail around what was then thought to be a large island.

We know nothing of the coastwise journey of this probable branch expedition, but the route that its members would follow is unmistakable. They would pass along the coast of Newfound-land and Labrador and enter Hudson Bay. Here, very likely, they would think they had reached the west side of the "island," because the east shore of Hudson Bay runs straight south for 1,000 miles. But when they reached the head of James Bay, they would find the coast again turning northwestward; and upon reaching the Hayes or the Nelson River they would under-stand that they were not circumnavigating an island, but were confronted by a continent, because these rivers are far greater in volume than any river in Europe.

By this time they may have come to the conclusion that their search for the lost apostates was in vain. The problem was now to return to their headquarters. Two courses were open. They could go back the way they had come, past unending ramparts of naked mountains. But this was a bleak prospect. An easier route, or at least one with more promise, was to follow this great waterway to its headwaters and there perhaps cross over to another river flowing eastward to Vinland, such a river as the St. Lawrence, the mouth of which they may have searched pre-viously. In planning such a course, they were only following the way of primitive man from the earliest times, a way also used by later explorers of America, such as Marquette and Joliet, La Salle and Tonty, Lewis and Clark. But they could not be sure of reaching their headquarters by such a course. Perhaps this river (the Nelson) came from a high tableland of mountains like the mountain plateau of interior Norway. In that case, they would have to return to their ships, and that possibility made it advisable to leave ten men in charge.

Meanwhile, these men who were left at the headquarters in Vinland had nothing to do but to find food for the reduced company. During this long period of waiting and praying for the welfare and return of their comrades, the erection of a church would seem a worthy and propitiatory task, pleasing to God and to their patron saint, the great St. Olaf, that they might bless their enterprise. So, with diligent and prayerful attention to every detail, they built the first house of worship in this new land. They put in the foundations, four feet deep, below the frost line. They were not satisfied to build a simple meeting house of logs enclosed by four plain walls, but had a more ambitious plan—a church which would be a memorial to both nationalities represented in the expedition, and which would thus make for better fellowship. In the eight cylindrical columns and circular arches, all neatly faced with white stucco, we see a construction which reflects the respect of the Norwegian members for the noble round church in Tunsberg. It was also well known to the Swedish members of the expedition—members of the King's Bodyguard—because Tunsberg was the "capital" of the few provinces that were left under King Magnus' personal dominion, after his son, Haakon, became King of Norway in 1355. There King Magnus had a big fortress and spent much of his time with his retinue. But, as this church at Newport was built in a wild country, inhabited by unpredictable savages, prudence would demand that it be fortified. The provisions for defense found in the upper stories are practically duplications of the upper fortified stories of the round churches in West Gothland, and in other parts of southern Sweden, which were familiar to the Swedish members of the expedition. The nave below could not be adequately defended, so they placed the altar in the second story. But with the vision of hope, they no doubt looked forward to the time when this fair land might be a crown colony, and therefore made provision for the future addition of an ambulatory. Lacking beasts of burden, all this was hard work, but it was a labor of love which shines out over the centuries. Figure 27 shows probable appearance of the Tower in 1362.

In this evidently long stay we find the only reasonable explanation for the position of the door and two windows. None of these openings in the wall of the Tower look out toward the village as it was located in Governor Arnold's time. Instead, they all face the sea, as indeed they should, since the chief concern of the group was for the return of their comrades from their distant mission. The doorway not only commands a view over the entire inner harbor, but also looks west by south toward the entrance to the harbor. As the south end of the island still is, and probably always was, devoid of native timber because of the strong gales from the Atlantic, the removal of a few trees near the Tower would provide a view of the ocean to the south. The same conditions and process would afford a view of the sea from the east window. All these placements indicate that the Tower was built by a party of explorers who were much interested in watching the sea approaches to their headquarters.

The conclusion that the Tower was built by the Royal expedition of 1355-1364 explains, moreover, the peculiar fact that the bases of the columns are not on the same level. These men probably had no intention of building permanent buildings when they left Norway and therefore did not take a spirit level with them.

But is the site of the Tower the best that could be chosen for the location of such headquarters? The choice of location would no doubt be made with great care, because it would be governed by a number of important considerations. We can visualize the following requirements:

1. Their first need would be a good harbor where their vessels could ride safely in all kinds of weather.

2. Their headquarters would necessarily be located near this harbor, and preferably on an elevation above it, so that the

occupants could watch for the approach of possible enemies or visitors.

3. It was essential that a dependable supply of fresh drinking water be available near-by.

4. Finally, they would presumably build their headquarters on a commanding spot, where it would stand as a guiding beacon, for the benefit of their absent members, and for future expeditions.

These are important requirements, and the location of the Tower fulfills them completely. The expedition's vessel or vessels would be anchored in the Inner Harbor of present Newport— as safe a haven as can be found on the entire Atlantic coast. The Tower stands within five minutes' walk of the shore and commands, or did before the present buildings of the city were put up, a view out over it. The water supply, a large spring, was only a short walk north of it. Finally, no more advantageous location could be found for a view out over the surrounding waters. Figure 24 is a sketch of the outline of the lower end of Rhode Island with the contour lines as given on a large-scale hydrographic chart. This map shows that the Tower stands on top of the plateau between Narragansett Bay and Easton's Inlet. Its site is near the southern tip of the narrow eighty to one-hundred foot elevation, with the land sloping away in every direction except toward the northeast. In that direction, there is a slightly higher elevation (100 feet), but as this is twice as far from the harbor, and also farther from the spring, it would not be as good a location as the one chosen. From this elevation the occupants of the Tower would have an unobstructed view for many miles out to sea—east, south, and west—if the timber near the Tower was cut down. Moreover, as the Tower was originally covered with stucco, its white walls gleaming in the sun would make an admirable beacon.

The fact that the builders were able to finish the erection of the Tower indicates that their relations with the Indians were friendly. The courtesy of the primitive Indians has been attested to by most of the early explorers. Verrazano, who in 1524 spent two weeks among the Indians of this same vicinity, is full of praise for their generous hospitality. It is therefore probable despite earlier skirmishes between Norsemen and Indians that the Indians on Aquidneck Island and the later Norsemen were on the best of terms. As the latter stayed there for several years, it is more than likely that intimate social relations developed between some of the members of the King's retinue and the dusky Indian damsels. This assumed intimacy may even perhaps explain the strange presence of an honored old Norse name among the Indians of this region several hundred years later. The account is incidental to present purposes and no conclusions may safely be drawn from it, but the story has been discussed in connection with Norsemen in America and it may as well be reviewed here.

In 1676, at the close of King Philip's War, a chief of the Narragansetts named *Magnus* was captured and put to death by the English. This chief was a woman, old in years at that time, a niece of "the prudent and peaceable" Canonicus, the most famous of the Narragansett chiefs, who was born about 1560. The question has arisen, how did she get the name of Magnus? It has no meaning in the Algonquian language, nor has any etymologist familiar with Indian linguistics been able to suggest any proper Indian term from which it may have been derived. Nor can it have been bestowed upon her by the colonists, because this name is not to be found among the several hundred English names preserved from that time. S. G. Drake quotes an obscure writer as suggesting that *Magnus* was derived from *Matantuck,* another term by which she was also called, but this theory may be rejected, as no phonetic law or tendency can be cited to support the theory that Matantuck, with the accent on the second syllable, would change to Magnus. According to

Dr. Frank G. Speck, Matantuck is derived from *Madahando* (with accent on the penultimate syllable), which is still in use, with the meaning of "a person-chief of renown." Her full name or title would therefore be Madahando Magnus, meaning "the great chief Magnus."

This chief Magnus is said to have been an old woman when she was put to death in 1676. She would, therefore, have been born many years before the first settlers came to Rhode Island in 1636. If the first settlers of any region known to have been visited by white men at a previous time found European implements among the primitive natives of that region, this discovery would be considered additional evidence of the visit of these earlier white men. If the discovery is a name, instead of an implement, and if the name can definitely be placed as European the connotation is just as obvious.

In this case no such definite placement can be asserted; but it is probable that there would be some intercourse between the natives and the white men during so long a stay. The members of this expedition were devout Catholics, engaged upon a religious mission, with the highest regard for the saving grace of the sacrament of baptism, and certainly these men would not suffer their own offspring to run the risk of eternal damnation by neglecting its baptism. The child would be given a Christian name, and if it were a boy, the likeliest name of all would be that of Magnus, the name of the popular king who had dispatched this Norse expedition upon its great enterprise. The Indians would have great respect for this name when told that it was the name of the great king of the white men, and it would very conceivably be passed on to succeeding generations.

It is reasonable to assume that a time limit was set for the return of the subdivision that was sent north. The venture was dangerous, and the men at the headquarters could not wait forever. But, as we know from the Kensington Stone, the subdivision met with disaster, and it is not likely that any of the men that went inland ever returned to Vinland. Eventually the men at the headquarters must have set out upon their return to Norway. But there is no indication that any of them reached home. Paul Knutson, for instance, who played an important part in the affairs of Norway and West Gothland before the expedition sailed west, is not later mentioned. Whether his part of the expedition was lost at sea on the return voyage or met its fate in the new land, all further trace of him disappears.

The only men of this valorous company who might have returned to Norway appear to be the ten men who were left in charge of the two ships at the mouth of the Nelson. They were left there to provide an exit for the men who proposed to return to Vinland overland in case that search party found no possible route. If these men started inland in June, as soon as the river was free from ice, the date of departure would give the "ten men by the sea" two or three months before it was necessary for them to leave Hudson Bay that year. After passing through Hudson Strait, they were not far from the Norse Settlements in Greenland, and they may have decided to put in there for lack of food supplies, or they may have been driven there by storm.

These were probably the men who brought the kayaks to Norway. If they reached Greenland they may have put into a harbor for the night in the Western Settlement. This settlement was now deserted except for periodical looting visits by the Eskimo. On seeing this one small vessel (the other had probably been left behind at Nelson River) with only a few men on board, the Eskimo may well have made an attack, and been defeated during an action in which four of their skin boats were captured. If later they reached Norway, the surviving members of the expedition would have had little news to tell. To be sure, they could have spoken of the excellent qualities of Vinland, but these were already recognized. They would have seen nothing of the great interior and would have known nothing of what had happened to the other men. They had sailed past thousands of miles of bleak rocky shores and spent two or three winters in exceedingly cold spots. None of this would be attractive news. But they would have had something important to show if they had captured some of the boats of these *Skrellings,* who were the cause of the emigration and disappearance of their countrymen. Thus these kayaks might well become religious symbols of the crusade and self-sacrifice of the men who had perished in their effort to bring the apostate Greenlanders back into the fold of the Church. So two of them were hung in the Cathedral of St. Halvard in Oslo, and two in the Cathedral in Trondheim.[74] The fact that these kayaks were permitted to occupy prominent places of honor in these cathedrals for generation after generation shows the veneration with which this great enterprise was remembered.

The outstanding achievement of this expedition is not the voyage across the sea to America 130 years before Columbus. The Norsemen had made such voyages hundreds of years earlier, and those trips were not as dangerous or as strenuous as their journeys far into the frozen arctic. But what makes the expedition almost unique in the annals of discovery is its serene mastery of its surroundings. When these men reached this new land of mystery—Vinland—they looked about them and selected the very best of all harbors for their headquarters. Instead of challenging the hostility of the natives by insolence and cupidity, as was the common procedure of the Spanish in the West Indies, they must have made friends with the dark-skinned people of the land, so they could live in peace. In what could only be calm confidence of success, they recalled the details of their beloved churches at home and proceeded to build one like them. Nor did they permit their isolated position to drive them to shoddy construction. Down to the solid rock they put the foundation, and with indefatigable industry they scoured the vicinity to find suitable stone, which they carried to the building site. Columns and arches, recesses and altar, fireplace, chimneys and loopholes were all carefully planned and so well constructed that after 600 years the Tower still stands in fairly good condition. And, when it was all done, they covered it, inside and out, with a coat of shining white stucco. A thing of beauty forbids profanation, and to the successive generations of wondering Indians, this strange structure must indeed have seemed the abode of a mighty spirit who was not to be offended. See Figure 25.

The same masterfulness also marked the men who were sent northward to search for the lost apostates. With the assurance of experienced seamen, they made the long journey past Labrador and into Hudson Bay. With amazement they must have looked upon a new continent taking shape. When they reached Nelson River, which spoke to them of a vast hinterland, they boldly left their ship to explore the interior of this great land. On reaching the region of the savage Sioux, they met with a serious disaster—ten of their irreplaceable men were killed and mangled. But even that catastrophe did not cause them to turn back. Through countless lakes and streams running hither and thither they persistently pushed their way toward the southeast, where, far beyond, lay their comrades and headquarters in Vinland. On the shores of lakes they camped and left their camp sites marked by mooring stones across Minnesota from northwest to southeast, until they reached the Mississippi at St. Cloud. There, unfortunately, the trail ends, for there was no need to use mooring stones on the great river—a tree on the bank would serve the same purpose.

The explanation of this indomitable efficiency lay in the character of the men who were selected for the expedition. When Columbus started on his westward journey to Cathay, he was accompanied by so many untrained hotheads and jail-birds that his plans for a peaceful conquest were irreparably wrecked, and Spanish affairs in Haiti became one of the worst muddles in history. In contrast, the men of the Paul Knutson expedition were probably as carefully selected as were ever the members of any exploring expedition to foreign lands or arctic regions. The king had instructed the commander to select some (perhaps the majority) of the men from the Royal Bodyguard, and these

were the most promising men of the king's realm. They were
the king's messengers, associates and councillors, a class of nobles
who later were advanced to knighthood.

And even if none returned from such an expedition, or even
if only these ten returned whose main experience of the new
lands had been along the barren shores of Labrador, one would
still think that a people with the energy and spiritual resources
to mount one such expedition would certainly have sent out
another at some future time, and that new voyages would have
led to more extended emigration. But it must be remembered
that the 14th Century was the time of the Black Death in
Europe, and that almost one-third of the population had been
destroyed by 1363 or 1364 (the earliest dates any possible survivors might have returned). The chief factor in promoting
emigration is the need of land on which to make a living. At
that time there was no scarcity of land as thousands of farms
lay idle, but there was a great scarcity of men to work them.
Many centuries passed before European population conditions
created the need of an outlet across the sea. The English discovered America in 1497, but more than a century passed before any emigration was attempted, and even most of these
earliest emigrations were motivated by religious rather than
economic reasons.

Norumbega

IN THE second half of the 16th century, when knowledge of the American mainland was in its infancy, and for a hundred years thereafter, the most prominent name on the Atlantic coast was Norumbega. It was the name of a city, and some of the cartographers, as for instance Mercator, emphasized its importance by adding towers and battlements to drawings of it. The earliest maps locate it on the south shore of New England, between Cape Cod and the Hudson River. Later it was used as the name of a river, a cape, and a region embracing all New England.

Students of Indian languages have thought much and written more about its meaning, but without success. In the *Handbook of American Indians,* the great symposium of Indian lore published by the Smithsonian Institution, we read that "according to Vetromile, the best recent authority on the Abnaki language, the correct Abnaki form is Nolumbeka, meaning 'a succession of falls and still waters,' used by the Indians to designate certain parts of the Penobscot River, and not the river itself."

Father Sebastian Rasles, author of an Abnaki dictionary, knows nothing of Nolumbeka, but thinks Norumbega may be the same as *Aranmbeg8k,* which means the head of the water, "au fond de l'eau," from *aranm*-au fond. J. N. B. Hewitt disagrees with this and maintains that *aranmbeg8k* means "at the

clay inlet." Still another Indian linguist, Gatschet, thinks that
Norumbega may be derived from *Nalabigik* or *nalambigi,* which
refers to a pool of still water, from *nala,* "a stretch," and
bigik, "at the mouth."

These linguistic interpretations are unsatisfactory, not only
because of the wide disagreement as to meaning, but also because they are devoid of any suggestion of how the term could
have become the name used for a reputedly large town and
the province around it. It is therefore better to turn to the
history of the region wherein the name occurs. As the existence
of the name Norumbega (to denote a village, river, and district)
is attested to by many explorers and affirmed by scores of
cartographers, it must have some historical origin.

Arthur James Weise makes the following categorical statement
about the meaning and location of Norumbega: [75]

> When the first French explorers sailed along that massive
> bulwark of trap-rock, now called the Palisades (near the
> mouth of the Hudson River), rising on the west side of the
> Grande River to varying altitudes from two to five hundred
> feet above the level of the stream, and ranging northward and
> southward a distance of more than ten miles, they were pe-
> culiarly impressed with its grandeur, and figuratively called it
> L'Anormee Berge (The Grand Scarp).

This, he believes, is the origin of the name, Norumbega. But
he does not say who these "early French explorers" were; nor
does he tell us when and where they gave this name to The
Palisades. Verrazano anchored in the lower harbor of New York
in 1524, but he did not get up into the river because of a
sudden squall. The earliest description of the Hudson River is
from 1609, but by that time the name Norumbega had been
applied to Narragansett Bay and River for almost a hundred
years.

The first mention of Norumbega in literature is in a French
document entitled *Recherches sur les Voyages et découvertes des
Navigateurs Normands,* written in 1539 and published in 1832.

The work is by Pierre Crignon, a writer in Dieppe, and contains the following passage as part of its description of the North Atlantic Coast:

> This coast was discovered fifteen years ago by Messire Jean de Verrazano who took possession of it in the name of King Francis I and Madame *Regente*. Many navigators, and even the Portuguese, call it Terra Francaise. It tends toward Florida. . . . This land is called Norumbega by the natives.

Pierre Crignon probably got his information directly from Verrazano because the latter, while in the service of King Francis, made his headquarters at Dieppe. Crignon, however, says nothing to identify the location of Norumbega, except that it was visited by Verrazano.

Fortunately, this lack is supplied by a great navigator only three years later. In 1542, Jean Alfonse was selected by King Francis to be the chief pilot of the great Roberval expedition. He visited Norumbega and describes its location in a manuscript of the cosmographer Raulin Secelart, now in the National Library, in Paris. The original is quoted by Weise (pp. 354-356):

> I say that the Cape of St. John, called Cape Breton, and the Cape of the Franciscan [Point Judith?], are northeast and southwest, and range a point from an east and west course, and there are 140 leagues on the course, and makes one cape, called the Cape of Norombegue [Cape Cod]. The said cape is in 41° of the height of the arctic pole. The said coast is all sandy and flat without mountains. And along this coast there are many isles of sand, and the coast is very dangerous because of banks and rocks. . . .
> Beyond [west of] the Cape of Norombegue, the river of Norombegue descends about 25 leagues from the cape. The said river is wider than 40 leagues of latitude at its mouth, and within this width is as much as 30 or 40 leagues, and it is full of isles which stretch out ten or twelve leagues, and it is very dangerous on account of rocks and swashings. The said river is in 42° of the height of the pole.

Up the said river, 15 leagues, there is a town which is called Norombegue, and there is in it a good people, and they have peltries of all kinds of animals. I think that the said river runs into the river Hochelaga [St. Lawrence] for it is salt for more than 40 leagues up, according to the statement of the people of the town.

Weise thinks that this statement about the water in the Norombegue being salt 40 leagues from its mouth, proves that the Norombegue was the Hudson, which is salt 120 miles (40 leagues) upstream under normal tidal conditions. But this statement rests on very poor authority, because Alfonse says he was so told "by the people of the town." As there is no reason to believe that he could talk Algonquian, and as the Indians certainly knew no French or Italian, they were unable to talk with each other except by signs and gestures.

The fact is that even when Alfonse spoke with people of his own country, he was not always understood. Thus he is quoted as saying that the Norombegue is "wider than 40 leagues (120 miles) at its mouth." This "40 leagues" appears to be an error for four leagues because the distance from Sakonnet Point to Narragansett Pier is only thirteen miles. Presumably Raulin Secelart, the writer of the report, misunderstood Alfonse, and the latter had no opportunity to check the written report (he died in 1548.) Shorn of this error, we have the report that about 75 miles west of Cape Cod a river was found having a vast estuary with many islands in it.

There is only one river west of Cape Cod which has a very large estuary with many large islands in it. This is the Narragansett and it is about 75 miles west of Cape Cod. Alfonse, who was the chief navigator of the expedition, took an observation and found that this estuary lay between 41 and 42 degrees north latitude. Narragansett Bay lies within these latitudes but the mouth of the Hudson is about 40° 20'. While Alfonse's report is faulty, these three facts—the observation made by him, his statement that the river Norombegue emptied into the sea through a vast estuary, and that its mouth lay 25 leagues west of Cape Cod—seems certainly to indicate that he was referring to the Narragansett River and Narragansett Bay.

A more definite evidence is that of Jean de Verrazano himself. Verrazano was the first explorer in post-Columbian times to make a long voyage along the greater part of the Atlantic coast of America and to leave a record of it. He was a Florentine sea captain making a voyage of discovery on behalf of King Francis of France. It was a quick voyage and a successful one. On January 17, 1524 he left the Madeira Islands. He reached the American coast at about latitude 34° north, followed the coast to 50° north, and was back in France in the middle of June of the same year. He made only one long stop, fifteen days, on the voyage, and that was at Narragansett Bay. Here he found such a fine, cultured tribe of Indians, "inclining to whiteness," that he devotes the greater part of his report to a description of their merits.

At this place Verrazano appears to have found a construction of apparently European origin which he called Norman Villa. It was on the east side of Narragansett Bay, near its mouth. It is first mentioned in 1526 on the map of Vesconte Majollo, who got his information direct from Verrazano. It is also mentioned in the same position on the map made a few years later by Hieronumus Verrazano, the explorer's brother, and also on the Globe of Euphrosinus Ulpius of 1542. Verrazano's discovery greatly excited the cartographers, and it was forthwith marked with the names *Noruega, Norbega, Nova Norbega* and *Norumbega* on fifty or more maps. A dozen expeditions went out to inspect this supposed city and its province. Among these was the ill-fated expedition of the famous Sir Humphrey Gilbert, sent by Queen Elizabeth.

There is the fact that no Indian derivation for the name Norumbega has been able to satisfy any general group of scholars of the Indian languages. There is also the fact that the Latin (and, therefore, clerical) name for Norway is Norvega. Norvega is often spelled Norbega because the v and the b can be so much

alike in writing, and in sound as well. It has already been
demonstrated that if the Newport Tower was *not* of 17th Century construction it must have been built by medieval Norsemen, and the arguments against the possibility of such 17th
Century construction are here re-submitted as conclusive. By
any reasonable evaluation of evidence there were Norsemen at
Newport on the shores of Narragansett Bay in the 14th Century.
What would be more likely than that they called their little
domain by the name of the home country just as the French,
the English, the Scotch and the Dutch called their American
domains New France, New England, Nova Scotia and Nieu
Niederlandt. Likewise, the Norse emigrants of the last century
gave the name of Norway to dozens of post offices and scores
of townships in America.

There is the additional consideration recognized by all logic
that the simplest competent explanation of any given phenomenon or series of phenomena has the weight of reason on its
side. No quantity of far-sought and much-disputed Indian deriva-
tions for the name of Norumbega can be given serious credence
in the face of the simplicity, appositeness, and historically supported presence of Norvega or Norbega as the root word. One
must conclude that the Norsemen were not only settled for some
time at Newport but that they left the church name of Norway
to the Indian language, to later history, and to the legends which
have grown up around it.

Perhaps the first Norse word that the Indians would learn
was *Norrmen,* the name of their white visitors, a possibility
which may explain the origin of the "Norman villa" mentioned
by Verrazano. The meaning of *villa,* in 16th century Italian
is given as "a manor or establishment with an ambitious man-
sion usually set on a hill, with colonnades, terraces and often
towers." What Verrazano saw could not, therefore, have been
an Indian village or a formation of nature. Nor could it have
been a shop or trading post. It must, rather, have been a structure of some dignity, most likely a building of stone showing

good lines. Obviously we must have here another reference to the Newport Tower, built by the royal expedition of 1355-1364 on this very spot on the east side of Narragansett Bay, near its mouth. Just as William Wood, a few years before the first settlers came to Rhode Island, saw or heard of the stone tower near the mouth of Narragansett Bay on the east side, and, thinking it was left by a prehistoric company of Englishmen, called it *Old* Plymouth, so Verrazano, on seeing its Norman columns and arches, and perhaps on hearing an Indian name for it, may well have thought it was the remains of a former Norse commander's house and called it Norman Villa.

But why is this villa first mentioned on Majollo's map and never in Verrazano's report?

We have several of his reports, but they are not verbatim copies.[76] In the main they tell the same story, but there are several minor incidents and facts which are mentioned in some versions but omitted in others. As both Majollo and the explorer's brother were told of this villa and its precise place on the map, they presumably got their information from Verrazano himself.

But there is another matter of importance to look into: what evidence is there to show that Verrazano's fifteen-day visit among these very friendly Indians was indeed in Narragansett Bay? Several other harbors, among them New York Harbor, Boston Harbor, and Penobscot River in Maine have been mentioned as probable locations.

Fortunately, Verrazano, being a navigator, is so precise in the description of his courses, distances and nautical observations that there can be no doubt about the identity of the places he mentions. He says he reached a low shore at latitude 34° and turned southward looking for a harbor, but finding none, turned northward again. Then he sailed northward for about 200 leagues along a low sandy shore until he "found a very pleasant situation among some steep hills, through which

a very large river, deep at its mouth, forced its way to sea."
The first place north of latitude 34° where a very large river,
deep at its mouth, runs into the sea between steep hills, is, of
course, the Hudson River estuary. He anchored his ship in a
good berth and set out in a small boat to inspect the harbor.
After rowing up about a half league, he found "the river formed
a most beautiful lake, three leagues in circuit"—the upper harbor
of New York. Unfortunately, his exploration here was cut short
by a sudden squall, which made it necessary to hurry back to
the ship. Then he continues: "Weighing anchor, we sailed fifty
leagues toward the east, as the coast stretched in that direction,
and always in sight of it." This shows that he was following the
Long Island coast eastward, because only at New York does the
shore turn eastward. "At length we discovered an island of triangular form," apparently Block Island, whose shape is markedly
triangular. From here, he says, it was about fifteen leagues to a
"very excellent harbor." This harbor could only have been Narragansett Bay, the sole "very excellent" harbor in that region.
Moreover, he says the latitude was 41° 40', a latitude which passes
right across the middle of Narragansett Bay. In comparison, the
latitude of New York Harbor is 40° 30'; of Boston, 42° 30';
and of Penobscot, 44° 20'. Finally, he mentions that the inner
part of the bay "enlarges itself to form a very large bay, twenty
leagues in circumference, in which are five small islands. . . .
Among these islands any fleet, however large, might ride safely,
without fear of tempests or other dangers." Verrazano's details
exactly describe Narragansett Bay.

This harbor was the only place, after leaving New York
harbor, where Verrazano had any intercourse with the natives.
Upon leaving them he writes:

> Having supplied ourselves with everything necessary, on the
> fifth of May we departed from the port, and sailed one hun-
> dred and fifty leagues, keeping so close to the coast as never
> to lose it from our sight . . . The people were entirely different

from the others we had seen, whom we had found kind and
gentle, but these were so rude and barbarous that we were
unable by any signs we could make, to hold communication
with them . . . [76]

It is plain that Norumbega's appearance on the maps and
in the records of the 16th century is due entirely to the information gained and reported by Captain Verrazano, partly by his
written report, and partly by personal narrative. Its location
is shown by his explicit description of his voyage as well as by
his observation of the latitude. It is also supported by the
statement of Jean Alfonse.

Finally, there is the physiographic evidence. A glance at the
map shows that anyone sailing from New York to the end of
Cape Cod, passing south of Long Island, will find only one big
river and one large and good harbor. Both are at Narragansett
Bay.

Throughout the 16th century there was no disagreement
among cartographers about the location of Norumbega. But in
1605, Samuel Champlain made a coastwise voyage from Fort
St. Croix, near Passamaquody Bay to Nauset Harbor on Cape
Cod. On the Penobscot River, called by him the Pentegoet, he
found a large village of Indians. Knowing nothing about Narragansett Bay, and thinking that this village on the Penobscot
was the famous Norumbega, he thus marked it on his map of
1612. Since it was believed that he knew more about America
than any other man before his time, his identification was
accepted by many cartographers.

A Lost Inscription

Pierre Gautier de Varennes, Sieur de La Verendrye, was a soldier of France and one of the most dauntless of that tough French breed of explorers that roamed the virgin continent. Born at Three Rivers on the St. Lawrence in 1685, La Verendrye served on the battlefields of France for several years, but chose to return to America where he became commandant of a fur-trading post on Lake Nipigon, the furthest west of all French frontier posts.

It was probably at Lake Nipigon that the lure of the West took possession of La Verendrye, for in 1731, on patent from the King but at his own expense, La Verendrye set out from Quebec with fifty men to explore a route to the South Sea. In 1732 he reached the western shore of Lake of the Woods on what is now the boundary between Minnesota and Manitoba. There he built Fort St. Charles as his headquarters and despite failure of supplies, mutiny, and attack by the Sioux, pushed further north and west building several other frontier forts.

In 1738, La Verendrye undertook a new expedition into what is now central North Dakota, and there, along the banks of the Missouri, in the territory of the now-extinct Mandan Indians, he discovered a pillar or cairn of stone in which was fixed a small stone inscribed on both sides with unknown characters. As he was unable to decipher the inscription and had seen nothing like it before, he brought it with him in 1743 when he made a trip

to Quebec. There he submitted the inscribed stone to the scrutiny
of some Jesuit scholars. They were likewise unable to read the
inscription; but on comparing it with illustrations of Tatarian
inscriptions which they found in books in their college library,
they found the characters "perfectly alike." Esteeming this discovery a matter of state importance, the stone with its mystic
inscription was sent to Paris to Count de Maurepas, Minister of
Colonies.

The record of this remarkable discovery is preserved for us
by Professor Peter Kalm, a member of the Swedish Royal
Academy of Sciences, who was sojourning in America about
that time. While here Kalm kept a diary of his observations
which later was published in three volumes.[77] In 1749 he visited
Quebec, where he not only heard the story of the discovery of
this inscribed stone from the Jesuit scholars in the city, but also
received an account of it from Captain La Verendrye himself.
Kalm's report, therefore, is practically first hand.[78]

> The history of the country can be traced no further than
> from the arrival of the Europeans; for everything that hap-
> pened before that period is more like fiction or a dream than
> like anything that really happened. In later time, however,
> there have been found a few marks of antiquity, from which it
> may be conjectured that America was formerly inhabited by
> a nation more versed in science, than that which the Europeans
> found on their arrival here; or that a great military expedition
> was undertaken to this continent, from these known parts of
> the world.
>
> This is confirmed by an account which I received from Mr.
> de Verandrier who commanded the expedition to the South
> Sea [the Pacific] in person, of which I shall presently give an
> account. I have heard it repeated by others, who have been
> eye-witnesses of everything that happened on that occasion.
> Some years before I came into Canada, the then governor-
> general, Chevalier de Beauharnois, gave Mr. de Verandrier an
> order to go from Canada, with a number of people, on an
> expedition across North America to the South Sea, in order to
> examine how far those places are distant from each other,
> and to find out what advantages might accrue to Canada or

Louisiana, from a communication with that ocean. . . . As
they came far into the country, beyond many nations, they
sometimes met with large tracts of land, free from wood, but
covered with a kind of very tall grass, for the space of some
days' journey. . . . When they came far to the west, where, to
the best of their knowledge, no Frenchman, or European, had
ever been, they found in one place in the woods, and again on
a large plain, great pillars of stone, leaning upon each other.[79]

These pillars consisted of but one stone each, and the French-
men could not but suppose that they had been erected by
human hands. Sometimes they have found such stones laid
upon one another, and, as it were, formed into a wall. . . .
At last they met with a large stone, like a pillar, and in it a
smaller stone was fixed, which was covered on both sides with
unknown characters. This stone, which was about a foot of
French measure in length, and between four or five inches
broad, they broke loose, and carried to Canada with them,
from whence it was sent to France, to the Secretary of State,
the Count of Maurepas. What became of it afterwards is unknown to them, but they think it is still (1749) preserved in
his collection. Several of the Jesuits, who have seen and handled
this stone in Canada, unanimously affirm, that the letters on
it are the same as those which in the books, containing accounts
of Tataria, are called Tatarian characters, and that, on comparing both together, they found them perfectly alike. Notwithstanding the questions which the French on the South Sea
expedition asked the people there, concerning the time when,
and by whom these pillars were erected, what their traditions
and sentiments concerning them were, who had wrote the
characters, what was meant by them, what kind of letters they
were, in what language they were written, and other circumstances; yet they could never get the least explanation, the
Indians being as ignorant of all those things, as the French
themselves. All they could say was, that these stones had been
in those places, since time immemorial. The places where the
pillars stood were nearly 900 French leagues westward of
Montreal.

It is evident from this account that this inscribed stone was
not an Indian pictograph. Pierre La Verendrye had spent about
fifty years in Canada, mostly among the Indians, and probably

had seen dozens of such pictographs. The Jesuits, likewise, many of whom had spent years among the Indians as missionaries, were also familiar with their pictographs. Indeed, the picture writing of the Indians has so little in common with the appearance of the writing of more civilized peoples, that even one who sees it for the first time would not confuse it with the alphabetic characters of other people. Professor Kalm states that the Jesuits, upon comparing the writing on the stone with illustrations of Tatarian inscriptions found the characters "perfectly alike." This comparison is helpful, but of course, it could not have been a Tatarian inscription, for the Tatars, living east of the Caspian Sea, with no known interest in seafaring and exploration, would be among the last peoples on earth to find their way into the interior of North America.

It happens, however, that Tatarian inscriptions and runic inscriptions have a remarkable superficial resemblance. Sir Charles Eliot, in his article on the Turks, in the Encyclopaedia Britannica, calls attention to this resemblance. The letters in both modes of writing are most often formed on a vertical staff, and they are mostly rectangular in form. Several runic signs have their duplicates in Tatarian characters which occur in inscriptions on the upper Yenesei and Orkhon rivers.

As the Jesuit scholars found these characters in an illustrated book on the Tatars, it may be possible to get a definite image of La Verendrye's inscription by consulting the illustrated books on Tatars published before 1743. While several books on the Tatars were published prior to this date, there was only one, according to the Librarian of Congress, which shows specimens of Tatar writing. This is Philipp Johann von Strahlenberg's *Das Nord—und Östliche Theil von Europa und Asia,* published in German in Stockholm, 1730, 4to. Strahlenberg was a Swedish officer, who for thirteen years had been a captive of the Tatars, and his book was by far the most popular of its kind, being translated and published in many editions, among them an

English translation in 1736, another in 1738, and one in French in 1757. This English translation was most likely the book on the Tatars in which the Jesuit scholars in 1743 found illustrations "perfectly like" the writing on the Verendrye stone. On *Tab. V*, section D of Strahlenberg's book, may be seen a Tatarian inscription containing fourteen different characters. Eight of these are common runic forms, and the other six are so suggestively runic that if this inscription were found in the North, valiant attempts would be made to translate it. In view of the fact that only an expert in runic or Tatarian writing would be able to distinguish between the two, there seems to be good reason to believe that La Verendrye found a runic inscription. This conclusion is strengthened by the fact that it was found in the same general region in the Northwest, which Norsemen, possessing the knowledge of runes, are reported to have visited. Its position when found, on top of a large stone or pillar, also suggests the practice of the Norsemen who reached the 73rd parallel in Greenland about 1300, where they built a cairn of stone and wrote their inscription upon a smaller stone, which they placed upon the cairn.[80]

Professor Kalm states that the site of these discoveries was 900 French leagues west of Montreal. This statement is not of much help in localizing the site, as the La Verendrye discoveries covered several thousand miles of territory west of Lake Superior, nearly all of which could roughly be included in the description "nine hundred French leagues west of Montreal."

It is possible, however, to limit greatly the area in which the cairn with the inscribed stone was found. Kalm states in the beginning of his account, that the La Verendrye with whom he talked in 1749 was in personal command of the expedition on which they found the inscribed stone. This dating excludes La Verendrye's three sons, for they were all in the West in 1749. La Verendrye Sr. must therefore have been the La Verendrye with whom Kalm talked. Now we know, from the senior La Verendrye's own published account, that he did not personally penetrate farther west than the first Mandan village, which was located somewhere in the northern part of what is now McLean County, North Dakota. This expedition left Fort St. Charles on the Lake of the Woods September 11, 1738, and proceeded to the site of the present city of Winnipeg, where La Verendrye had built a station called Fort Maurepas. The explorers then went up the Assiniboine River to the site of the present city of Portage La Prairie, where La Verendrye built another station, called Fort La Reine. From here, La Verendrye and his men, accompanied by a large number of Indians, traveled southwestward to the Turtle Mountains, and after following a circuitous route reached the village of the Mandans on December 3, 1738. Somewhere near the Mandan village they must have seen the large pillars which they believed had been erected by human hands. "At last," says Kalm (that is, near the end of their journey), "they met with a large stone, like a pillar, and in it a smaller stone was fixed, which was covered on both sides with unknown characters." This significant pillar and inscribed stone must therefore have been found in the vicinity, and probably to the north or east, of the first village of the Mandans.

This mystic inscription was sent to Count de Maurepas and probably baffled the Count and his advisers as much as it had bewildered the learned Jesuits in Quebec. While something was known of Tatarian inscriptions, the day of runic interpretation had not yet arrived. The stone was sent to Paris, where it should have received the attention of scholars. In 1911, shortly after hearing about this stone, I lost no time in visiting Paris. I made the rounds of all the museums, but none of the curators had ever heard of it. In 1928, on my next trip to Europe, I engaged in further research, but in vain. In 1950, through the aid of a Guggenheim Fellowship, I spent much time in Paris and Rouen, France, and in Canada, searching for records dealing with Count de Maurepas, but without important results.

Other interesting but inconclusive evidence of Viking occupation, has been turned up in the East, in the vicinity of
Newport.

The first of these—like La Verendrye's unverified account—
concerns a report of the discovery of what is described as an
ancient Norse boat.

In 1911 Mr. Barthinius Wick, an attorney of Cedar Rapids,
Iowa, much interested in history, came to Newport to study
the Tower. Among the men he talked with was J. P. Hammond,
a highly respected old settler, who told him that when the
Ocean Drive was built across the outlet of Lily Pond about
1866, remains of a small strange vessel had been uncovered in
the sand and clay of the marshy pond. He and Edward Kearney
and some other men had all inspected it. Mr. Hammond describes the vessel in a letter to Mr. Wick in the following
words: [81]

> As near as I can remember, she was about twenty-five feet
> long, with considerable sheer. The stem was quite prominent,
> and deeply, though roughly, carved. The stern was narrow
> and wedge-shaped, with peculiar rough carving thereon. She
> was deep or high-sided and had quite a narrow flat bottom.
> The boat was evidently built for speed and rough service, as
> her timbers were good and strong. . . . She must have been
> there a good many years, for her timber was as black as bog
> oak, and it takes time to color wood like that, so I conclude
> that the boat must have lain there undisturbed for centuries.
> We could only guess as to its origin, but in 1893 a real viking
> boat appeared in the Newport harbor. It had crossed the
> ocean and was on its way to the World's Fair in Chicago.
> It was the general agreement of those of us who had seen the
> boat unearthed at Lily Bay that in type it agreed closely
> with this viking boat.

At the upper end of Lily Pond an antique iron arm-ring was
found in the soil. It is just big enough to slip over the hand, and
it has a double spiral formation. If it were gold plated, it would

be just like the arm-rings which it was customary for the gentry of the Middle Ages to wear.

Of greater importance is a short runic inscription in Martha's Vineyard. This was found in 1922 on a rock in the woods of Mr. Godfrey Priester, about two miles southwest of North Tisbury. Mr. Priester is (or was) a fastidious gentleman of leisure who lived in Palm Beach, Florida, but spent his summers at Martha's Vineyard. He had a hired man, a recent immigrant from Ruthenia, and it was he who found the inscription while working in Mr. Priester's woods. He copied it on a piece of wrapping paper and brought it to Mr. Priester. This is how the copy on the coarse wrapping paper looks:

ᚦᚠᚱᛁᛘ

These are runic characters, but they make no sense when translated:

T ᛉ L I M

However, it is possible that the Ruthenian made some slight mistakes as he no doubt knew nothing about Norse runes. If we extend the vertical line of the second character upward a trifle, and if we insert a dot in the fork of the last character we get

ᚦᚦᚱᛁᛘ

This is a phonetic spelling of *Thollef,* a very common Norwegian name, but rarely used in Sweden and Denmark.

Of special interest is the runic ᛘ, the last letter in the inscription. As far as is known, *the only other existing inscription containing this form of the v is the Kensington inscription,* where it occurs ten times. But my book on the Kensington Stone, where this rune is first mentioned, did not come out until ten years after the Martha's Vineyard stone was found. This fact therefore points to the conclusion that the inscription dates from the 14th century, when this form was in use, unless some runic expert was at work.

The latter possibility fades, however, when we consider the external evidence. Only two men had anything to do with the finding of the inscription and the preservation of it. One was the Ruthenian laborer who copied the marks on it. It is not conceivable that this rustic had mastered the mutations of medieval Norse linguistics or solved the mystery of unstable runes. The other is Mr. Priester, who received the copy in 1922. There is nothing to show that he is an expert on this difficult subject, but even if he were, there is the consensus of those who know him that he is temperamentally disqualified for such misrepresentation. An aristocratic recluse with a passion for music, fastidious in his mode of life and much averse to publicity, would scarcely attempt to fake an inscription which would gain him nothing but possible ridicule.

We can well understand its origin if we assume that it was made by a member of the royal expedition of 1355-1364. This company of men spent many years in their headquarters at Newport Harbor, only thirty miles away. It is reasonable to assume that some of these young men would make trips in various directions to see what was to be seen. And, just as it is common for travelers of the present to scratch their names at places they visit, so also was it in medieval times.

I have given a complete report on all circumstances of this inscription, including a linguistic analysis, in *Scandinavian Studies,* a publication of the Society for the Advancement of Scandinavian Studies, Vol. 21, No. 2 (May 1949), pp. 79-88, and those who are interested can trace the details there. Since the find has received some attention, I mention it here, but in the absence of the stone itself, this reported find lacks much of being good evidence.

The Earliest Map
of America

IN THE Royal Library in Copenhagen are two old maps which show what is probably the earliest cartographical representation of America. One is by Sigurd Stefansson, who was Rector of the episcopal school at Skalholt in Iceland. This map is dated 1570 (see Figure 27). The other map is by Johannes Poulsen Resén (1561-1638), Rector Magnificus of the Royal Danish University and Bishop of Sjælland, Denmark. He was a man of outstanding scholarship, much interested in cartography. His map is dated 1605 (see Figure 28). It is so much like Stefansson's map that it is generally believed that the Resén map was a copy of the other.

This is an erroneous conclusion. Bishop Resén states in an annotation on the map that it was several centuries old (*ante aliquot centenos annos*),[82] and there is no reason to suppose that a man of his learning and stature would make false claims about it. Moreover, the map shows a number of dated discoveries by Davis, Frobisher and others which took place just a few years before the date on the map, and even one which took place the same year (1605). In view of these datings it would be absurd for the Bishop to claim that the map was several hundred years old. Bishops and university presidents dislike

[270]

nothing more than to be considered absurd. We must therefore find another explanation.

Nor is another explanation difficult to find. The cartographers of that time—and, for that matter, of all time—were obliged to build on the accepted work of previous map makers. Each new map therefore consisted largely of old data, to which was added such new facts and discoveries as were ascertained by each successive cartographer. Resen merely followed established procedure. He took an ancient and crudely drawn map of unknown date, showing countries which he had heard of, but had never seen depicted on any map, and inscribed on it (or on a copy of it) all the new discoveries of which he had information. The date, 1605, is therefore merely the date of his revision. Being an honest cartographer, the Bishop did not claim to be its author, nor did he make any changes in it, except to add new discoveries. The map made by Stefansson is likewise a copy of the same ancient map, but he gives no credit to the unknown map maker to whom he is indebted. The suggestion that Resén's map is a copy of Stefansson's is also untenable because the former is much more complete than the latter.

Resén's map, moreover, depicts a number of geographical details which were not known in 1605; which did not, indeed, become recognized until well into the 19th century. Among these details are the correct positions of both the Eastern Settlement (Österbygd) and the Western Settlement (Vesterbygd) on the southwest side of Greenland. In Iceland at that time it was the general belief that the Eastern Settlement lay on the east side of Greenland and that the Western Settlement lay to the west, as shown on Bishop Theodor Torlacius' beautiful map of 1668 (see Figure 29). Bishop Gudbrand Torlacius' map of 1607 shows the same conception. Stefansson evidently had no faith in this detail of the old map he was copying and therefore omitted mention of the location of the settlements. In Denmark even less was known about Greenland and America because the Icelandic manuscripts describing the discovery of

Greenland and America were not brought to Denmark until 1662. Not until Captain Graah, in 1829 and 1830, had spent two years pushing through the ice-covered eastern shore and demonstrated that the Norsemen could never have lived there, was there any doubt in the general opinion that the Eastern Settlement lay on the east coast of the land.

Another remarkable thing about Resén's map is that it shows good knowledge of Long Island Sound. This sound is supposed to have been discovered in 1609, but here we find it very well drawn on this much older map. Even if Resén's details are argued to be an addition to the old map, they still antedate any known discovery by four years. At the eastern end of the sound we find some islands just where they should be, and the western half of the north Long Island shore shows the same indentations as are shown on the Dutch map of Cornelis Hendrixson, dated March 27, 1614. Moreover, the location of these features correspond closely with existing geographical facts. This knowledge of American geography is so surprising for that early date that the reader will hesitate to believe the map was made as early as 1605 and even long before that time. He will think that there must be some other explanation. However, there is no other possibility, as will be shown below.

The Norse settlements in Greenland were destroyed by the Eskimo in the 14th and early part of the 15th century. There are three firm dates for the process of this destruction. The first is 1342, when the people of the Western Settlement, because of the repeated assaults of the Eskimo, emigrated to America. Before long, the Eskimo tried the same sniping attacks in the Eastern Settlement that had been successful in the Western, and in 1379 they killed eighteen Norsemen and took some prisoners. There were probably many such small attacks on the widely scattered homesteads of the far-flung fjords. This warfare finally culminated in a great naval attack by the savages in hundreds of kyaks who devastated one fjord after another, destroying the homes and churches, killing hundreds of people, and capturing many prisoners. This assault in force happened about 1418, but news of it did not reach the church authorities in Europe until thirty years later. There exists a report of it in a letter by Pope Nicolaus V in 1448, in which he states that this disaster took place thirty years earlier.[83] The Pope makes a strong plea to the bishops of Norway to bring spiritual aid to the survivors who were without priests, but if anything was done as a result of this plea, we have no record of it. The attack of 1418, therefore, seem to have been the deathblow to the Greenland colony which for almost 500 years had carried on, far out on the extreme edge of the known world, under the most adverse conditions.

Time went on, and the succeeding generations forgot Greenland. To ninety-nine out of a hundred of the older people it had been little more than a name, and now even that was forgotten. But about a hundred years after the last mentioned attack, the Archbishop of Trondheim in Norway, Erik Walchendorf, became interested in Greenland. As the former diocese of Greenland belonged to his archbishopric, all the church taxes of Greenland (paid *in natura*) passed through this office, and he found in the archives of the episcopal residence many old papers dealing with a large and active religious community in an unknown land far across the sea. It must have been a startling revelation. He became so interested in rediscovering this lost colony that in 1516 he organized a search expedition in which he personally intended to take part. Walchendorf even obtained the Pope's absolution for all its members. King Christian II, however, refused to let him go, probably because Walchendorf asked for a ten years' monopoly of Greenland's commerce. Later the Bishop seriously offended the King by speaking against the royal concubine, and he had to flee for his life.

During the next half century nothing was done to carry out Bishop Walchendorf's plans to rediscover Greenland, but in 1568 King Frederik of Norway-Denmark became interested in the project, and fitted out five successive expeditions—all unsuccessful. The difficulty was that no one knew where to look for Greenland. When Pope Nicolaus in 1448 wrote to the bishops of Norway to give aid to the Christian people of Greenland, he says that Greenland was "an island said to lie on the extreme border of the northern ocean, north of Norway."[83] Actually, that part of Greenland which was inhabited by the Norsemen lies directly west of the *southern* part of Norway. This far northern location of Greenland was the opinion of "the learned" in the 15th and 16th centuries, but in Norway and Denmark it was believed that it did not lie north of Norway, but northwest. Therefore we see that all the expeditions sent out by King Frederik, of which we have any record, sailed east and north of Iceland and then northwest until they were stopped by the arctic ice.

In the meantime, Queen Elizabeth of England had sent out several expeditions in search of a northwest passage to the Orient, and John Davis in 1585-86 had penetrated far up the so-called strait that bears his name. There, on the east side, he had seen an unknown land. One of his officers, named James Hall, believed this was Greenland, and in the years 1605-1607 he was hired by the King of Denmark to pilot three expeditions to that location. But as the greater part of the west coast of Greenland is uninhabitable, they found no evidences of former Norse occupation. As noted, moreover, it was the belief of everyone that the main settlement in Greenland, known as the Eastern Settlement, lay on the east coast of Greenland. Even in Iceland, where a clearer tradition obtained about the Greenland colonies, and where the old sailing directions were recorded in existing documents, it was believed that the main settlement lay on the east side. Expedition after expedition continued to be sent off to try and break through the icebound seafront on the east coast. We have a comprehensive report on these efforts of 400 years to find the homes and churches of this neglected colony.[84]

The only possible explanation of the fact that this old map gives a correct picture of the location of the Greenland colonies, is therefore that Bishop Resén was right when he said it was several centuries old. Such a dating brings us back to the time when the Greenland settlements still existed and had some connections with the outside world. But that is not enough. The map shows so much knowledge of American geography, that the one who drew the map must have spent considerable time in America, or obtained his information from one who had. We know of very few coastal voyages along the south shore of New England before 1605. The most important of these in post-Columbian times was that of Verrazano who had followed the south shore of Long Island and knew nothing of the great sound north of it. Nor was he aware of the geography of Greenland. He could not therefore have made this map.

Five hundred years before Verrazano, Thorfin Karlsevni of Iceland with a large company of men sailed westward from a point on what must certainly have been Cape Cod, following the shore, until he came to a fjord with a swift current. He went up this fjord and found it highly pleasing with mountains near by. This is a good description of the Harlem River at the north end of Manhattan Island. Here he built his headquarters, intending to settle there permanently. He tarried for three years until the hostility of the natives compelled him to leave. It therefore seems possible that the map was made by him and copied by later members of his family as a memento of their ancestor's great explorations, although the preservation of the map over such a long period seems unlikely.

There is at least circumstantial evidence that Karlsevni did sail on Long Island Sound. But all possibility that the original map was his must fade when one examines the impossible shape of Iceland as shown on the map (see Figure 3A). For several centuries Thorfin's family was one of the most cultured and eminent in Iceland, and no intelligent Icelander would make such a caricature of his island. In contrast, Stefansson's map (see Figure 27) shows Iceland very correctly, as does Thorlacius's, although the partial reproduction in the present volume (Figure

29) shows only the northwestern tip of Iceland. It is therefore evident that the man who drew this map was neither an Icelander nor acquainted with Iceland.

These facts show that a group of Scandinavians, not acquainted with Iceland, but well informed about Greenland, visited the shores of New England and Long Island Sound, not later than about 1400.

There is only one expedition which in personnel, purpose, time, and field of operations fulfills all these conditions. Once again the weight of the evidence points clearly to the royal expedition of 1355-1364, sent out by King Magnus Erikson to find the people of the Western Settlement of Greenland. This map may, indeed, be the firmest existing evidence that the Hudson Bay boat-guard, or some part of it, actually did return.

Apparently the purpose of the man who made this old map was to give some information about Vinland where he or his informer had spent several years. If it was indeed the boat-guard who first drew this map, it could, of course, be argued that Hudson Bay should appear in greater detail, for it was there the possible survivors remained with little to do but fish, hunt, and explore. But Hudson Bay must certainly have struck them as desolate and worthless territory, as nothing to return to for any reason. Very likely, however, the map-maker might have wished to pass on information about Vinland the Good where he, or his informant, had spent many months. He is not interested in sketching the coasts of Helluland and Markland, and merely shows their general location with reference to Vinland. But when he comes to represent Vinland itself, his cartography becomes detailed. He outlines the shape and orientation of Cape Cod, the promontory of Vinland, then he draws a fairly correct map of the south shore of New England with some bays, islands and headlands, all of which was known as Vinland.[85]

In presenting Resén's map (Figure 28), nothing has been added, but all the recent discoveries which he marked on the map and his long annotations have been omitted in order to show the map in its probable original form. Both maps at present show latitudinal parallels, but these do not harmonize with each other, which indicates that they were added later. Graded maps did not come into use until after the beginning of the 15th century, because of the lack of instruments for taking observations. Claudius Clavus, the Danish cartographer, was the first to make graded maps.

Reminiscences of the
Paul Knutson Expedition

IN REVIEWING our information about the royal expedition of
1355–1364, we are confronted with the fact that very few
of its members appear to have returned to Europe. We learn
that the expedition, at the time the Kensington inscription
was written, was widely separated in three parts. One group of
twenty or thirty men was endeavoring to return from Hudson
Bay to the headquarters in Vinland by an overland route. Of
these, ten men were killed in the camp by "the lake with two
skerries." The survivors almost certainly did not return to the
headquarters in Vinland; not even conjecture can follow them
with any assurance beyond the point where the St. Croix enters
the Mississippi. A second group of ten men had been left in
charge of the vessels at Hudson Bay. The third and probably the
largest group remained at the headquarters in Vinland. Sir Paul
Knutson, the commander, probably remained with this group,
and it is likely that they perished at sea, because Sir Paul, whose
name is often mentioned before 1355, is not mentioned later.
The indications, therefore, are that only the second group of ten
men, in whole or in part, could have had returned to Norway.

To the evidence of the kayaks that were hung in the two
cathedrals, and which has already been discussed, certain other

evidence may be added as indication that these men did indeed return.

First, there is the fact that the death of Bishop Arni of Greenland in 1349 did not become known in Norway until 1364. It follows that some ship from Greenland must have arrived in Norway in that year. Since shipping from Greenland had become non-existent at this time, and since it would be at just about this time that the boat-guard party did return, the fact that Arni's death was belatedly recorded in 1364 and that the new bishop was appointed in 1365 indicates a definite source of information which many schclars, Storm and Nansen among them, have accepted as conclusive evidence that some part of Knutson's expedition returned in 1363 or 1364.

Second, there is the map made by Claudius Clavus, the first cartographer of any importance in the Middle Ages and, as mentioned above, the first (1424) to make a map of Greenland having approximately the correct shape and orientation. Claudius Clavus is also the source of the information given by Archbishop Olaus Magnus concerning the kayaks captured by a royal battle fleet.

Clavus's first map shows only the eastern half of Greenland. Later, when he was appointed royal cartographer to the King of Denmark, he made a map showing the western half as well. Three details of this map are pertinent to the question of whether or not some part or all of the Hudson Bay boat-guard returned to Norway:

1. In an annotation on the map, Clavus mentions the skinboats as being in a Norwegian Cathedral and as having been captured by the Norsemen when the natives of Greenland tried to sink the Norwegians by boring holes from below the water line. This incident, moreover, is mentioned on many maps.[87]

2. The map not only shows that Greenland was wedge-shaped, but is the first to give a fairly good outline of the west coast up to the 72nd parallel. We know, from Archbishop Magnus's report

on the kayaks in the Oslo Cathedral, that the men who brought them sailed along the (west) coast of Greenland. It is, therefore, more than possible that Clavus got this information from their record.

3. The map of Clavus gives the latitude of the southern end of Greenland as 59° 15′ which is only a half degree short of the true position. If Clavus did not personally visit Greenland and make this observation, it must certainly have been made by a competent navigator.

Now it is true that Clavus claims to have visited Greenland. But all geographers are agreed that he could not have done so, because he does not give a single Norse place name, nor does he mention any Norse occupation, although that was still in existence in Greenland in the beginning of the 15th century. We have the record of a big wedding in Greenland in 1408 with guests from Iceland, and we have two papal letters mentioning that church service took place in 1418.

The fact is that Claudius Clavus was not a scrupulous scholar but a cartographical rogue who played extravagant tricks on his colleagues. There is an outstanding example of his lack of probity in the coastal names which he inscribed on his second map of Greenland. All the early map makers had one fault in common: in order to magnify their reputation for learning, they marked the coastlines of new countries with a bristling array of fictitious names of towns, rivers and promontories. Clavus was just as vain as anyone, but he used another system. Instead of using a lot of meaningless nouns, he used the successive words of a Danish folk song. Dr. Björnbo has shown that, beginning high up on the eastern coast on the Clavus map of Greenland, reading downward to the south end, and upward on the west coast, the words of the following folk song are inscribed as place names in quaint 14th century spelling (perhaps slightly distorted so as not to make his joke too obvious): [88]

Ther boer eynh manh ij eyn Grönelands aa	There lives a man by a Greenland bourn
Occ Spjellebodh mundhe hanyd heyde.	And Spjellebod he is named.
Meer hawer han aff uldesildh	More he has of a lousy hide
Een hanh hawer flesk hynth feyde.	Then he has of bacon fat.
Nordhum driwer sanden paa.	Northward drifts the sand.

This silly doggerel still adorns thousands of copies of Clavus's maps in many countries. It probably pleased his erratic fancy to think of learned scholars struggling to find a kernel of meaning in these strange words.

Despite Clavus's trickery, his second map of Greenland and other parts, dated 1467, showed large areas of land previously unknown and gave their proper locations. This map was copied innumerable times and exercised a great influence on the cartography of the 15th and 16th centuries. As he also (in his annotation on the map) endorsed the idea that Tartary (China) could be reached by sailing west, he undoubtedly had a considerable share in promoting the efforts made in 1476 (and discussed in the next chapter) to reach the Orient by sailing west or northwest, and which finally culminated in the voyage of Columbus in 1492.

While Clavus was a Dane, his maps were highly esteemed in southern Europe. Lucas mentions that a number of copies of the Clavus maps were made in Florence, Italy in the 15th century,[89] and are still to be seen in its Biblioteca Nazionale and the Laurenziana. Also, there was Toscanelli in Florence, on whose advice Columbus chiefly depended. Is it too much to assume that Toscanelli in turn was indebted in part to the maps he found in his own town?

These details from Clavus' second map, along with the fact that Clavus himself obviously did not sail these waters, must point to the conclusion that someone arrived in Norway with new cartographical information about Greenland at a time when shipping had all but ceased. Moreover, this 'someone' must have been a person who had instruments which enabled him to make fairly accurate astronomical observations, from whom Clavus later borrowed his information about Greenland, including the approximately correct latitude of the south end of Greenland.

Is it possible that any member of the Royal Expedition of 1355-1364 could take astronomical observations? It is generally understood that the quadrant and the astrolabe were not invented until a hundred years later, and without an instrument of this kind it would have been impossible to make the observations mentioned by Clavus. Columbus had an astrolabe in 1492, but Dr. Morison says "he was unable to use it on his First Voyage, and there is no evidence of his taking such an instrument on any other."

At the time of the Royal Expedition (ca. 1360) there was one man who was known as "the man with the astrolabe." He was Nicholas of Lynn, England, and he made one for John of Gaunt, Duke of Lancaster, who at that time was the foremost patron of art and literature in England. Apparently Nicholas was a famous traveler, and he wrote a book about the wonders of the islands of the northern seas called *Inventio Fortunata,* which is now lost, but is mentioned by many writers. Among them are Ferdinand Columbus and Bartolome de Las Casas, the historian of Columbus. He is also cited by Chaucer in his *Treatise on the Astrolabe.* The following is part of a statement in *The Dictionary of National Biography*:[90]

> Hakluit states that Nicholas of Lynne made a voyage to the lands near the North Pole in or about 1360. His authorities, Gerardus Mercator and John Dee, who make no reference to Nicholas by name, derive their information from James Cnoyan, of Bois-le-Duc, a Dutch explorer of uncertain date. Cnoyan's report, written in 'Belgica lingua' is lost. Mercator made extracts from it for his own use, and sent them in 1577 to John Dee. These extracts are preserved in the British

Museum. From them it appears that Cnoyan's knowledge was obtained from the narrative of "a priest who had an astrolabe." The narrative was presented to the King of Norway in 1364. According to this priest's account, an Oxford Franciscan, who was a good astronomer, made a voyage in 1360 through all the northern regions, and described all the wonders of those islands in a book which he gave to the King of England, and inscribed in Latin "Inventio Fortunata."

As this synopsis does not in all details agree with the original statements of Mercator and Dee, the latter are given below. The following is a translation of Mercator's inscription on the margin of his map of 1569.

Touching the description of the North partes, I have taken the same out of the voyage of James Cnoyen of Hartzevan Buske. . . . The most part, and chiefest things among the rest, he (Cnoyen) learned of a certaine priest in the King of Norwayes court, in the yeere 1364. This priest was descended from them which King Arthur had sent to inhabite these Islands, and he reported that in the yeere 1360, a certain English Frier, a Franciscan, and Mathematician of Oxford, came into those Islands, who leaving them, and passing further by his Magicall Arte, described all those places that he sawe, and tooke the height of them with his Astrolabe, according to the form that I (Gerard Mercator) have set downe in my mappe, and as I have taken it out of the aforesaid James Cnoyen.

The mathematician John Dee, contemporaneous with Mercator, apparently had access to the same source (Cnoyen), and he writes:

Anno 1360 . . . a frier of Oxford, being a good Astronomer, went in companie with others to the most Northern Islands of the world, and there, leaving his company together, hee travailed alone, and purposely described all the Northerne Islands, with the indrawing seas; and the record thereof at his returne he delivered to the King of England. The name of which booke is Inventio Fortunata, which book begins in its description at 54° and goes as far as the pole . . ."

We learn from these reports that Nicholas of Lynn was a member of a company of men who were visiting or exploring the northern islands. Apparently this group had a camp near latitude 54, because that is where Nicholas' explorations began. This latitude suggests Hudson Bay where there are many large islands north of latitude 54. Here the company divided and some of the men went with Nicholas to explore the northern islands.

This appears to be a definite reminiscence of the expedition sent out by King Magnus. Its mission was to find the lost Greenlanders, and this purpose would eventually lead the company up into Hudson Bay. We know from the Kensington Stone that this expedition in or about June, 1360 camped somewhere on the southwest shore of the Bay, not far from latitude 54. We further know from the same source that this company here divided, twenty men going into the interior, while ten men were left in charge of the (two) vessels so as to provide an exit for the explorers if and when they returned. As the best time to make the passage through the perilous Hudson Strait is in Fall, after the ice in the Foxe Channel from the previous winter has passed through the strait, Nicholas and his companions would have had several months for their exploration.

In this exploration of Hudson Bay we find an explanation for the sketch of Hudson Bay, called *Mare Glaciale,* shown on a Gemma Frisius globe of 1537 (see Figure 32).[152] Hudson Bay is supposed to have been discovered by Henry Hudson in 1610, but here, on a globe made seventy-three years earlier, there is an outline of it which is so good that the one who made it must certainly have sailed all over the Bay. Captain Fladmark, who first called my attention to this globe, called it "a most excellent map of Hudson Bay." That is putting it rather strongly, but when compared with maps of other and well known seas and countries, the delineation is quite good and indicates that the one who made it must have sailed all over the Bay. It is also shown, but less correctly, on a map by Johan Ruysch dated 1508, and on the Behaim globe of 1492 (Figure 33).

Apparently Nicholas was most interested in the aberrations of the compass, because Ruysch's map bears the following (doubtfully translated) annotation on the margin:

> In the book "De Inventione Fortunata" it may be read that below the arctic pole there is a surpassing area of magnetic rock 33 German miles in circumference. Below this is the *mare sugenum* (the out-pouring sea) which pours out water like a vase through openings below. Around it are 4 islands. . . . Extensive desolate mountains surround these islands for 24 days' journey, where there is no human habitation.

This magnetic pole center with its four surrounding islands is to be seen on many later charts. As the center of the magnetic area lies almost due north of Hudson Bay, it would be natural that Nicholas would be interested in its phenomena—the first study of the magnetic pole in history, and some 130 years before Columbus discovered that the magnetic needle did not always point to true north. The *mare sugenum* (this word *sugenum* indicates a sucking or whirling sea) was probably Hudson Strait which with its forty-foot tides is one of the most dangerous waters anywhere on earth.

The detailed description of the magnetic pole, of which Ruysch's note is merely a much condensed summary, indicates that Nicholas attempted a personal inspection of the magnetic pole area, which lies near 70 degrees north and 91 degrees west. It may seem doubtful that he could have penetrated that far north, but we have records of several other Norse penetrations much farther north in that same general area in the late Middle Ages. In Chapter 12, above, mention is made of the large accumulation of Norse artifacts on the island of Inugsuk on the 73rd parallel which marks this as a hunting station maintained for a long time. A little farther north is the island of Kingigtorsuak where a runic inscription was found dating from 1330. We also have a brief mention of the voyage made in 1266 or 1267 to learn where the Eskimo came from. That group penetrated into Kane Basin (about 80 degrees north). Here, too, Captain Nares found several Norse cairns proving that the Norsemen had been there several hundred years ago.

There is another point or two to clinch the reliability of the narrative about Nicholas of Lynn. The earliest report on him comes from James Cnoyen who, it is said, got his information in 1364 from a priest at the court of the King of Norway. This priest, it is said, was not a native Norwegian, but was descended from the people who long ago had settled on the northern islands. Now it happens that the best informed man by far concerning Greenland was Ivar Bardson, who was *born in Greenland*. He evidently returned to Norway with the survivors of the Paul Knutson expedition and had the best opportunity to learn of their adventures. In 1364 he was at the King's court to report the death of Bishop Arni in Greenland. He therefore appears to have been the first to report on the activities of Nicholas of Lynn. The same year he (Ivar) was given a benefice near Bergen.

It is not at all unlikely that Nicholas of Lynn was a member of the Royal Expedition. Lynn was the principal port in England through which the Norwegian trade was carried, and many Norwegian merchants were established there according to Alexander Bugge.[90a] In 1312 a merchant in Lynn levied a lien against no less than nine Norwegian vessels in the harbor of Lynn because of some claim he had against Norway. Between Lynn and Bergen, the chief port of Norway, there was much commerce so that news passed quickly from one to the other. Gisbrikt, the Bishop of Bergen, was an Englishman and may have known or heard of Nicholas, the learned Friar. The Bishop was no doubt much concerned about the welfare of this crusade for the preservation of the Faith, and as Sir Paul, the Commandant lived in Bergen, he had abundant opportunity to confer with him about the choice of a navigator. Such a great journey into unknown lands as was planned must have had a powerful appeal for Nicholas of Lynn, a man filled with scientific curiosity, and as this expedition was in need of a well qualified navigator, familiar with the latest devices, his presence would be very welcome.

We now have reports on the Royal Expedition of 1355-64, coming from no less than four widely separated sources. These are: first, a Norwegian record in the form of King Magnus's commission of 1354 to Paul Knutson; second, the Swedish record of Archbishop Olaus Magnus's report of 1555 on the preservation of the kayaks captured by the expedition while stopping at Greenland; third, an English record in the references to Nicholas of Lynn and in the citations from his work and history; and fourth, an American record in the Kensington inscription. These memoirs do not in any detail contradict, but corroborate each other in the following points:

1. All four documents agree that the expedition was planned to visit American waters in the latter half of the 14th century.

2. The English report and the Kensington inscription both mention that the expedition reached Hudson Bay in or about 1360.

3. Both of these reports agree that the expedition here divided in two parts.

4. The Norwegian report (Sir Paul's Commission) and the Kensington inscription agree that the expedition was binational in character.

5. The same and also the Swedish report agree that the expedition was religious in objective.

6. The English and the Norwegian data agree that the expedition returned in 1364.

Finally, a reminiscence of a different kind has been called to our attention by the late Philip Ainsworth Means, and may be appended here as incidentally interesting. It is found in the *Songe du vieil pelerin,* a literary work by Sir Philippe de Mezieres (1327-1405). This writer in his youth was an ardent crusader, and at the age of nineteen won his spurs of knighthood in the battle of Smyrna. Later he entered the service of

Peter, Count of Tripoli. When Peter became King of Cyprus and Jerusalem in 1360, Philippe became his chancellor. Together they went to many countries in Europe, including Norway, endeavoring to organize a new crusade against the Turks. The Abbe Cardon, an admirer of Philippe, says that in 1366 the latter made a second visit to Norway. Philippe mentions Norway both in the *Songe* and in his *Oratio tragedica*.[91]

As Means says: "The *Songe du vieil pelerin* was written in . . . 1389 and dedicated to the youthful King Charles VI of France." N. Jorga describes it thus:

> It is one of those allegorical voyages of which the Middle Ages were so fond. Queen Truth, wishing to observe their customs, visits the whole of Europe. . . . Contemporary customs are described in the work in a very lively fashion, and it is without doubt an historical document of the first order. The advice given therein is not less interesting.

The passage referring to Iceland, Greenland and America is paraphrased by Means as follows:

> The rich and precious Queen Truth left Prussia with all her fair company and passed to Yselant [Iceland] where she was so well entreated and so much honored by the Christian master of Yselant that she gave the country her blessing. Thence, led by an ardent desire for knowledge, the Queen and her ladies went to a far northern land very remote from other inhabited countries. This land was Godelant [Greenland]. The Queen and her ladies made their usual inquiries as to the customs of the country, and they found much which made them melancholy.
> From there they went to the kingdom of Norway and to that of Sweden and to that of Denmark, and they were sad to find that the Kings had the habit of fighting with one another. . . . They found that one of the three kings, he of Norway, had an enormous realm, and that part of it was on an island in the sea so far away from Norway and beyond Godelant that certain ships which he was wont to send thither to collect the tribute of his subjects had to take three years to go and come again. And on the ocean road they found so

many marvels, phantoms, and deviltries that it is astonishing
to hear of them.

Means comments thus on the above passage (*Newport
Tower,* 219):

> If the distant land beyond Greenland here referred to by
> Philippe de Mezieres . . . be not a secret surviving colony in
> Vinland, I am at loss to know what it can be. The "secret"
> nature of that colony may be guessed from the manner in which
> Philippe's Norwegian informants went out of their way to make
> the country sound unpleasant and the road thither full of
> terrors. This is a time-honored method of discouraging un-
> welcomed curiosity from foreigners. Since the royal ships used
> to go there in spite of distance to collect taxes, there must
> have been a considerable settlement in that distant possession
> of the Norwegian Crown.

It is doubtful if Means is right when he says that this proves
the existence of a "secret" colony in America in the 14th century. But the various circumstances that are mentioned are very
true of the Scandinavian countries in the 1360's. Sir Philippe
mentions four things: First, the Kings of Norway, Sweden and
Denmark were making war on each other—this was true in the
1360's. Second, that conditions were peaceful in Iceland—also
true of 1360, though after 1361 peace was an uncommon fact
in that restless island. Third, that in Greenland "they found
much which made them melancholy." In view of the fact that
a large part of the population had given up the Christian faith,
and the Western Settlement had been laid waste by the Eskimo,
Queen Truth had reason to feel melancholy. Finally we have
the fourth item, that the "island" far beyond Greenland belonged to Norway. Up to the time when the Paul Knutson
expedition reached Vinland, it could not be said that this region
was a part of the King of Norway's realm. But Sir Paul had
presumably taken possession of Vinland in the name of the
King, as was customary. We may, therefore, add one other
corroborative bit of evidence for the probable return of the

boat-guard in 1364, for we see by this that a land beyond Greenland belonging to the King of Norway was more or less known to be a fact in the latter half of the 14th century.

Philippe de Mezieres' statement that it required a voyage of three years to go to Vinland to collect taxes and return again seems to be a misconception on his part. Sir Philippe may have inquired if there was any sailing to this land beyond Greenland, and he might have been told that the King's men (members of the King's bodyguard) had recently returned on the royal vessel after an absence of several years, and he may have assumed that the "King's men" went there to collect taxes.

After the death of King Peter in 1369, Sir Philippe became councillor to King Charles V of France and served as such until the King died in 1380. Sir Philippe was, therefore, a highly respected nobleman, and we may assume that he sent copies of his Songe to many monarchs and high dignitaries, who in this way could have learned of the existence of new countries in the west. Whether or not Sir Philippe's allegory can be argued as pertinent to the Knutson expedition, the information contained in it cannot help but be interesting, the date considered. Additionally, the fact that Philippe was in a position to spread this information through Europe, may very well have helped motivate later voyages of discovery. It was on exactly such bits and hints of information that cartographers such as Toscanelli built their maps and speculations.

The Norwegian-Portuguese
Expedition to America
in 1476

AMONG THE men who have greatly influenced the aims and
energies of their fellow men in a material sense, there are few
who surpass Marco Polo (1254-1325). Before his time the
world was not envisioned as a great globe of far-flung states
and empires, filled with diverse peoples, strange products, and
alluring potentialities. Rather, the known world in the late
Middle Ages was only a dozen minor nations in the western
half of Europe, oscillating between stagnation and violence, and
doubtfully held in check by an ecclesiastical pontiff.

But then came Marco Polo, the world's number one traveler,
who told of twenty-four years' sojourn in great and wealthy
countries never heard of before. He told of China, enormously
rich, "most fertile in gold, pearls and precious stones, where
they cover the temples and royal residences with solid gold." He
described the great stone palaces of Siam and told of the vast
abundance of precious spices. He spoke of Japan and Java,
Burma, Indochina and India—all open for trade, where fortune
awaited men with enterprise.

This was long before the printing press was invented, so these revelations were not flung out to the multitude over night. But they had a tremendous appeal to man's greed and kindled a fire of new ambitions in the hearts of men. They suggested a new commerce with distant nations which resulted in vast maritime enterprises, the discovery of new continents, and the horrors of the slave trade.

In the beginning this progress was slow. It seemed that the only way to get the riches that Marco Polo said were to be had in the East was to do as he had done. So caravans were organized which crossed the desert, climbed the mountains, and pushed wearily on for 10,000 miles, just as did their distant kinsman 500 years later in the California Gold Rush. But the toil was tremendous, and it was not possible to carry many bags of spices on horse or camelback. Moreover, the dangers were innumerable, and most of the Argonauts found, not riches, but an inglorious death on the journey.

As the overland journey was so difficult, what about going by water? That was a question which it took a long time to answer, for the men of the Middle Ages had a most wholesome respect for the sea. Moreover, the cost of fitting out one or more vessels with their crews and cargoes for barter was a most serious handicap to a doubtful enterprise. But finally a man appeared who not only possessed the means, but also the courage to take up the battle with the sea. This was Henry, Prince of Portugal (1394-1460), who with singular devotion used all his efforts to open a seaway to the Orient by circumnavigating Africa.

But the seafaring men were timid about going southward because of the old and ominous belief that the equatorial zone was too hot for man to endure. It was claimed that the vertical rays of the sun were sure death to human life. Because of this myth, the explorations southward were slow and fainthearted. A short advance beyond the achievement of the previous voyage was all that the doubtful captains dared to make, and then an excuse was always found for returning. When Prince Henry died in 1460, the numerous expeditions he had promoted had not yet reached within 600 miles of the equator. The African continent seemed endless, and it was not until 1488 that Bartholomeu Diaz rounded the Cape of Good Hope.

To further stimulate speculation, in 1450, a grandiose statement to the Pope was made by King Christian I. This monarch was huge in body, pompous in manner, and given to making large claims. He said that his kingdom of Norway lay near to, or was connected with the country of the Tartars (meaning China). The Pope in his reply is reported to have said that this statement had created much discussion among his "astrologers."[94]

With our greater opportunity for gaining knowledge, we are inclined to smile at the naive conceptions of 500 years ago. But in those credulous and superstitious times, people were in no position to pass judgment on things beyond their immediate horizon, and Sir John Mandeville's tall stories about his travels were generally accepted at face value. It was therefore believed in the latter half of the 15th century that Greenland was an extension of Asia. Thus, we see a good delineation of Greenland on the map made by Cantino in 1502, on which the cartographer has an annotation wherein he twice says that "it is the opinion of cosmographers that this (the southern point of Greenland) is the extreme point of Asia."

Feeling doubtful of ever reaching the Indies by circumnavigating Africa, Prince Henry began to ponder over the Northwest passage which later became so notorious. But it evidently led through a region of ice and cold, which his sailors feared just as much as they dreaded the equatorial heat. In order to accomplish an exploration in that direction, it was necessary to get the aid of a people accustomed to such a climate. He therefore devised a long-range program of courteous service to the Danish-Norwegian King, Christian I, with the object of getting that king to attempt an exploration of the seas west of Greenland. Dr. Sofus Larsen, Chief Librarian of the Royal University Library in Copenhagen, has related in detail the various courtesies shown to Danish noblemen by the Portuguese court at this time.[95] But Prince Henry died suddenly in 1460, and for a time his plans were laid aside.

King Alfonso shared his late uncle's keen interest in reaching the Orient. Feeling the need of expert advice, he communicated with an astrologer and cosmographer of high renown, Paolo Toscanelli of Florence. Toscanelli was most helpful and sent him a map and a letter dated June 25, 1474, in which he assured the king that a voyage of 5,000 nautical miles due west from Lisbon would bring him to Quinsay, a large city in China, greatly praised by Marco Polo.

Morison says: "Neither Alfonso V nor his son did anything about this extraordinary letter, whose echoes we shall find in Columbus' journals of every major voyage." But Morison must have missed the record of the letter for King Alfonso wrote to King Christian soon thereafter to persuade him to fit out an expedition. Alfonso probably supplied the necessary funds, while Christian provided the ships and the men, and this expedition, as we shall see, sailed two years later. One Portuguese nobleman was to accompany the expedition as observer. King Alfonso would no doubt have preferred to follow Toscanelli's advice to sail straight west, in which case it would have been another and more important Norse discovery of America. But King Christian did not approve of this course. Didrik Pining, the Norwegian skipper in command, knew the way to Greenland, and as Greenland was supposed to be the eastern extremity of Asia, the greater part of the northern route would be coastwise (so Christian thought) and therefore safer.

Alexander von Humboldt was the first in modern times (1836) to call attention to this expedition, but the data was then in such faulty shape that little investigation followed. In 1909, however, Dr. Louis Bobe published a letter dated 1551 in which this voyage is mentioned, and which also states that it was undertaken at the request of the Portuguese King, Alfonso V. The letter was written by Carsten Grip, the Burgomaster of Kiel, a man who evidently was interested in geographical research, in reply to a letter from King Christian III of Denmark. The letter in translation reads thus:[96]

> I have this year seen a map found in Paris, showing your Royal Majesty's land, Iceland, with a description of all the strange things there to be seen. It states that Iceland is twice as big as Sicily beyond Italy, and it further states that the two skippers Pining and Pothorst were sent out with several ships by Your Majesty's grandfather, Christian I, at the request of His Majesty, the King of Portugal on an expedition to the *new islands and the continent in the North.*

Christian I was King of Denmark from 1448 to 1481, and the only "islands" lying beyond Greenland which up to that time had been discovered were Vinland, Markland and Helluland, mentioned in the sagas. The term, continent, may have referred to the conjectural Asia of which Greenland was thought to be the tip and which Toscanelli had mentioned, or it may possibly be an echo from the Knutson expedition, some of whose members would have been the first to comprehend that they had found a continent.

This letter of Carsten Grip and other material led Dr. Larsen to give the subject a thorough study. In 1920 he published a book entitled *Danmark og Portugal i det Femtende Aarhundrede,* in which, with much detail, he presents evidence to show that this expedition was sent out in the 1470's. The book was translated into English and French in 1924 with the title *The Discovery of America Twenty Years Before Columbus,* which is a better title. His thesis has been generally accepted as having proved its main claim.

Larsen's argument, and particularly his dating of the expedition, is based principally on a passage in P. Antonio Cordeyro's *Historia Insulana* which reads as follows:

"As the vice-royship of Terceyra was thus vacant on account
of the death of the first vice-roy, Jacome de Bruges, thereupon
there landed at Terceyra two noblemen who came from the
land of stockfishes which they had gone out to discover by
order of the Portuguese king. One called himself Joao Vaz
Cortereal and the other Alvaro Martins Homem. Now, as soon
as they had procured information about the island, it pleased
them so much that they returned to Portugal and petitioned
that they might have it, i. e., the government of it as a reward
for their services, and as our infante Dom Henrique had already
died then and had been succeeded as governor of the Order of
Christ by the infante Dom Fernando whose widow the infanta
D. Brites was still alive, and as such was the guardian of her
son the duke, Dom Diego, who was a minor, this infanta rewarded the two noblemen who applied for the vice-royship of
Terceyra by dividing it between them both, in two vice-royships
of which one comprised Angra, the other Praya, just as that of
Madeyra was divided in two; Funchal and Machico. Therefore the deed of gift of the vice-royship of Praya, made out to
Alvaro Martins Homem, must be among the archives of the
castle at Praya. The deed of gift to Joao Vaz Cortereal is extant; I have seen it in an old register in the archives of the
castle of Angra on page 243, and therein the deed of gift to
Alvaro Martins Homem is mentioned.[97]

Harrisse, the historian of Gaspar Cortereal, writing some
years before Dr. Larsen's work appeared, has expressed doubts
of the validity of some of the allusions to Joao Cortereal's
voyage, and especially about the reliability of Cordeyro, because
the latter had gotten much of his information from Gaspar
Fructuosa, an unskilled historian. However, Larsen has answered these objections so convincingly as to leave this reader
completely satisfied.

For that matter, the 18th century testimony of Cordeyro and
Fructuoso is immaterial, because the fact of Joao Cortereal's
discovery is mentioned a couple of centuries earlier. Larsen
has called attention to the fact that Kunstman's Atlas, published in 1859, contains a reproduction of an atlas by Vaz
Dourado, the original of which, dated 1571, is found in the

Record Office of Lisbon. On sheet two of this Atlas is found a map of a part of America, and here is shown a point of land marked *Teso de Joao Vaz,* and a bay called *b(aia) de Joao Vaz.* As Larsen says, "the place and name in conjunction render it beyond doubt that here we have an allusion to Joao Vaz Cortereal." In addition, Jörgen Lechler has pointed out that no less than five earlier maps record the discoveries of Joao Cortereal.[98] These five are:

1535 La Riccardiana:	Terra do Ja Vaz, B. de Ja Vaz
1541 Desliens:	Terra de Jeha baz
1546 Desceliers I:	G. de Ja. Vaaz
1550 Desceliers II:	Terra de Jehan Vaaz
1568 Fernao Vaz Dourado:	Terra de J. Vaaz

There are, besides these, numerous other early and more complete mentions of this discovery, some of which will be given below.

Certain difficulties cloud the record, however. The names of the commanders of the expedition, one must note, are not given by Cordeyro. They are first mentioned by Carsten Grip, Burgomaster of Kiel, in answer to the king's request for certain books and maps. On the Paris map which mentions the commanders they are said to be Pining and Pothorst.

This is the first and last time that these names are mentioned in connection with this enterprise. Instead we find a number of references to an expedition to America at approximately this time, in which the commander is always given as Jon or Johannes Skolp, and the date not as 1472 but 1476. Here are some of them:

In 1533 the priest Francesco Lopez Gomara published a work entitled *Historia de las Indias,* by which he means a history of America. In speaking of Labrador he says: "Here also have come people from Norway under the pilot Johannes Scolvus, and the English with Sebastian Cabot." Later he adds: "Much knowledge and experience has been gained about how one sails from Norway passing right below the North Pole and then south along the coast to China."

Fridtjof Nansen has added another reference to our knowledge of this expedition. In an English State document from about 1575, there is a brief mention of all the early attempts to find the Northwest Passage. After a mention of Cabot's voyage in 1497 and of Caspar Cortereal's in 1500, it says: "To find the passage from the North Sea to the South Sea (the Pacific), we must sail to the 60th degree, that is, from 66 to 68. On the north side of this passage was John Scolvus, a pilot from Denmark in 1476."[99] This description precisely fits the eastern end of Hudson Strait which in the Middle Ages was thought to be Ginungagap, the connecting link between the inner and the outer ocean.

Cornelius Wytfliet, a Dutch author, writes in 1597: "But the honor of America's second discovery (after the Zeno brothers) belongs to Johannes Scolvus Pilonus who in the year 1476 sailed into the northern strait under the Arctic circle, and came to Labrador and Estotiland."

On a globe made by Gemma Frisius, in conjunction with Gerhard Mercator, about 1537 there is an annotation north of the strait marked *Fretum trium fratrum* (the Bay of St. Lawrence) which reads: *Quij Populi, ad quos Johannes Scolvus peruenit circa annum 1476* ("The Quii People to whom Johannes Scolvus penetrated about 1476"). This name *Quij* has puzzled all commentators. It is given as the name of a tribe in the far northern part of America. I believe we have here the name of the Cree Indians who occupied the region south of Hudson Bay and northwest of the Bay of St. Lawrence. Their full name is variously spelled Kristenaux, Quenestinos, Kilistinos etc., but they were commonly called the Cree, which vocally, is much like Quii.

We also have two references made in 1605 to Johannes Scolvus on Resén's map. One is at the southern point of Greenland, the other at a land west of Greenland. Both of these notes read: "Here came Johannes Scolvus in 1476."

The earliest surviving reference to the expedition of 1476 is found in a letter dated July 14, 1493, written by Dr. Monetarius in Nuremberg to the Portuguese king on behalf of Martin Behaim. In this letter Monetarius mentions that the Duke of Moscow "a few years ago had discovered the great island of Greenland, the coast of which stretches more than 300 leagues, and where there is still a numerous colony of the Duke's subjects."[99a] This can only refer to the Pining-Skolp expedition following the coast of Greenland for many hundred miles on their voyage up to the Hudson Strait. Monetarius' mistake in saying that Greenland belonged to Russia was probably due to the fact that Behaim (following Nicholas Germanus) placed Greenland north of Russia.

Summarizing the above, we have eight references to Joao Cortereal's voyage of discovery, briefly mentioned on maps. We also have seven or eight other more complete references to its Norwegian commanders and to the fact that the expedition was of Portuguese origin. These references are found on Dutch, English, French, German, Portuguese and Spanish maps and documents, and their widespread recurrence indicates that they were derived from early reports that had wide publicity. One of these maps mentions that the expedition was under the command of Pining and Pothorst, while six mention Skolp as commander.

Didrik Pining is a well-known person in Norwegian history. He came from the same district in Norway as Paul Knutson, the commandant of the expedition of 1355-1364, and at various times held many important offices. He was a military commander, Chief Judge of Gulathing, Admiral of the Danish-Norwegian fleet in the Baltic Sea, and Governor of Iceland. This last office appears to have been his reward as commander of the elder Cortereal's expedition. In his later years he was especially famous as the persistent and relentless enemy of the Hanseatic League, which the people of the Scandinavian countries looked upon as the great octopus which had crushed all their commercial efforts in the 14th and 15th centuries. Like other resourceful and tireless gentlemen of those days, Pining was a famous freebooter, fighting not only under his country's flag, but also in the service of England.

Johannes Pothorst was Pining's constant companion at sea. Of Johannes Skolp nothing is known except what is related above. There is only one family by the name of Skolp in Norwegian history, so it is likely that he belonged to this prominent family whose home was in Söndmöre in western Norway.[100] Skolp and Pothorst are probably two names of the same person. There is some evidence that Johannes Skolp was knighted in reward for his services on the expedition of 1476, and that as the name Skolp had a plebian sound, he was given another, Pothorst, which the king, being of Germanic stock, favored. The Pothorst escutcheon appears on a vault in the Maria Church in Elsinore which was then the principal seaport of Denmark.

The question remains: Did this expedition take place in 1476, the date mentioned by six different early writers, or in 1472 (or 1473)? Larsen's sole authority for the earlier date rests on Cordeyro's statement that Joao Cortereal and Alvaro M. Homen were appointed vice-roys of Angra and Praya early in the spring of 1474 as reward for their explorations in "the land of the stockfishes." But Cordeyro's testimony is unsatisfactory because much of what he says is incorrect. Homen was not a member of the expedition because, as Larsen shows, he had been in temporary charge of Terceira for several years. Cordeyro's surmise that Cortereal was appointed vice-roy of Angra as a reward for his exploration of lands in the west is therefore of little value.

The 1472 date for the expedition not only lacks supporting evidence, but is unlikely because of King Alfonso's preoccupa-

tion with the war against the Moors. In 1471 he invaded
Morocco and carried on an intensive and successful war by
which he gained the title *Africano*. In 1475 that campaign was
crowned with victory, and he returned to Lisbon with much
honor and riches. This time of great elation was therefore a
highly auspicious time for him to seek new honors in exploration. Furthermore, it is not likely that the king would first send
out his expedition and then later inquire about the wisdom
of doing so. The date of Toscanelli's letter (1474) therefore
seems to prove that the date 1472 is wrong.

In any event, the expedition started with a Portuguese observer on board. For this mission the king needed a man of
competence and discretion, and Joao Cortereal, one of his officers in the African campaign, to whom he had entrusted the
governorship of Terceira was probably just such a man. Moreover, as he was under obligation to the king, he could not well
say no. More likely, he would be eager to go, because the thought
of discovering new lands carried with it many possibilities. As
his three sons were now grown men, they could take his place
during his absence.

When Cortereal returned and reported that no sea-way to
China was found, King Alfonso's hope of a northwest passage
was blasted. The enterprise had been a failure. Moreover he
was in most difficult circumstances. In 1476 he lost the war
against his wife's brother-in-law, King Ferdinand, and was
compelled to abdicate. Mortified and weary of mundane affairs,
he soon withdrew into a monastery to meditate on the futility
of life.

But Cortereal had other visions. Personally he did nothing
more. He was getting old, and as he had a well-paid job of
much honor, there was no incentive for him to undertake
further dangerous journeys. But he had three sons, and his
reports about the new lands which he had seen in the west were
evidently so promising that these sons spent the entire family
fortune in paying the expenses of fitting out expedition after

expedition to find them. At first there seemed no reason for hurrying, but when the Spaniards overran the islands of the Caribbean, and especially when Cabot found his way to the very location of the elder Cortereal's discoveries, no time was to be lost if they were to hold the lands he had discovered.

In this devotion of the sons to their father's dream of exploiting a new continent, we have excellent proof of the truth of his discovery. Gaspar Cortereal, the youngest of the three, led two expeditions to rediscover the lands found by his father, while his brothers put up the money. On May 12, 1500, King Manuel (1469-1521) obligingly signed a deed of gift, wherein Gaspar and his heirs were granted extensive rights on the islands and on the continent which he, at his own expense and risk, intended to *rediscover* or search for. The term *continent* is highly significant because it indicates that the elder Cortereal must have penetrated up the St. Lawrence River, whose vast flood of waters would convince him he had found a continent. Nothing is known of the results of Gaspar's first voyage, but in 1501 he set out again, this time with three ships. Two of these returned, but the third, on which Gaspar sailed, was wrecked.

On January 15, 1502, King Manuel issued a deed of gift to Miguel Cortereal, a brother of Gaspar, granting him half of the lands discovered by Gaspar, as well as those discovered by himself. With indomitable purpose Miguel set out with two vessels, but he was never seen again. As Dr. Larsen says:[101]

> Old Joao Vaz and his sons all undoubtedly cherished a hope, that this far off fairyland, in time to come, should prove a source of wealth and fame to the family. These enterprises cost the lives of two of Joao Vaz's sons besides involving the family in great financial straits, but in return they threw a luster of fame over the aristocratic old family.

Despite the failure of the Cortereals to realize their hopes, there is good reason to believe that the expedition of 1476 greatly expanded the cartographer's knowledge of America, an expansion amply evidenced by the new discoveries shown on

Behaim's globe of 1492, the first known globe of the Middle Ages (See Figure 33).

Behaim's globe may at first appear to be an utter confusion, but careful consideration will show that it portrays new information accurately. To begin with, one must ignore the indicated location of the Pole. Behaim had no knowledge of the location of the Pole because no astronomical observations had yet been made in the Arctic regions. All he had to guide him was the uncertain knowledge of his times concerning the location of various parts of the northern world in relation to other known parts. He had no means of knowing on which side of the Pole the various "islands" lay. Divested of this confusion, the northern portions of Behaim's globe can be seen to be quite accurate, with one exception.

Beginning at the bottom of Figure 33, one sees *Scotlant* in position, and a proper distance to the east, the Jutland Peninsula. North of Jutland, one sees a large triangle marked *Nordwege* and *Swede,* the usual delineation of the Scandinavian Peninsula in Behaim's time.

But now there occurs an enormous error: Greenland is positioned immediately north of Norway across a narrow gulf! This misconception, it must be noted, turns up on most fifteenth century maps, among them the 1466 and 1482 maps of Nicolaus Germanus, the 1490 map of Henrik Martellus, the Laon globe of 1493, and the "King" map of 1502. The error seems to have been introduced by the energetic and scholarly Pope, Nicholas V, who, in a still extant letter of 1448, referred to Greenland as "an island lying on the extreme border of the northern ocean, *north* (italics mine) of Norway." Martin Behaim, in deference to pontifical authority and in the uncertain knowledge of the times, misplaced Greenland in conformity to Nicholas V's utterance. Had he placed it 90 degrees farther west, where it belongs, the remaining parts of the map would have fallen into proper place.

West of Greenland is Davis Strait, indicated on Behaim's globe as a gulf, and west of this gulf is Labrador. Behaim had probably heard of its towering sea coast because he marks it as mountainous. The long Hamilton Inlet of southern Labrador is also plainly marked on the globe. Southeast of Labrador, Behaim indicates an area of islands and narrow passages. Newfoundland, whose deep inlets were long thought to be straits, is customarily so depicted by early map-makers. Adjoining this area is a large block of land which probably represents Nova Scotia.

If the reader will turn Figure 33 so that the upper left hand corner points straight down, he will see at once that Nova Scotia is in proper position below a very good outline of the Gulf of St. Lawrence. If he will ignore the intruding polar circle, he will see the gulf bordered on the north by the straight east-west coast of Labrador with Newfoundland in position on the east, Nova Scotia on the south, New Brunswick and Gaspé on the west, and the wide estuary of the St. Lawrence properly located in the northwest corner of the Gulf. I am indebted to Captain R. Fladmark of the Norwegian merchant marine for calling this interesting map to my attention.

The fact that Behaim's globe, showing such detailed knowledge of the American shoreline, is dated 1492, must certainly tend to dramatize the fact that the lands Columbus sailed to "discover" were already rather extensively known. And to the information contained on Behaim's globe, one must further add the existence of detailed knowledge of Hudson Bay and of the American coast from Nova Scotia to Manhattan Island.

The many details of the shorelines beyond Greenland, and especially of the Gulf of St. Lawrence, as shown by Behaim do not appear on any earlier map, but it must be noted that Martin Behaim was in a particularly favorable position to learn of the most recent discoveries in these areas. In 1486 Behaim went to Fayal in the Azores and there married the sister of Joao Cortereal's son-in-law, remaining in the Azores four years. Living so close to Governor Cortereal and with family access to him, he was ideally situated to learn about the lands discovered by

Cortereal, and Behaim's details of the outline of the Gulf of St. Lawrence—known for many years as *Gulfo Quadrato*—may well have been taken from a map made by the elder Cortereal when he, with Pining and Skolp (Pothurst), explored the gulf.

This expedition of 1476 appears to have been the last to bring tidings from Greenland until its rediscovery about 250 years later. In 1891, Reverend Luca Jelic of Dalmatia read a paper before the *Congres Scientifique Internationale des Catholiques* in Paris on the subject "The Evangelisation of America before Columbus." Much of the Reverend's dissertation is of no value because he was not familiar with the history of Vinland or Greenland, but he presented a hitherto unknown document from the papal archives—a letter of Pope Alexander VI replying to a petition from a Benedictine monk named Matthias to be appointed Bishop of Greenland.[103] This petition had been sent to the previous Pope, Innocent VIII (1484-1492), but had not been acted upon.

In making the appointment the Pope, as usual, repeats much of the applicant's letter, and from this we learn that Greenland is a large island which can only be reached in August because of the surrounding ice. Because of this barrier the applicant believed that no ship had reached Greenland during the previous eighty years and that no bishop or priest lived there. The result was that most of the inhabitants had given up the Christian faith, of which they had no other memory than an altar cloth (*corporale*) which once a year was displayed and which had last been used about a hundred years before when the former bishop consecrated the Lord's Supper.

The circumstances mentioned are true and historical. The last ship, known to have been to Greenland, returned to Norway in 1410 or as stated, "about eighty years ago," and the last officiating bishop died in 1383 "about a hundred years" earlier. The letter also indicates that news from Greenland had recently been brought to Europe, a detail that points directly to the Pining-Skolp expedition.

The Genesis of the Cabot and Columbus Voyages

JOAO CORTEREAL returned from America in 1476 to be met by the news that King Alfonso had entered a monastery. After Alfonso's abdication, Portugal undertook no further western exploration for a number of years. Nor, in Denmark, was Christian I much interested in the western wilderness despite his earlier grand claims to the Pope of a kingdom abutting Asia, and despite his earlier willingness to participate in a journey with Alfonso—for which Alfonso probably put up most of the cash. Cash, as a matter of fact, must have been very much on Christian's mind. As much a spendthrift as an idle braggart, Christian by this time was pawning his kingdom province by province to pay for his extravagances, and was in no position to fit out expeditions to distant and non-negotiable lands.

The merchants of Bristol, on the other hand, found the reports of new discoveries very interesting. Bristol was the principal port in the British Isles for the Icelandic trade in fish, wool, and other products en route to the British Isles and to France, Spain, and Portugal. Icelanders would be frequently in port there and they would certainly boast of their ancestors' discoveries in Markland and Wineland. Most of this talk could have been passed off as sailors' yarns by the people of Bristol, but now the Icelanders could report that they had actually talked with men of Pining's crew who had actually been to Markland. For that matter, Bristol was a thriving port, and some of the men from Pining's crew might very naturally have passed through to tell their stories in person. This Markland, or Woodland as it would be translated, was commonly supposed to be the same as *Brazil,* a name derived from the sapan wood of southern Asia. Many medieval maps show a mythical island named Brazil in the remote Western Ocean. Markland, then, was this island, and it was said to lie only a short distance from Vinland.

This promise of riches, straight west from Iceland, prompted a wealthy merchant named John Jay and some other men to send out a convoy of several ships in 1480. Thomas Lloyd, called "England's most scientific mariner," was the commander, but the expedition was not successful. For nine weeks it struggled forward, hindered by storms and calms. Then a persistent storm from the west drove the ships back again. Other attempts were made to cross the ocean, but nothing is known about them except that they were all unsuccessful until John Cabot (1450-1498) made the attempt.

Cabot was born in Genoa, but moved to Venice after reaching maturity. Little is known of his life in Venice, except that he was an importer of spices. The business could not have been very successful, because in 1490 he moved to Bristol, which was very far from the spice market. He learned some English, remained in England, and heard of the existence of a land in the west and of the vain attempts to reach it.

He must have been a man of forceful personality and great initiative because he succeeded in getting a commission from King Henry VII in March 1497, authorizing him to explore the sea wherever he chose to go, east, west, or north. So liberal a commission must have been thought quite an achievement for a recent immigrant who had not yet learned to speak fluent English. He departed in May, 1497 in one ship with eighteen men on board. A month later they discovered land, and they had little doubt that they had reached the land of the Great Khan in Cathay. It was perhaps some part of Nova Scotia. On August tenth, Cabot returned to England and was rewarded by the King with the post of Great Admiral.

Cabot immediately began to prepare for a second voyage. A number of Bristol merchants cooperated in fitting out five vessels for the purpose of exploring and colonizing the new lands. In the spring of 1498 the expedition set forth, but almost immediately ran into severe storms. One of the ships put into an Irish harbor and got back to England; but no further news was heard of the others. Thus perished John Cabot, a sturdy man and a great explorer.

We have now briefly reviewed 500 years of western seafaring history. In spite of the ravages of time and the loss of many records and maps, there is still much material left to show that the Norse discovery of America continued as a living tradition down to the time of Columbus.

Did Columbus know anything about Norse discoveries?

It is fairly safe to say that up to the end of 1476 he knew nothing of them. He was then only twenty-five years old, a weaver of cloth and a common illiterate sailor, apparently without any ambitious plans for the future. In 1476 he left the loom and enlisted as a seaman on board a vessel sailing in a large Genoese convoy which periodically made commercial trips to Lisbon, Flanders, and England. Shortly after entering the Atlantic, this convoy was attacked by a war fleet of thirteen vessels. A number of vessels were sunk, including the one on which Columbus was serving, and he was finally cast up on the shore of Portugal, clinging to a spar. He made his way to

Lisbon. Being a penniless sailor, he probably spent his time among poor folk.

That same year, 1476, Cortereal returned from his great trip to the western continent, but it is likely that Columbus heard nothing about it at that time. As a poor sailor, he would very probably be serving on some ship at sea. Or even were Columbus in Lisbon, Cortereal may have come overland from Copenhagen, not arriving till well into 1477. In any case, being a lone traveler, Cortereal may have kept his discovery a secret for the time being. The great pains his sons later took to protect a discovery they seemed to look upon as a family secret might suggest that Cortereal did not hurry to spread the news.

Columbus mentions in his writings that in February, 1477 he went to Iceland. This reference has been interpreted by many as indicating that Columbus went there to learn about the Norse voyages to Vinland. His statement about this journey reads thus:

> I sailed in the year 1477, in the month of February, a hundred leagues beyond the island of *Tile* (Iceland), whose northern part is in latitude 73° north, not 63° as some would have it be. Nor does it lie on the meridian where Ptolemy says the West begins, but much further west. And to this island, which is as big as England, come English with their merchandise, especially they of Bristol. And at the season when I was there, the sea was not frozen, but the tides were so great that in some places they rose to 26 *braccia*.[104]

Here, however, the line of speculation becomes rather confused. There would be nothing extraordinary in the fact that Columbus went to Iceland; he was after all a sailor, an especially venturesome one as we know, and sailors sail the seas. Nevertheless, his account raises many questions that have led scholars to doubt its accuracy.

If he did indeed go to Iceland, the most probable date of arrival would be sometime early in 1477, a matter of only a few months after the arrival from America of the Pining-Pothorst expedition. The arrival of these men with new word from those far lands of legend which Icelanders had not visited for generations, was a dramatic event, and the ports must have been alive with excited comment. If Columbus arrived on the scene at that time, the Icelanders' talk would have been for Columbus a dramatic introduction to the subject of western exploration, and certainly the turning point in his life.

Nevertheless there remain the doubts raised by the inaccuracies of his account. The account itself was written many years later, and contains tremendous errors. He presumes to correct the latitude of northern Iceland and is wrong by more than six degrees. He describes a tide of 26 *braccia*. A *braccia,* literally, "an arm," was computed at 22.9 inches. Columbus claims to have observed a tide at Iceland which rose fifty feet in February, when even the spring tide there is only thirteen feet!

Moreover, Columbus claims to have sailed a hundred leagues *beyond* Iceland. Considering that his league was computed at 3.18 nautical miles, he would have reached the vast Greenland ice-pack long before he had sailed that distance whether he sailed west or northwest from Iceland. And how could a sailor before the mast undertake such a voyage? There is certainly no likelihood that the captain would risk his ship in that unknown sea of ice-floes.

Many historians have argued the absurdity of this account as evidence that Columbus never made the journey but simply invented it as a piece of self-aggrandizement. Columbus' excellent biographer S. E. Morison cites several examples of his willingness to invent yarns that would present him as an intrepid voyager who shunned no danger. Other historians have argued that errors in Columbus' account were the result of faulty memory in the long interval between the voyage and the writing of his account, some of these errors being assisted by a certain amount of pure boastful invention. As Morison points out, however, there is no reason for rejecting Columbus's statement that he did sail to Iceland.

Whether the voyage was fact or fiction, it seems to have been sometime between 1477 and 1481 that Columbus wrote to Toscanelli for information on how to reach the western lands. Toscanelli was kind enough to send Columbus a copy of the documents he had earlier sent to the king. That letter and map, as Morison shows, were his guide and credo on all his later voyages.

In the meanwhile, Columbus must have advanced himself considerably. Within three years of his reported voyage he married the daughter of Bartholomew Perestrello, Governor of Porto Santo, which lies about thirty miles from Madeira, and he and his wife lived in Funchal on Madeira for some years. The marriage was fortunate for his future career, for here on Madeira, living in reasonable comfort, Columbus had the opportunity to study and to prepare for his great enterprise. Here he mulled over what had become known via Cortereal and the Pining-Pothorst expedition, and poured over Toscanelli's letter and map. He was sure he was right about the possibility of reaching eastern Asia. The Norwegian-Portuguese expedition had reached it. And even more certainly there was the chart and letter of the great scholar Toscanelli. Columbus' faith in Toscanelli never wavered.

The Pining-Pothorst expedition had reached a great land in the west, which all concerned, including Columbus, believed was Asia. But the expedition had not found Cipangu, Cathay, or the land of spices, because it had sailed too far to the north. But there, before him, lay Toscanelli's letter which explained that the correct course was straight west, or perhaps a little south of west. That letter, plus the huge but helpful under-estimate by Columbus of the breadth of the western ocean, led him to success.

Out of the turmoil and incomprehension of the Middle Ages arose America dimly, like a newborn world. Bold, indeed, were its first white visitors, Leif and Thorwald Erikson, Thorfin Karlsevni and others, for who knew what powers of evil here held dominion? They were followed by other land-hungry men who dauntlessly built their homes in the new land, some to fall as victims of the Red Men, while others prospered, and their ecclesiastical lord, Bishop Erik Gnupson, followed them, solicitous for their spirtual welfare.

To the more discreet Norsemen who remained in Greenland, America was for a long time only a vast timber reserve where they got the lumber needed for their homes, churches and various implements. But the time came when the entire population of three outlying Greenland parishes, harried by savage Eskimo, were compelled to seek refuge in America. Of their sad fate little is known, but the King of Norway, whose subjects they were, sent out a great expedition to bring them help, both temporal and spiritual. Members of that expedition left the Kensington Stone inscription—a memento of perhaps the most adventuresome enterprise of the Middle Ages.

And thus we see the early history of America slowly evolving and always dominated by Norse enterprise. In spite of the devastation of time, we follow it from century to century, faintly inscribed on fading charts and faulty manuscripts. And, when finally the more southerly countries of Europe became conscious of the existence of a great land in the west, it was to the Norse sea captains they turned for help in finding that land.

Linguistic Aspects of the Kensington Inscription

When the Kensington Stone was found more than a half century ago, its inscription was rejected as a fraud by some philologists because they could not read the date on the stone. They found the word *Vinland* and therefore assumed that the inscription purported to mention some event in the 11th century, when Vinland was discovered. That discovery took place in 1003, and as the language of the inscription manifestly is not of that period, they rejected the Stone as a hoax. Ten years later, when the study of the inscription was revived, it was shown that it was dated 1362, and that the early rejection was therefore based on false evidence. As the date in the inscription is the starting point for all evaluations of its faults and merits, these early judgments may therefore be ignored as being inconsequential and arbitrary.

Since that time the language and runes of the inscription have been subject to much careful study and many articles for and against the inscription have appeared. The following scholars have published articles attacking the inscription as a fake: G. T. Flom, Marius Hœgstad, Harry Andersen, Erik Moltke, K. M. Nielsen, Sven B. F. Jansson, and Erik Wahlgren. Their total number of pages, not including reprints, is 97.

The following philologists have defended the authenticity of the inscription: Hjalmar Lindroth, Andrew Fossum, Knut Söderwall, O. E. Hagen, William Thalbitzer, Gustav Indrebo, F. S. Cawley, and S. N. Hagen. Their total number of pages, not including reprints, is 140. Nor does this include 75 pages in my first book, *The Kensington Stone,* the first detailed study of the language and runes of the inscription.

Let us now see what are the fatal philological facts which prove that this old weather-beaten inscription is a delusion and a snare.

The most criticized word in the inscription is *opdagelse.* This, word, it is claimed is an anachronism. It could not have been used in 1362 because it is not found in Söderwall's dictionary of medieval Swedish.

It is an error to conclude that a word did not exist in the medieval Swedish if it is not found in this excellent dictionary. As Professor Söderwall did not live in the Middle Ages, his only sources of information about Sweden's medieval vocabulary were the preserved books and documents of that period. This literature was rather limited in scope, and there are many words which he could not include in his dictionary because they are not mentioned in the old writings. As an example there is the word, *eldstál* (fire-steel), which was used in the flint-and-fire-steel process of making fire. This steel was an implement which no house in the Middle Ages could be without. But it is not mentioned by Söderwall, because it does not occur in the old writings, which are mostly conveyances of land.

Professor Söderwall had no doubt that *opdage* was in use in the 14th century. I spent a couple of hours with him in his study, and he gave me the following statement:

> As far as I know, this word is not to be found in the meager literary fragments of the 14th century. But that proves nothing. As you probably know, these fragments consist chiefly of legal documents and homilies, and it is therefore not strange if a word of such comparatively rare import as *opdagelse* is not

found in such writings. The Old Norse word for this idea was *leita landa,* but this expression had become obsolete when the great change from Old Swedish to the Swedish of the late Middle Ages took place about 1300. As *landaleita* was dropped, some other term must have been adopted to express the same thought. The only word we know which fills this function is *opdage.*

It has been claimed that this word is of German or Friesian origin. But "it is not necessary to cross the creek to get water." The verb *daga* is an old Norse word in the meaning of "becoming day," "to reveal." We find it thus used in *Alvismal,* a mythical poem some hundreds of years older than 1362. Here trolls are spoken of as being *dagadr-uppi* or revealed by the coming of dawn. *"Uppi* ertu nu dvergr um *dagadr,* nu skinn sol i sali" (*Alvismal,* 36).[105] Transposing the words of the first clause, we have: *"Tu ert uppidagadr"* = "You are revealed." In *Grettis Saga,* 141, we read: "En Bardaelingar segja hana hafi *dagat uppi* þa þau glimdu" = "But the Bardalings said she was revealed when they wrestled." It has been claimed that the meaning "discover" in *opdage* was influenced by the German *entdecken.* Inasmuch, however, as the earliest citation for *entdecken* in Grimm's dictionary in the sense of "discover" is from Klopstock (1724-1803), this claim can hardly seem reasonable. The Norsemen were many centuries ahead of any other northern European nation in discovering new lands and would therefore be the first to use words to describe this activity. As they had a word of cognate meaning a thousand years ago, it was not necessary to borrow from other languages. We have a cognate word in the English *discover,* which is derived from the old French *découvrir,* "to be uncovered," "to come to light." No one can tell when these words changed from intransitive to transitive usage, and they probably did not change simultaneously in all parts.

There is nothing German about this word except the suffix— *else* (German—*nisse,* English—*ness*). But this suffix had been adopted in the Scandinavian countries from the German a century before the date on the Stone. (In *Vestgötalagen,* Ms. of 1285, we find *optagelse, opfarelse, opstandelse, fulkomelse,* etc.)

Another objection to the inscription is the allegation that it contains a number of English words. These alleged foreign "intruders" are *from, mans, of, illy* and *ded.*

From. The preposition *from (fråm,* Eng. *from)* occurs three times. Twice it is spelled *fro* and once *from.* This latter form occurs sporadically from the earliest days of Swedish literature down through the Middle Ages. It is mentioned by Falk and Torp in *Etymologisk Ordbog* as occurring in the old East Scandinavian. Söderwall called my attention to a number of medieval Swedish passages in which this preposition in the spelling of *fram* occurs.[106]

It may be objected that in the passages referred to the word is spelled *fram,* whereas the inscription has *fråm (from).*

The difference is merely dialectic. Professor Axel Kock has shown that long *a* when joined with a labial consonant had a tendency in the 14th century toward *å* and *o.*[107] In another place he writes: "During the 14th century the long *a*-sound changed to a sound more like long *å*; this transition was completed toward the year 1400."[107]

As there was no rune for the letter *å,* the runemaster has used the rune for *o.* Kock cites numerous examples from the 14th and 15th centuries of words with an *å*-sound which were written with *o,* such as *motte* for *måtte, forstondit* for *forståndit, gorden* for *gården, monga* for *många,* etc.[107]

The only pertinent criticism raises the question: inasmuch as the writer knew the normal form *frå* or *fro,* why did he also use *fråm?* Is not this illogical? Illogical it certainly is, but illogic of a sort which abounds in the writings of the Middle Ages. In a letter of 1341 we find *fra* and *fron* used only two lines apart. In a *Guide to Pilgrims* written about 1425 we find *fra, fran* and *från* used interchangeably.

Such laxity in the use of word forms is characteristic of the early days of writing. Professor Hagen cites an analogous case from Chaucer. "In the Prologue to the Canterbury Tales, line 404, 'There was noon swich *from* Hulle to Cartage,' may be compared with line 408: '*Fro* Gotland to the Cape Fynystere.' Nobody asks why Chaucer used both *from* and *fro* within the narrow space of five lines."[108]

Mans. In the sentence "(wi) har 10 *mans* we hawet," some critics found evidence to show that the inscription was written by a Swedish-American "because he uses the English plural form of mans." This is shallow criticism because there is no such plural form in English. *Mans* is the genitive singular of *madr* (English *man*), but it is also used in the meaning of people, *folk* and the genetive *mans* then often takes the function of the nominative or accusative as is seen in some of the illustrations given below. Professor Finnur Jonsson was much surprised when he was told that philologists in Oslo believed this was an anglicism. It happens that *mans* is used even now in Iceland as a term denoting *folk*—a number of people: "That voru malægt 250 *mans* og foru med gufuskibit."[109] In *Flateyjarbok* (ca. 1380) it occurs frequently coupled with terms denoting a number of people: "Olafr Konungr uar tha j nidarosi ok hafde med ser fiolda *mannz*."[110] "Fiolde *manz* fell thar of Aeirekssonum." It was also used in West Gothland in 1349:[111]

Han ok hans æruinge skal that goz ænnær like aghæ meth swa skiæl at theer guire mik ater swa mangæ peningæ som twer gother *maenz* of hans weghne og twer af mine sighia. (He and his heirs shall have the property with the understanding that they shall give me back so much money as two good men on his part and two on mine shall determine, etc.)

Of west. The phrase *fro Vinland of west* has been translated by some critics *"from Vinland of the West,"* and they see in this an anglicism. As there never was a Vinland of the East, this translation does not make good sense. But the author of the Kensington inscription knew his medieval language better than his critics. *Of* is a preposition meaning over, across, through, and round about. The following passages from writings of the 13th and 14th centuries illustrate this:

Of allan Noreg (over all Norway).

Vestr for ek *of* ver (westward I fared across the sea).

Han for *of* Biskops syslu sina (he traveled round about his diocese). These and many similar illustrations may be seen in Vigfusson's *Icelandic Dictionary* and Fritzner's *Ordbog over the Gamle Norske Sprog*.[112]

Ded. Most critics believe that this is a misspelling of the English word *dead.* They point to it as an illustration of the tendency of immigrants in America to mix English words with their native speech. It is true that such mixing is common, but there is a certain system about it. Words pertaining to their daily life such as farm, barn, stable, dinner, bedroom, factory, good time, etc., are quickly adopted into their native speech, but this is not the case with sacred or serious words such as God, savior, church, death, grave, government, etc. This is a rule I have never heard violated.[113] Professor Kock has given a much better and no doubt correct explanation of this spelling of *ded* for *död.* (The ö has the sound of *u* in urn). He points out in his history of Swedish phonetics that there was in the writings of the Middle Ages a frequent substitution of *e* for *ö,* such as *hera* for *höra, bredr* for *brödr, lena* for *löna, grea* for *gröa,* etc.[114] Rydquist also gives a large number of illustrations of this tendency.[115] In a letter written in 1390 by Queen Margaret we find two examples of this. One is her spelling of the name of Lödöse (she spells it *Ledese*). The other is her spelling of the same word which is criticized in the inscription. The sentence reads: "Effther the henne husbonde her Jens Herne *ded* er" = "because her husband, Sir Jense Herne, is dead."[116] Opponents of the inscription dispose of this annoying comparison by saying that the Queen (or her secretary) made a mistake. But if the writer of the letter could make a mistake, why could not also the writer of the inscription?

Illy or *illu*. It is not possible to say with certainty whether the rune for the last letter in this word is a *u* or a *y*. Neither of these letters occur elsewhere in the inscription. If it is read as a *u*, the critics are satisfied because there are two versions of the Lord's Prayer of the 14th century in which the form *illu* occurs. Nevertheless, I am inclined to think that the rune stands for *y*.

This word *illy* occurs in the prayer, "Ave Maria, save us from evil!" In this prayer we have a significant glimpse of the medieval attitude in the face of sudden death. These ten men who had been slain by the natives had had no opportunity to confess their sins and receiving final absolution. They were greatly in need of the prayers of their friends and fellow men. We, therefore, see how their solicitous comrade couples together the two most popular prayers of the Middle Ages, the Ave Maria and the Pater Noster, by citing the first words of the former and the last clause of the latter. In this way he hoped to enlist the good will of all who passed that way and read the invocation to join their supplication to his and thus cut short the punishment in purgatory of the ten victims.

The critics, through some strange linguistic aberration, chose to ignore the fact that this *illy* is a good old Norse word and claim that it is the English word *ill*, which the runemaster has somehow misspelled. In *Flateyjarbok*, Ms. of 1387, we read of *Ulfr in illi* (Ulf the evil) and *Torgrim ille*.[117] A Norwegian boundary description of 1268 reads: *Madr het Arne illi* (A man named Arne the evil).[118] These examples are in the nominative, and the word in the inscription is in the dative which properly took the ending *o* or *u*, as in the Lords Prayer of about 1300: *Frälse oss af illu* (save us from evil). However, it appears that the *u*-ending changed to *i* in some dialects later in the same century. This is illustrated in the refrain of a ballad harking back to the Black Plague of 1350:

"Hjælpe oss Gud å Maria Möy (Help us God and Virgin Mary
   Å frælsæ oss alle av illy"   And save us all from evil.)[119]

As no part of this inscription has escaped the stern scrutiny of the learned critics, this short and humble prayer has also been weighed in the balance and has been found wanting. The editor of a Swedish Historical Quarterly recently asserted that the inscription could not be authentic because this prayer was not in accordance with Catholic usage in the 14th century. He insisted that people at that time honored and worshipped the Virgin, but did not pray to her. He does not seem to know that this prayer, which originally was the greeting given in Luke 1:28 and 42, in the 14th century was given this form:

Ave Maria, Mother of God!
Pray for us sinners, now and in the hour of death!

This form is well-known to all Catholics. As further evidence we have the ballad above which has survived through many centuries of Lutheran domination, in which there is a prayer to the Virgin in every stanza. Archbishop John Ireland was so impressed with the proper medieval usage of this prayer that he publicly pointed to it as good evidence of the authenticity of the Kensington inscription.[120] Another Catholic historian, Professor James J. Walsh, author of *The Thirteenth, Greatest of Centuries,* gives the inscription similar endorsement for the same reason.[121]

Daghrise (pronounced *dagrĭsě,* a unit of distance equal to about 75 English miles) is another word which a few extremists claim is English. They say that the writer meant to write *reyse,* but was so steeped in English that he attempted to express the diphthong in *reyse* by the English spelling *rise.* This is a very laborious argument which leads nowhere. The English *rise* is a verb which has nothing to do with voyage or journey. Moreover it has only one syllable while *reyse* has two. One will therefore look in vain for such mixing in the speech of Swedes in America. It is particularly inapplicable to Olof Ohman, the finder of the stone who continues to be labeled by such critics as the "forger" of the inscription. He came to America as a grown man only seventeen years before the stone was found. He never learned to read or write English because he lived in a Swedish settlement, where only Swedish was spoken. On Sundays he heard a Swedish sermon, and his reading was confined to a Swedish newspaper. Likewise, when he went to town he bought his groceries from a Swedish merchant.

It is not necessary to go so far afield for a proper explanation. The man who wrote the inscription meant to write *rese,* a familiar word to all classes of Swedes, both in modern and ancient times. But the phonetics and spelling of the 14th century were rather lax. The invention of printing had not yet come along to standardize spelling and vowel sounds were not uniform in all parts of Sweden. Professor Adolf Noreen recognizes the existence of wide local variations in his discussion of the vowel *i*: "In several foreign languages, *as in Swedish dialects,* there is found a loose i-sound, formed somewhat further back (in the mouth), which often approaches *e.*"[121a] This spelling of *i* for *e* occurs frequently in 14th century documents. In Queen Margaret's letter of 1372 to King Håkon we find *bider* for *beder, ider* for *eder, smyd* for *smed, bytale* for *betale,* etc. As late as 1620 Captain Jens Munk writes *rinsdiur* for *rensdyr* (*Navigatio Septentrionalis,* p. 16), and the learned linguist, Ole Worm, writes *thry* for *tre* (*Fasti Danici,* liber III, 125). It has been objected that the *i* in these examples is short, whereas the *e* in *rese* is long. But, as Professor S. N. Hagen has pointed out, "-*rise* in the two instances in which it occurs is the second member of a compound, thus lacking the full stress of the simplex." Moreover, the *i* in the pronoun *ider* in the Queen's letter is long.

A more plausible argument is the claim that the language of the inscription, phonetically, is too modern to be of the 14th century. It does not sound like the hundreds of letters which have survived from that period.

This is quite true, but these letters do not truly represent the speech of the people. In the Middle Ages there were very few people who could read or write. The bishops were therefore instructed to appoint one or more monks to act as *Notarii publicii* in each district to draw up contracts, conveyances of sale, or testamentary gifts to the Church, for a fixed compensation. These scriveners constituted a professional class who took their accomplishments very seriously. In order to impress the common people with their learning and dignity, they adopted a stilted style based on the more sonorous language of the past. Aside from the names, the opening sentence was always the same: "Ollum monnum þeim som sea eda höjra þetta bref senda Paal Jonsson og Peter Berg quedia gudh ok sina." Then follow the details in as antique a wording as possible. Thus, the notaries gave the parties concerned an assurance that the document was drawn up in the most approved and time-honored form and was therefore above reproach and fully dependable, just as many legal documents, even now, are drawn up in clumsy and well-nigh obsolete language.

This antiquated style was favored by the professional scriveners into the 16th century, although it is recognized by many philologists that linguistically it was a thing of the past even in the 14th century. Professor Munch, writing of the 14th century, says:

> The melodious and highly inflected Old Norse language was being displaced by a less elegant transition language, marked by lacerated verb forms and the lack of strict grammatical rules and therefore probably not written the same way by any two writers . . . The regular grammatical inflections which distinguish all old languages were the first to be discarded . . . The neglect of inflectional endings and the substitution of particles or the use of certain modified sentence structures became characteristic.[146]

We see proof of these statements in letters written by persons who were not members of the notarial fraternity, but wrote their own letters. The following is a letter written in Oslo in August, 1371, by Henrik Henrikson who was the King's chap-

lain and later became Chancellor of Norway. The original
is preserved:

> Min aldrakæreste herra Konung Hakon, Jech helsar yder
> med gudh oc med min ödhmyuke thienest, Kungjör jach jder at
> erkebiscopin aff throndeim dödhe innan gaar vm nat hær
> j Oslo, oc herra Sigurdher comber ey aff siengenne fore
> öginowerk . . . Min Kære herre jach bider jder ffore Gudz
> döth sculd oc jder eghen heder sculd at j varin mich ey
> oblidhe fore nokon min darscap sculd elle bradha ord sculd,
> hawer iach eet hult hierta til jder hafft.[147]

The following is the beginning of a long letter, partly Swedish
and partly Norwegian, written by Queen Margaret to her
husband, King Hakon, in 1370 (or 1372). The original is
preserved:

> Idher min aldrakæriste Herra helser jak Margarete inner-
> ligha med Gudh, Kungör iak ider at jak ma væll, Gud late
> mik thet sama til idher spöria, vita skulin i thet min kære
> herra, at jak ok mine thjenæra liidhum stora nöödh vm mat
> oc dryk swa at hwargæ iak ælla the fangom vara nöödthorfft.
> Oc thy bider iak ider min kære herra at j finnon ther nokra
> vægha till at thet moghe bættras, at the som med mik æra
> ey skulu skylias vider mik fore hungers skuld . . . [148]

Another illustration, this time in a Norwegian letter, of what
Munch says about lacerated verb forms and lack of inflections
is found in a letter written in Oslo in 1401 by Sir Gaute Ericsson.
The original is preserved:

> Jæch Gaute Ericsson riddara kjænnæs thet med thætta mit
> opnæ breff um allæ the breff hwat helder the luda wpæ,
> lææn, penninga eller sysler eller giæld eller scyld som jæk
> her til hafur haft eller hafur af min herre Konung Magnus
> oc Konung Hakon . . . mælær jæk dödhæ oc gantze maktlösæ
> hvoræ the æræ eller finnæs, swa at the her æftær engin macht
> hafæ. . . . Men the tw breff som jæk nu fik af for(nævn)-
> de min herre Konung Eric oc min fruæ drotning Margareta
> . . . the sculæ blifuæ widh theræ macht wpa bodhe sidher
> æftær thy som de ludæ. Til meræ bewaring (af) allæ thissæ

forskriffnæ stykkes tha hafur jach mit inciglæ mædh wilghæ
og wit scap latit hengis for thettæ breff.[149]

The following is a letter written in West Gothland in 1372.
The original is preserved:

Konog Magnus ok konog Hacon med Gutz naat Konogga
j Norreghe ok Suereke helsar jak Tubbe Erekson odmiu med
guth Kunger jak jther thes at jak ær scild af Örabro, ak ligger
jak ok bithar een suar af thetta bref vm j vilen mina thyænest
haua ok vilen j mik nokot vnna j Vestrogötland, til Noreghes
vil jak ey ok jak Kan ey legge vacta for thy jak hauer mykct
folk huat j vilen mik göra thet Kungören mik med thenna
brefförara vel hauer jak andra vtuægha vtan jak vil eygh annot
bigripa for een jak hauer hört jthar villia.[150]

These letters written by a Royal Chancellor, a queen, a member of the Royal Council, and a military commander are sorry
specimens of orthography and syntax and prove the truth of
Munch's statement that there was no common standard of
writing. If read aloud, they show a wide difference from the
inflected notarial style and have a modern sound much like
that of the Kensington inscription.

The fact is that all these meticulous examinations of the inscription have failed to produce any evidence that it could not
have been written in the 14th century. There are certain peculiari-
ties—misspelled words, lax phonetics and doubtful grammar—but
there are none which can be proven incompatible with oral usage
at the time of the date it carries, which was before the printed
page had begun to standardize the written language. Thalbitzer,
O. E. Hagen, S. N. Hagen, Söderwall, Lindroth, Indrebö and
Fossum, all recognized Scandinavian philologists, have found
no reason to doubt the authenticity of the inscription because
of linguistic difficulties.

Even the most persistent critics are now becoming aware of
the futility of their criticisms and admit that they have not yet
proven their claim. The following are the statements of two

of the most recent critics. Dr. Erik Moltke of the National Museum in Copenhagen writes:

> There are many opinions on both sides. Some experts say that the inscription is genuine while others say it is false, and it would be difficult to appraise one expert's qualifications above another. One thing, however, is certain, and that is that it has not been proven that the inscription is false, nor has it been proven that it is genuine. Speech is a peculiar living fish, and it is not given to many desk-philologists to get a true grasp on it. What do we know about the spoken language of the 14th century? Very, very little, and that little which we think we know we quarrel about. We must therefore turn to the runes, and there, I believe, lies the solution.[122]

Dr. K. M. Nielsen of the Royal Library in Copenhagen, a very thorough philologist, writes:

> It would seem comparatively easy to determine by literary criteria whether the inscription is from the 14th or the 19th century. Objectively it can be shown that it does not agree with the existing manuscripts of the 14th century. But this does not prove that it cannot be from that time. One is here depending on a subjective opinion. The determining factor is the possibility of finding among these criteria one or more upon which one can safely build.[123]

This is a rather meager result after fifty years of energetic research by able scholars. K. M. Nielsen admits this and says:

> The mystery of the Kensington Stone has not yet been solved. Holand has made an impressive contribution to show that the inscription can be from 1362. It must therefore be the task of future research to show how it could have been made in modern times. To solve this problem it is necessary to examine the form of runes in use in Sweden in the 19th century and likewise the dialect in the region where Ohman came from. Only then can the philological and runological problems be said to be solved.
>
> If the inscription was made in the 19th century, then it seems that the runemaster can be no other than Ohman himself.[124]

It has been shown above that Ohman could not have written the inscription. He was a man able to read a Swedish newspaper, but illiterate in English and without linguistic or historical knowledge. The Minnesota Historical Society's Committee, which in 1909-10 thoroughly investigated the circumstances of the discovery of the stone, fully exonerated Mr. Ohman from any complicity in the creation of the inscription. The statement of the committee is as follows:

> Not one of all who have interviewed Mr. Ohman, whether believers or non-believers in the authenticity of the inscription, has seen any reason to question his veracity.[125]

One fact of importance which all linguistic critics overlook is the dialectal mixture in the membership of the Paul Knutson expedition. The Kensington inscription mentions the presence of eight Goths and twenty-two Norwegians; but there is no probability that these twenty-two were from the same parish in Norway. Quite likely there were some from the vicinity of Tunsberg in the southeastern part of Norway, where the king had his principal residence, and where the ambitious young men of the neighborhood had the best opportunity to reach the attention of the king. Paul Knutson, the Commander, was from western Norway (Onarheim near Bergen), and as the king authorized him to select the members of the expedition, it is likely that he would select some men, whom he knew as capable and trustworthy, from his own neighborhood. Membership in the King's Bodyguard was eagerly sought by all nobles and prominent men for their sons because it was about the only way to reach knighthood and worldly eminence. Very likely there were also some Danes from Skåne in the company, because the king had recently won this fertile Danish province, and he would favor the appointment of young men from that region as a means of maintaining the allegiance of its prominent men.

For seven years these young men from diverse parts of the Scandinavian countries had been together in close fellowship on shipboard and in camps. Indeed, the period was much longer, because many of them had been together as members of the King's Bodyguard for many years *before* the expedition started. Such close relations would result in considerable mixture of speech. We have a similar situation in the Scandinavian settlements in America. These settlements are seldom made up of people from one single parish in the old country. Usually there are two or more groups from different parts. Little by little there are changes in the dialect of each, caused by words borrowed from one another. In studying the linguistic problems of the Kensington inscription, this probability of dialectical mixture must be carefully noted.

The Runic Symbols

Runes are a type of alphabetic characters in wide use in the Scandinavian countries, Germany and England for a thousand years. The most generally accepted theory of their origin is that they were derived from the Greek alphabet in cursive writing. The Goths and kindred tribesmen in their wanderings early in the Christian era are supposed to have invented these characters in imitation of Greek writing from the shores of the Black Sea and then brought them back to their kinsmen on the Scandinavian peninsula. This early alphabet had twenty-four characters divided into three "eights." The Kylfer Stone (see any large encyclopedia) shows the complete alphabet. Eventually the alphabet was simplified by using one sign to represent two or more sounds, such as *p* for *b* and *p*, *k* for *g* and *k*, and *i* for *ı*, *e* and *j*. In this way, between the 9th and 11th centuries, a shorter alphabet of sixteen characters, known as the "younger" alphabet, came into common use. In this period runic epitaphs on stones became very popular and developed into a fine art.

After Christianity was established in the North about 1050, the Latin alphabet came into general use, and runic writing became rare. Moreover, these late inscriptions show many new forms. *Codex Runicus,* for instance, a law book of 200 pages, written in runes about 1275, has many new forms. We have an inscription, written by King Waldemar of Denmark in the first half of the 13th century. It contains only six short words, but there are four runes which in form are different from those in other inscriptions of the same period. These and many

similar deviations are discussed by Professor P. G. Thorson.[126]
It is therefore not strange if an inscription as late as the Ken-
sington Stone (1362) should show a number of singular forms.
These new forms are ᚷ ᚲ ᚠ ᛉ ᛆ ᚦ ᛒ

In the late Middle Ages, the people of the Scandinavian
countries kept track of their holy days and other dates by means
of a perpetual calendar which consisted principally of runic
letters. These were inscribed on a flat stick of wood about two
inches wide and upwards of three feet long, known as a
runstav. Dr. Moltke, a prominent runologist in Copenhagen,
believed that the faulty runes on the Kensington Stone were
derived from a late specimen of one of these perpetual calendars,
supposedly brought in by an early settler. He says:[127]

> If we inspect these calendars, we find, especially in those
> from the 16th and 17th centuries, that they operate with
> greatly degenerated runic alphabets which have forms not un-
> like those of the Kensington Stone. *There cannot therefore
> be the slightest doubt* that the writer of the Kensington inscrip-
> tion has constructed his alphabet from the alphabet of such a
> Swedish runic calendar.

This statement is without support because there is no evidence
whatever that the criticized forms on the Kensington Stone
were borrowed from a late runic calendar. This calendar consisted in part of the sixteen standard runes of the "younger"
alphabet, plus three new signs   ᚠ ᚷ ᚦ   , making a total of
nineteen signs for the nineteen years of the moon cycle.[128] In
1328, these nineteen runes were still without change as shown
by Ole Worm in his *Fasti Danici* published in 1643. They continued sporadically with very little change in form until the
beginning of the 17th century, when there was very little knowledge of the literary use of runes, and the signs on the runic
calendars became mere symbols, subject to more or less accidental modifications in the making of new runestaves.

On the Kensington Stone we have the standard runes which
were in use up to the 14th century with two or three changes.

The carver of the Kensington Stone has forgotten the correct form of runic *K* and has substituted the Latin K; likewise, his *a* is different and his *y* is upside down. He also uses dotted runes for *e* and *g* which came into general use in the 12th century, but which are not found on the runic calendars. Finally he needed some *umlauts,* and for these there were no runic archetypes. He was therefore obliged to introduce several new signs shown above. Moltke has been unable to show any connection between the criticized runes on the stone and the runic calendars, early or late, although he insisted that "there cannot be the slightest doubt that the Kensington runemaster has constructed his alphabet from the alphabet of a late runic calendar."

I give below the ancient alphabet of sixteen runes, together with the runes on the Kensington Stone, and the Latin equivalents of both; also the new runes that were added to both:

	The old *futhork* of sixteen runes	Dotted runes added in the XII century
Runes in use about 1200	ᚠᚢᚦᚨᚱᚲ:ᚺᚾᛁᛅᛋ:ᛏᛒᛘᛚᛦ	ᛏᛂᛒᛒᛂᛂ
Latin equivalents	*f u th o r k h n i a s t b m l R(y)*	*e d g p œ ø*
Kensington runes	ᚠᚡᛂᚨ ᚱ ᛅᚴᛁᚼᛐ ᛏᛒᛘᚱᚤ	ᛏᚼᛒᚷᛂᚠ
Latin equivalents	*f w d o r k h n i a s t b m l y*	*e g p œ ø j*

Moltke has a separate objection to the rune for *n* ᚾ
This is the form we find in most of the very numerous Swedish inscriptions of the 11th century. After that time very few inscriptions were made and they show some changes, including the *n* which is usually written ᚿ . Here, says Moltke, we find that "a rune which became extinct in 1100 is used on a stone dated 1362!"[129]

Moltke forgets that if the inscription is authentic, the carver did not get his runic lore from any learned book on runes because there were none in the 14th century. Nor were there any local runemasters, because we have no Swedish inscription from the 14th or 15th centuries, except on the island of Gotland and in Skane. But round about in the woods and fields of most parts of southern Sweden could be seen dignified memorials from former days, and here he could get his alphabet. He was presumably one of the eight Goths mentioned in the inscription and a native of West Gothland. Recently all the inscriptions in that province have been photographed and published.[130] Of these 98 readable inscriptions, 81 have precisely the same form of the *n* as is found on the Kensington Stone, and only 17 use the sign demanded by Moltke. It therefore seems reasonable that the carver of the stone would use the more common form.

For a while Moltke seemed to think that the runic calendars had an answer for everything. Rather brashly he declared that "The runic numerals prove *superabundantly* that the inscription is of a late (16th century) origin."[131] However, as it was not difficult to disprove this and the other two arguments, he finally rejected this thesis in the following words:

> Have we then shown that the inscription is false? Not at all; for while the degenerated calendar runes appear to belong to the 15th and 16th centuries, we cannot ignore the fact that Ole Worm's calendar was from 1328. We have reached that borderland of doubt which is the particular element of this inscription. The alphabet does not seem probable for the 14th century, but on the other hand it is impossible to disprove it.
>
> Precisely to the same point do we come when we turn to the numerals. Even in the late medieval inscriptions, dates are expressed either by Roman numerals or the number is written out with runes . . . , but Holand has succeeded in finding in the parchment literature examples of very early use of Arabic numbers.

Concerning his objection to the form of the letter *n* (ᛁ) he says: "It is not wise to lay emphasis on this form."

But in spite of these admissions, Moltke is by no means ready to admit the authenticity of the inscription. He has one argument which he thinks is conclusive. It is the presence in the inscription of the letter ᚠ in ᚼ ᛁ ᚠ ᚷ ᚱ *(skjar)*. He writes:[132]

In his eagerness to present as complete an alphabet as possible, the Kensington scribe has also constructed a *j*-rune. That he should not have done, because it happens that the letter *j* is a recent addition to the Latin alphabet, as is also the letter *v*. Both of these letters were invented by the French philosopher, Petrus Ramus, in the 16th century. . . . He took them from the Hebrew alphabet and added these two greatly needed consonants to the Latin alphabet.

Adolf Noreen, the master-philologist in Sweden, has pointed out that *j* as a consonant was in wide use in the 14th and 15th centuries.[132a] Von Friesen,[133] Kock,[134] and G. Vigfusson in his dictionary also mention that *j* as a consonant was in use in the Middle Ages in the Scandinavian countries. Most writers, however, continued to use *i* and *j* for both vowel and consonant. I have translated the ⸋ as consonantal *j* because that is its function at present. In this discussion it is immaterial how it was used. The important question is: was there such a letter or is it an invention of the runemaster?

The answer is that this letter was in general use in the 14th century. In *King Waldemars Jordebog* from about 1300, the writer's name, Jon, is written with a sign ⸋ which is a copy in reverse of the sign under discussion. Reversed runes occur frequently. In the Kensington inscription we find that both the *k* and the *g* are reversed. This means nothing except that it does not indicate that the runemaster got his knowledge of runes from books.

However, the runemaster may not have reversed the sign. In Norway, Sweden and Iceland the form with the oblique line on the right was common. In the Flatey Book, largely compiled by a Norwegian, Magnus Thorhallsson, this sign in cursive writing is found on every page.[135]

This sign ⸋ is also found in cursive form in many letters from the 14th century. As an illustration may be cited Queen Margaret's letter of 1370, where it occurs twenty-two times.[136] Below is shown a photostatic copy of the two first lines divided into four parts. The sign appears twice in the first line, once in the third and once in the fourth. Its form in cursive writing ( ) is clearly shown in the first letter of the first word, *Idher* (you). The curve to the left is merely ornamental and means no more than the curve to the left in the modern cursive capitals *B R* and *P* . If this curve is omitted, we have , the same as the sign in the inscription, the oblique line and the cross line being made by one swing of the pen.

Idher min aldrakærista herre helsar jak

Margareta innerligha med gudh. knngör iak

idr at jak ma væll Gud late mik det sama

til idr spöria. vita skulin I thet min Kære —

This character or is no longer in use, and is so little known to philologists that they thought it an invention of the runemaster. Its presence in the inscription is therefore excellent proof of its authenticity. Where could a forger have found this sign?

Moltke is wrong when he says that *v* was not introduced into Scandinavian usage until late in the 16th century. *V* or *w* (differentiated from *u*) is found on practically every page of the Flatey Book Ms., completed in 1387. Professor Storm mentions that an ancient *gildeskrå* (guild ordinance) from Trondheim, dating from the second half of the 13th century, always uses the *v*-sign. He gives a photostatic copy of the document.[137] A similar *v* is found in a letter from Bishop Nikulas of Oslo from the same period, and on many gravestones of the 14th century.[138] The writer of the Kensington inscription has placed his *v* across

the top of the runic staff, but as this resulted in an m-sign Υ ,
he has placed a dot in the left angle of the $v \psi$ to differentiate
it from m. Incidentally, as the sound of Norse v is something
between v and w in English, this rune in transliteration is sometimes expressed by a v and sometimes by a w.

Another much criticized rune is the $\ddot{\otimes}$, because it has two
dots above instead of one. But this does not seem to be any serious
indictment in view of the fact that the Hanseatic League which
controlled most of the business in southern Sweden and Norway
used an o with two dots above to designate $\ddot{o}$.

In the 14th century the letter $\ddot{o}$ was in a transitory form.
Manuscripts of that period show no less than ten ways of writing
this letter, and there are some writers who use two or three
forms on the same page without any difference in sound.[139]
The most common forms were o with one dot above, o with an
oblique bisecting line and a circumflex above, and o with a
cross in the middle. The first was the simplest and should therefore have become the dominant survivor, but it did not. Why
was this?

The explanation can only be found in strong foreign influence. In Germany at this time it was becoming customary
to mark *umlauts* (vowel mutations) with two dots above,
$\ddot{a}$, $\ddot{o}$ and $\ddot{u}$.[140] In the 1300's the Hanseatic League had an over-
whelming influence on commerce in the North, and the German
accountants presumably used the double dots in their invoices.
In this way they would become known to those members of the
King's Bodyguard whose daily task it was to keep the king's
large household supplied with food, clothing and equipment of
all kinds. It is therefore probable that the runemaster has
taken the $\ddot{o}$ with which he was familiar (an o with a cross
in the middle) and added the two dots that the bookkeepers
of the Hanseatic League were using. The rapid dominance
in writing of this sign ($\ddot{O}$) can only be explained by its German
origin through the Hansa representatives who dominated the
commerce of Sweden and Norway.

The ⼗ in the inscription is also a loan from the Latin alphabet, as it is precisely like the *k* in 14th century manuscripts, except that it is in a reversed position. Likewise the *y* (⼭) reflects the (⼴) of the same period. But as this is the runic sign for *g*, the runemaster has added another dot and also a line across the staff to differentiate it.

The origin of the runic *a* (✕) is somewhat doubtful, but it seems probable that the early ⼂ later changed to ✕ . This happened in some districts in Sweden, notably in Dalarne. However, this does not explain the presence of the little "hook" on the upper right side. In expressing the *umlaut* of *a* with ✕ , he is again following the new style of double dots introduced by the Hansa merchants.

In inscriptions in the "younger" alphabet the sign ᛒ was used for both *b* and *p* up to about 1200. After that time p is represented by both ᛒ and ᚲ . In the inscription the form is ᛒ , which indicates a local variant.

It is not strange to find some incorrect runes in this inscription. Most of the 3,000 rune stones that still remain have some erratic forms. The famous Kingigtorsuak Stone of Greenland, dating from 1333, contains only fourteen words, but four of its runes are different from those in common use in the 14th century. Yet no one has therefore impugned its authenticity. The Kensington inscription is what could be expected from that time. In the 14th century runic writing had become obsolete and was of interest only as an antiquarian curiosity. Among these men of West Gothland who were members of the King's Bodyguard and took part in the expedition, there were perhaps one or two who were interested in runic writing. However, in 1362 it was seven years since they had left their homes, and during that time there had been no opportunity of refreshing their knowledge of runic writing. Some of these quaint characters would therefore be forgotten. It would be interesting to know how many students of today, having taken a classical course in college, would seven years later remember all the

forms of the Greek alphabet. It may seem strange that the
explorers in these circumstances would use the runic alphabet
at all. But it possessed one merit of great importance. As it consists mostly of straight lines, it was much easier than the Latin
alphabet to inscribe on stone.

Those who argue against the authenticity of the Kensington
Stone have been much troubled by the scarcity of possible forgers
of the inscription. They realize that their work is not completed
until they can point to a plausible person as the creator of "the
hoax." If the stone had been found in an old, settled community,
the finger of suspicion would have had free range; but the situation in a pioneer settlement on the edge of the wilderness, where
every settler was well known to his neighbors, was different.
Where could one find a historian, a runologist, and a 14th century
linguist, all in one, in such a place? Since Olof Ohman was the
finder he became naturally suspect. To be sure, Ohman had been
thoroughly investigated by the committee of the Minnesota Historical Society and many others, and had been exonerated by
all (see p. 175). But even then he continued to be mentioned. There simply was no one else available for suspicion.

Moltke, for example, does not mention that Ohman had
been investigated and exonerated. As Ohman was needed to
serve as the villain, the only thing to do was to build him up
as a learned trickster. In Moltke's last article he makes the
following statement:[141]

> Ohman was not the dull-witted farmer Holand wants to
> make him, but rather a man with a remarkable interest in
> mysticism and history, and who owned antiquarian books which
> are not mentioned by Holand, although he has examined
> Ohman's library, *books that shed no little light* on the peculiar
> runic inscription and its orthography.

Here Moltke makes a very serious charge without presenting
any evidence. Incidentally, I have never alluded to Ohman
as being dull-witted. On the contrary, I have always said he

was intelligent, but with very little education—a total schooling of nine months.

A graver charge is Moltke's statement that "Ohman owned antiquarian books   . that shed no little light on the peculiar inscription." Moltke knows that this is not true because his co-worker, John A. Holvik, investigated and reported on these alleged runic books Here is the true story:

When I visited Ohman in 1907, he told me he had tried to learn what the inscription said. He heard that Andrew Anderson, who married a cousin of Mrs. Ohman, had a book which contained some signs like those on the stone. This book had belonged to Sven Fogelblad, the former minister (see p. 347) who had died in Anderson's house. Ohman borrowed this book and found the signs referred to, but they did not help him. The next year I visited Ohman and examined his library. The book he had mentioned was a Swedish grammar, but I could not see that it could have been of help in making the inscription.

When Winchell in 1909 went to Kensington to investigate the discovery of the stone, I told him about the grammar, and he bought it from Ohman. As Winchell could not read Swedish, he looked about for someone who could help him. He was told that John A Holvik, a student in the Lutheran Seminary in St. Paul, had been studying in Oslo. He asked Holvik to report on the possibility that this grammar may have helped a supposed forger to make the inscription. Holvik gave it a careful inspection whereupon he made a proper and detailed report which concludes as follows:[142]

> To summarize: The difference in rune systems, and the so-called "errors" in the inscription, with some parallel correct forms in the book, make it evident that there is no connection between the inscription on the Kensington Stone and the book bearing the name Sv Fogelblad.
>
> Yours truly
>
> J. A. Holvik.

Since Holvik was selected for this job, partly because he was known as an unbeliever in the authenticity of the Kensington inscription, Moltke's claim must be dismissed as unfounded. Moreover, because he knew of Holvik's report, it having been printed in the official committee report, and again in my first book on the Kensington Stone, his statement must further be labeled reckless.

Aside from this borrowed grammar book examined by Holvik, Ohman's "library" consisted of only one book in addition to a bible, a hymnbook and a few elementary school books. This other book is entitled *Den Kunskapsrike Skolmästaren—The Well-informed Schoolmaster*. It was compiled by Knut Rosander for the purpose of aiding people who, like Ohman, had had very little schooling. It contains chapters on arithmetic, grammar, elementary history, agriculture etc. In the chapter on grammar there is an illustration of the runic alphabet—precisely the same as that shown in Fogelblad's grammar. But this alphabet would be of no help in writing the Kensington inscription because the latter contains no less than sixteen runic characters which are not found in the grammar or in Rosander's book—nine runic letters and seven runic numerals.

What then remains of Moltke's vision of "antiquarian books that shed no little light on the peculiar runic inscription and its orthography?"

Disappointed in the minister's grammar, Ohman in his own humble way sought other means to learn the contents of this mystic inscription. He made a copy of it and, as noted on page 163 above, asked J. P. Hedberg in Kensington, to send it to the editor of a Swedish paper in Minneapolis.

Hedberg's letter and the photostat of Ohman's copy were filed in the archives of the Minnesota Historical Society in 1925. In 1949, Holvik found this printed copy and immediately claimed it was not a copy but a draft of the inscription! This story was printed in many papers. It seemed to me so utterly absurd that an alleged faker would obligingly publicize his own draft within two months of the time when the stone was found that I did not bother to comment on it. But as it is continuously repeated in Moltke's publications,[143] I shall here briefly discuss it.

Holvik claims that the copy or "runepaper," or "draft," as he calls it, contains seven words using different rune-forms from those on the stone. He also finds seven words showing differences in spelling.

It is not easy to copy a long document containing strange characters without making mistakes, a fact well illustrated by Professor Oluf Rygh of Oslo University who early in 1899 attempted to copy the inscription from a print form. In this I think he had an advantage over Ohman, because Rygh had the print form on his desk, while Ohman could not get the stone so close. Yet Rygh made more mistakes than Ohman.[144] I quote below Holvik's and Moltke's reasons for believing that Ohman's "runepaper" is a draft and not a copy of the inscription. Alternating with them are Rygh's mistakes.

"1. On the runepaper the word for *from* is written *FRO* the first time it appears and *FROM* in the fourth line, while the stone has *FRO* in both places."

Rygh made precisely the same mistake.

"2. On the runepaper the word for *röd* is written with an H-rune after the vowel. There is no H-rune in the same word on the stone."

Rygh again makes the same mistake and in addition makes two more in the same word. He spells it *rohde;* it should be *röþe.*

"3. The word for *blood* is spelled with a complicated character for the *umlaut* of O, [Ö] which is an incorrect spelling in any Scandinavian language at any time."

This is quite true; no one drafting an inscription would write *blöd* because there is no such word. It shows that the copyist did not understand the runes and made a mistake. As these three examples are all that Holvik and Moltke give, it may be presumed that these are the most damning. But so far one might just as well claim that Rygh's transcription was a draft as much as Ohman's supposed runepaper. In the first and second criticized words both men made the same mistake, and the third is plainly not a part of a draft as Holvik has shown.

There are other proofs that Ohman's runepaper was a copy and not a draft of the inscription. One is found in the first line (see Figure 34). It will be seen that the last four letters, ᛁᛒᚦᚷ , have been rubbed out and then rewritten in the next line. There must have been some reason for this. If the runepaper was written as a draft there was no reason for rubbing them out because there is no change in the letters and there was plenty of room. But if the runepaper is a *copy* of the inscription we see why these letters were moved to the next line. The copyist evidently planned to make an exact copy, line for line, of the inscription. Too late he discovered that these four letters belonged in the second line, and he therefore erased them. But he soon found it too difficult to duplicate the spacing on the stone, and then used his own spacing. As in the inscription, however, he did manage to get his copy into twelve lines.

In the inscription are a number of omissions of small words (as indicated by the parentheses below). This haste is certainly explainable by the ominous circumstances under which the inscription was carved, and is interestingly confirmed by Mr. John K. Daniels' observations on the sculpting technique of the rune-carver as noted on p. 176, above. These omissions are: line 6, "we were (out) and fished"; line 7, "(we) found 10 (of our) men"; line 9, "save (us) from evil"; and line 10, "(we) have 10 men." These omissions are all duplicated in Ohman's paper, as they naturally would be in a copy. If, on the other hand, Ohman's paper was not a copy but a draft, it could certainly not be argued that the omissions were the result of working under threatening pressures, and indeed they become inexplicable on any grounds.

A similar careless error occurs in the inscription in the case of the word *wed,* which is used twice but is misspelled *we* the second time, and here too the error is repeated in the copy.

But it seems rather ridiculous seriously to discuss the merits of this runepaper in view of the circumstantial evidence of the age of the inscription. There is the age of the tree, whose roots clasped the stone, which shows that it had been in its finding place long before the first white settlers came to this part of Minnesota; there is the testimony in the inscription that the hill on which the stone was found was an island; finally there is the unanimous testimony of all the geologists who have examined the inscription that its weathering showed it had been exposed to the sun, wind and rain for a long period.

Accusations Against
Ohman and Fogelblad

The man who was the first to tarnish the names of Ohman and Fogelblad by publicly accusing them of having perpetrated a fraud upon the public was Rasmus B. Anderson. He was at one time a professor in the University of Wisconsin and later edited *Amerika,* a small Norwegian weekly, published in Madison, Wisconsin. The following article, written in English, appeared in his paper in the issue of May 27, 1910, and was reprinted in the *Minneapolis Journal* of June 2, 1910. It makes entertaining reading.

THE KENSINGTON RUNE STONE
ONCE MORE

Draw Your Own Conclusions

On the 17th of this month I lectured at Stanley, in the western part of North Dakota. In a drugstore in that city, a gentleman came and shook hands with me and deluged me with compliments. If he had been an Irishman I would have been sure that he had kissed the Blarney stone. The stranger was dressed in the plainest working clothes and the spots of dry mud showed that he was fresh from work. He was a very intelligent man and well educated. He could quote Swedish poetry and Greek and Latin words and phrases with absolute accuracy. He was well up in history, poetry and philosophy. I admired him not because he showered compliments on me and gave me a cigar, but because he, a man of so great intelligence and education, did not feel above common work. I asked him who he was. He told me his name was Andrew Anderson, that he was a Swede, that he in his younger days had been a student at the celebrated Upsala University, and that in 1882 he had quit the university, packed his books and emigrated to America settling in Hoffman, Minn., where he now owns a nice farm. He had for years worked on Jim Hill's railroad and was now at Stanley as foreman on a dump on the great railroad magnate's road.

Hoffman, Minn.! I asked him if that was not near Kensington and if he knew a man by name Olof Ohman, on whose land a rune-stone had been found. He said he was a neighbor of Ohman's, and that he and Ohman were brothers-in-law. Olof Ohman had come from Helsingeland in Sweden in 1875 and had settled near Kensington. He is a well-to-do man. He was educated as a mechanic in Sweden and is well skilled in the handling of all kinds of tools. Ohman is not a college-bred man, but has always been a great reader. His favorite books are Alex. V. Humboldt's "Cosmos" and a work in Swedish called "The Gospel of Nature." Then I asked Mr. Anderson what he knew about Rev. Fogelblad. He answered: "Rev. Fogelblad made his home at my house and died there about ten years ago." This Fogelblad, Anderson claimed, left the Lutheran Church because he could not endorse its tenets, but the fact is, he was deposed on account of his dissolute habits. He was a graduate in theology of the Upsala University and came from Sweden direct to Minnesota where he lived as a literary tramp. Anderson and particularly Fogelblad were well versed in the runes. Anderson had brought with him from Sweden a book by the great scholar Fryxell on the Swedish runes. This book he loaned to Ohman, and the three, Fogelblad, Anderson, and Ohman frequently discussed the runes when they were together, Fogelblad writing long sentences in runic on paper and explaining them to Ohman. He wrote a book called "The Age of Reason." It has no important bearing on the subject, but I may add that the three, Fogelblad, Ohman and Anderson were all proud to consider themselves wholly emancipated from the dogmas of the Christian faith.

Thus we here have Olof Ohman, who settled near Kensington in 1875 and on whose farm the notorious rune stone was found at the root of a young tree in 1898, Rev. Fogelblad, who came to Minnesota about the same time and Andrew Anderson, who settled there in 1882. All three were deeply interested in runes and either one of them was capable of producing the rune-stone in question.

From a runic, linguistic and historical standpoint the Kensington rune-stone is a fraud on the face of it.

Mr. Andrew Anderson, whom I can best describe as a diamond in the rough, did not in my long and interesting interview with him admit that either one of the three had had anything to do with the much advertised Kensington rune-stone, but he gave me some significant winks. We parted in the small hours of the morning as the best of friends.

Now, gentle reader, draw your own conclusions.

RASMUS B. ANDERSON.

May 24, 1910.

This article came to the attention of Professor N. H. Winchell, State Geologist, who investigated the report. The following article by him was printed in the *Norwegian-American,* published in Northfield, Minnesota, under date of June 10, 1910.

St. Paul, Minn., June 6, 1910.

Norwegian-American,
    Northfield, Minn.

You may have seen a short article written by Mr. Rasmus B. Anderson, published in "Amerika," of Madison, Wis., and copied in several other papers, giving account of an interview with Mr. Andrew Anderson, now of Stanley, N. D., but formerly living at Hoffman, near Kensington.

According to Mr. R. B. Anderson's statements and inferences, there is not only a possibility but a probability that the Kensington stone was a fraudulent production by one of three men, or by them all, and that Mr. Andrew Anderson, one of the three named, significantly winked at Mr. R. B. Anderson as if to admit the accusation.

On seeing this publication in "Amerika" I wrote to Mr. Andrew Anderson asking him if the facts stated by Mr. R. B. Anderson were true, and also for his opinion of Mr. Fogelblad and of his probable agency in the production of the rune stone. I have received from him the following letter, by means of which after correcting the article in "Amerika," it is hoped the gentle reader will form his own conclusion on what is left.

N. H. WINCHELL.

Stanley, N. D., June 3, 1910.

N. H. Winchell,
    St. Paul, Minn.

DEAR SIR:

Yours of June 1st at hand and contents noted. Yes, I got a copy of Mr. R. B. Anderson's paper, "Amerika," because I subscribed on it. I can't understand how Mr. Rasmus B. Anderson could write such an interview. I never told him half of what he got into his paper. I told him that if Fogelblad had written the runes they would have been correct. I said that Fogelblad could possibly have written the inscription on paper, and Ohman could have chiselled the runes on the stone, as he is a mechanic of trade. But I never said that he done it. I further said that I didn't believe in it at all, that they had created the stone, or "runes." I told him that Fogelblad was too honest for such a thing as that. Fogelblad had nothing to do with such a reproduction. Ohman wouldn't be able to produce an inscription of runes; so that settles it for all time. I have written "Amerika" in the Swedish language, and corrected his mistakes, and I do hope he is honest enough to give it space. I have also written "Svenska Amerikanska Posten," and I wish that paper would publish my article, and that will settle this controversy, as far as me concern. Anderson made a student of me too from the University of Upsala. He got so mixed so he seems to not know what he is talking about. This is all I got to say this time. It is hard to write in a railroad camp after quitting time where it is about 75 men talking at the same time, but I feel justified to be able to give you this information.

Yours for truth,

ANDREW ANDERSON.
Care J. Newville.

P.S.—I do believe the stone to be genuine.

Kensington, Minn., June 6, 1910.

Prof. N. H. Winchell,
    St. Paul, Minn.

My intention has been not to take part in any discussion of the Kensington rune stone, for the simple reason that I do not understand the farfetched arguments which the learned offer in regard to the same. But when such shamelessness and untruth find their way into public reports in the newspapers, I must fight for the truth.

A. Anderson has quite badly fabricated a piece of news which is without parallel. The truth is that Anderson has never been a student. He has never seen Upsala, much less been a student. That he before the interview with Rasmus Anderson could repeat Swedish poetry, if he was drunk, is not denied, but if he is at home in the Greek and Latin languages he must have acquired them since he left his family a year and a half ago. I know with absolute certainty that he was unable to do it. He possesses no more scholarship than I do. Perhaps he has had a better opportunity to attend the common school in Herjedalen than I had in Helsingeland. I would like to see the book which Anderson had with him, published by Fryxell, on Swedish runes, and which he loaned to Ohman; also that the three, Fogelblad, Anderson, and Ohman "frequently discussed the runes when they were together, Fogelblad writing long sentences in runic on paper and explaining them to Ohman." That is the most barefaced untruth that ever has been told and put into print, and also that Fogelblad has written a book called "Age of Reason." That book is not to be found except in Anderson's cracked brain. Also that Anderson and I are brothers-in-law. That is something which I do not understand can be so. The truth is that my wife and his wife are cousins. That is all. O. Ohman came from Sweden in 1879 to Douglas county and worked at several places in the county. That is true. That farm which he (Anderson) owns in Hoffman does not exist either. His family lives in a smaller house in Hoffman and live by their own work. He never possessed the good trait of caring for his family. He has had enough with supporting himself. That he has for years worked on Jim Hill's railroad and is now

working as foreman at Stanley, that is also not true. Whatever
he may become, he will never be foreman more than a few days.

Respectfully,

OLOF OHMAN.

Sven Fogelblad was born December 10, 1829, in Sweden.
He studied theology and the necessary classical studies that
went with it in Upsala. His first public appearance is some
time before 1860 when we find him as a curate under Reverend
Mr. Rolander in Tomberg parish in West Gothland.

He emigrated to America about 1870. Here he was almost
persuaded to re-enter the ministry as pastor of a Swedish congregation at Litchfield. But at the critical time his old enemy,
drink, tripped him up.

His first appearance around Kensington was about 1885-90.
He is described as a short, thickset man of about seventy
years of age, always cheerful and neat. He had no permanent
home, but as itinerant schoolmaster used to sojourn for a few
weeks at different farmhouses, getting fifty cents a month for
each child taught. His classes used to number six to eight pupils,
giving him an income of four to five dollars per month, which
was all he needed for clothes. When the times and the seasons
were inconvenient for schooling he used to quarter himself upon
a farmer. He was extremely lazy, and was never known to
have assisted in the harvest or carried in a pail of water or an
armful of wood. He preferred to repair old pipes, bind books,
make kitchen knick-knacks, etc.

In spite of his laziness the farmers were always glad to see
him because of his wealth of local news. He knew of births and
deaths and other doings far and wide, and was the forerunner
of the village newspaper. Moreover he was always absolutely
reliable in all his gossip, conscientious and kindhearted in all
his narratives, and clean and agreeable in person. He was without any ambition and never studied. He wrote neither books nor
pamphlets, his literary efforts consisting of humble doggerels,

which rarely if ever were printed. He, however, boasted to several that upon one illustrious occasion long ago in Sweden he had written an article for which a paper had paid him ten *kroner* (about $2.70).

On the whole, he appears to have been a tenderhearted, superficial person in general, with a deep conscientiousness which prevented him from squaring his creed with the doctrine of the Church, wearing his sorrows as well as his joys upon his sleeve, inspiring confidence in all by his openhearted ways.

He had been visiting for a year with a nephew in Scott county when, in 1897, he returned to Kensington to visit friends. On approaching the house of one Andrew Anderson, he suddenly felt ill, whereupon he went in there and died July 12, 1897, after a three days' attack of an unknown malady.

Those who knew him best in Grant and Douglas counties are Messrs. Oslund, Thompson and Simonson of Red Rock Lake, Hendrickson of Hoffman, Ekberg of Herman, and Moen, Carlson, Bentson, Ohman and Oberg of Kensington, all among the most respected farmers of that section. To these persons and many others I put the following questions:

Did you ever see or hear of Fogelblad making runes on window casings, doors, or elsewhere? Did he ever speak of American discovery, or of Scandinavians having visited this section long ago? Do you believe he could have had a hand in making the Kensington inscription?

To all of these questions I received an invariable and unequivocal "no." Not one had seen him make runes, not one had heard him speak of Scandinavian explorers in Minnesota, not one believed he could possibly have had anything to do with the Kensington Stone. Some of these persons at that time doubted the stone's genuineness, but, no matter who had chiseled it, they said, they were sure Fogelblad was innocent. He was, they said, too honest and conscientious to have perpetrated a fraud; he had no aptitude whatever for practical jokes and deceptions; he was too lazy to have executed it, and too garrulous to have concealed it if he had. Furthermore, it is plain from the limitations of his early training and later opportunities that he was entirely ignorant of the fine runological, paleographic and linguistic points involved in this inscription. Finally, he did not make his appearance around Kensington until about sixty years after the tree above the stone had wound its roots around it.

The only possible reason for connecting this poor old man with this supposed forgery seems to be the fact that he was dead and therefore could not deny the accusations against him.

The Minnesota Historical Society's committee concludes this investigation with the following paragraph:

> The small collection of books left by Mr. Sven Fogelblad at his death, at the home of Mr. Andrew Anderson, was found, on inquiry by the Museum Committee, to have been disposed of in part to Rev. M. A. Nordstrom, of Riverside, California [formerly pastor of the Swedish Congregation near Kensington]. In order to push the investigation of this question still further, inquiry was made of Mr. Nordstrom as to the existence of any works on runes, and especially by Fryxell on runes, in the collection owned by Fogelblad. Mr. Nordstrom replied, after some delay due to change of residence, that the books got by him were on philosophy, that Fogelblad had no work by Fryxell, and added that, in his opinion Fogelblad could not have made the inscription.[1]

The late historian and critic, P. P. Iverslie, took such a prominent and helpful part in the investigation of the Kensington rune stone that his name should at least be mentioned in this survey. I will, therefore, here add his pungent summary of the widespread discussion concerning Ohman's, Fogelblad's and Andrew Anderson's alleged complicity in the origin of the inscription.

> Here are some illustrations of how rumors concerning the Kensington inscription arose and multiplied to an amazing degree.

---

1 Minn. His. So. Colls., XV, p. 280.

1. A runic alphabet of sixteen characters in a Swedish grammar grew to become a big book on runes written by Fryxell.

2. A man by the name of Hans Voigt many years ago worked for a man by the name of Gunder Johnson and while there made some scratches on a board to illustrate his faulty memory of runic characters. Ohman also worked there. When the rune stone was found, Johnson recollected the incident, but through a confusion of identity said that Ohman had written the runes. And now pieces of wood and other articles inscribed with runes multiplied with amazing rapidity. According to gossip Ohman was as if possessed by a rune-writing devil and wherever he went he scratched runes, on sidewalks, on fences, on granaries, etc. According to report the rune devil also took possession of Fogelblad and he, too, wrote runes on all sorts of articles. And finally the devil seized a third man, Andrew Anderson, who also became possessed of the spirit of runic expression. Profoundly impressed, Professor Flom in his pamphlet makes the following precious remark:

"From Anderson comes the information that he, Fogelblad and Ohman would often sit studying and discussing runes, presumably from Fryxell and the runic book or books that Fogelblad and Anderson had."

The runic books by Fryxell and others which Fogelblad and Ohman are said to have possessed did not exist and the discussion must therefore have centered about the sixteen runes in the Swedish grammar. We hear of making a mountain out of a molehill, but to make such a huge mountain out of sixteen runes as to give material for endless discussion is certainly a more remarkable event. The above sage remark by the learned Dr. Flom, which he calls a "fact" is based on an apocryphal "interview" in the paper *Amerika* whose claims are denied by both Ohman and Anderson.

3. All the education Andrew Anderson had was received in a rural common school. But Professor Anderson makes him out to be a student from Upsala University, well versed in Greek, Latin, history, Swedish literature and familiar with runes. And all this is repeated by Flom with the most naive credulity.[151]

Notes

1. Riant, Count Paul, *Expeditions et peleringes des Scandinaves en Terre Sainte au temps des Croisades*. Paris, 1865.

2. Translated by G. M. Gathorne-Hardy in his *Norse Discoverers of America*, Oxford, 1921, p. 25.

3. This sketch of Erik Thorwaldson and his discovery of Greenland is based on the biographical account in Ari the Learned's *Landnamabok*, completed about 1120.

4. For a discussion of Norse units of distance (nautical), see W. Hovgaard, *The Voyages of the Northmen to America*, New York, 1914, Chapter IV. See also Gathorne-Hardy, *Norse Discoverers of America*, Oxford, 1921, pp. 198-211.

5. Bjarni could not have reached Baffin Land if he had tried, because Hudson Strait in late fall is barricaded by an icepack extending southward into Davis Strait more than a hundred miles. Bjarni returned to Iceland to spend the winter, probably late in October. He remained there perhaps a week to learn of the great migration and his father's new home. This long drift southward and the return northward must have taken at least a month, and he would not reach the "third land" until near the end of November. According to *Sailing Directions for Newfoundland*, Washington, 1942, this would be about a month too late to reach Resolution Island. "The pack ice from Baffin Land reaches Hudson Strait in late October or early November and is here joined at Cape Chidley about the first of November by the heavy floes from Fox Channel" (pp. 42-43, 599). It adds that these floes are impenetrable and often a hundred miles wide. It would therefore be impossible to reach Resolution Island with its glacier because it lies *north* of Hudson Strait, not to mention sailing around this island.

6. Most commentators have thought that this Gudrid who with her husband Thore was rescued by Leif was the same as Gudrid, the daughter of Thorbjorn, who later married Thorfin Karlsevni. This is an error. Gudrid was a common name, and the Gudrid who was rescued fom the wreck was the daughter of an Icelander named Ingjald who is mentioned in Gisle Surson's saga, who journeyed to Norway where she married Thori and went to Greenland with him. See *Grönlands Historiske Mindesmerker*, II, 583.

7. The *Flatey Book* says that Bjarni Herjulfson sailed for four days in a *northeasterly* direction in his voyage from Helluland to Greenland.

Hauk's Book says that Thorfin Karlsevni spent a whole winter with Leif Erikson in Greenland and presumably was told more than once of the location of the various western lands seen by Leif. The book claims that when Thorfin left the Greenland settlement he did not sail northwest to Baffin Land, but *south*, and there he found his Helluland.

The Saga of Erik the Red (a variant of the *Hauk's Book* account) says that Thorfin upon reaching Helluland changed his course from *south* to southeast.

An early geographical statement, said to have been written by Abbott Nicolaus of Thingeyri who died in 1159, reads as follows: "*South* from Greenland is Helluland, next to it is Markland; then it is not far to Vinland, which some men think is connected with Africa." (*Grönlands Historiske Mindesmerker*, III 220-26.)

Another description from the 13th century reads: "From Greenland to the *south* is Helluland." (*Ibid.*)

Björn Jonson (ca. 1600), who had access to old records now lost, writes: "Opposite Greeenland lies Furdustrand *hit mikla* (i.e. the big), where there is such hard frost that the land is not inhabited. *South* of this land is Helluland, which is called Skrelling Land, and from there it is not far to Vinland." (*Ibid.*)

In *Örvar Odd's Saga* it is said that Helluland lies *southwest* of Greenland. While this saga is a medieval work of fiction, the writer would naturally conform to the geographical conceptions of his time, otherwise his readers would judge him ignorant of well-known facts. While Helluland lies mainly south of Greenland, its (southeastern Newfoundland's) true position is five degrees west of south, so the statement in *Örvar Odd's Saga* is correct.

With these facts before us, there should be no doubt that Helluland was the southeastern part of Newfoundland.

8. The following is a list of the various areas, which have been thought to be the Norsemen's Vinland by the more prominent writers on the subject, and a bibliography of the writers defending each location.

1. CAPE COD AND VICINITY

Rafn, C. C. *Antiquitates Americanae*, Copenhagen, 1837.

Fiske, John. *Discovery of America*, I, Boston, 1892.

Lodge, Henry Cabot. *North American Review*, CXIX, 177.

Hovgaard, W. *The Voyages of the Northmen to America*, New York, 1915.

De Costa, B. F. *Pre-Columbian Discovery of America*, Albany, 1890.

Babcock, W. H. *Early Norse Visits to North America*, Washington, 1914.

Gathorne-Hardy, G. M. *The Norse Discoverers of America*, Oxford, 1921.

Gray, E. F. Leif Eriksson, *Discoverer of America*, London, 1930.

Jones, C. H. L. and Raddell, T. H. *The Markland Sagas*, 1934.

Brögger, A. W. *Vinlandsreiserne*, Oslo, 1937.

Hennig, Richard. *Terra Incognitae*, Dusseldorf, 1938.

Lechler, G. *Die Entdecker Amerikas*, Leipzig, 1939.

Haugen, Einar. *Voyages to Vinland*, New York, 1942.

Holand, H. R. *Westward From Vinland*, New York, 1940.

Pohl, F. J. *The Lost Discovery*, New York, 1952.

Löve, Askell, *The Plants of Vineland the Good*, Winnipeg, 1951.

Herrmann, Paul. *Conquest By Man*, London, 1954.

2. FURTHER SOUTH

Mjelde, M. M. *The Norse Discoveries of America*, London, 1921.

Naess, Almar. *Hvor Lå Vinland?* Oslo, 1954.

3. EAST SHORE OF NEW ENGLAND

Horsford, E. N. *The Landfall of Leif Erikson*, Boston, 1892.

4. EASTERN MAINE

Reman, E. *Norse Discoveries and Explorations in America*, Berkeley, 1949.

5. SOUTHERN NOVA SCOTIA

Storm, G. *Studier over Vinlandsreiserne*, Oslo, 1887.
Fischer, J. *Die Entdeckungen der Normannen in Amerika*, 1902.

6. NORTHERN NEW BRUNSWICK

Hermannsson, H. *The Problem of Wineland*, 1936.

7. ST. LAWRENCE RIVER

Steensby, H. P. *Norsemen's Route from Greenland to Wineland*, Copenhagen, 1918.

8. NORTHERN NEWFOUNDLAND

Mallery, A. H. *Lost America*, Washington, 1951.

9. The first mention of grapes, found by the Norsemen who discovered the American mainland, was made in 1070 by Adam of Bremen, Rector of the Cathedral School in Bremen, Germany. He obtained his information from King Sven of Denmark, who told him of the discovery of an "island" in the west where grapes grew wild "which made the best of wine." (*Gesta Hammaburgensis*, Ch. IV, p. 38.) He also mentions that a cereal was found growing wild which the Norsemen called self-sown wheat.

For no apparent reason some commentators have rejected the plain statements in the old narratives of Adam of Bremen and the Norse chroniclers and suggested that the grapes were probably currants or perhaps some kind of cranberry, and that the wheat was plain dunegrass. It is difficult to understand why these humble plants which were well known in Greenland and Iceland should have caused much excitement in the minds of Leif and Tyrk. Dr. Askell Löve, Professor of Botany in the University of Manitoba, who is an Icelandic Canadian, has now clarified the identity of these plants. based on the original terminology in Icelandic, the language in which Leif's narrative was written His conclusions are that the *self-sown wheat* was wild rice, a food product of great importance in the diet of the Indians of the eastern part of the United States (see A. E. Jenks, *The Wild Rice Gatherers of the Upper Lakes*, 1900). The *vinber* he identifies as the *Vitis Labrusca*, a sweet grape "not unlike the European grapes. This species is distributed from southern Maine to southern New England." The wild rice "grows near the coast up to southern Maine and southward to western Florida." As the northern limits of these two plants is southern Maine, their identity is of much importance in determining the locale of the region called Vinland. Dr. Löve's paper is printed in *The Icelandic Canadian*, 1951, Vol. 10, pp. 15-22.

10. A. C. Parker says "Corn cribs are an Indian invention and for general construction have been little improved by white men." (*New York Museum Bulletin* 144, p. 36, Albany, 1910.)

11. The first Catholic mission in the northeastern part of the United States was built on this meadow at the extremity of the headland in 1613. Father Biard writes that they found an open field there of about twenty-five acres. It was customary for the Indians to keep such meadows green and tempting

to the deer by burning off the dead grass each spring, and this promontory may therefore have been a conspicuous landmark when Thorwald saw it.

12. This is found in *Hauk's Book*. The best translation is by A. M. Reeves in *The Finding of Wineland the Good*, 1890, 28-52.

13. The reason for this long detour was the fact that Gudrid was the owner of Sandness, the largest farm in the Western Settlement, and it was natural that Thorfin would be interested in seeing it. About a hundred years later, this farm became the see of the first Bishop in Greenland, Erik Gnupson. In 1121 he sailed from here to Vinland. It is not known what islands are referred to by "Bear Islands."

14. An Englishman named Daniel Denton, New York, 1670, gives the following description:

New York is settled in the (south)west end of the aforesaid island, having that small arm of the sea, which divides it from Long Island on the south(east) side of it, which runs away Eastward to New England and is navigable, though dangerous. For about ten miles from New York is a place called Hell-Gate, which being a narrow passage, there runneth a violent stream, both upon flood and ebb, and in the middle lieth some Islands of Rocks, which the current sets so violently upon, that it threatened present shipwrack; and upon the Flood is a large whirlpool, which continually sends forth a hideous roaring, enough to affright any stranger from passing further.

We also have a report on the same streamfjord, written a few years later by two Hollanders ("Journal of a Voyage to New York in 1679–80 by Jasper Denckaerts and Peter Slyter" and translated for the Long Island Historical Society by Henry C. Murphy, 1867, pp. 135-36; 374-75).

A little eastward of Nieu Haerlem there are two ridges of very high rocks, with a considerable space between them displaying themselves very majestically and inviting all men to acknowledge in them the majesty, grandeur, power and glory of their creator. Between them runs the road to spyt den duyvel . . .
Hellgate is nothing more than a bend of the (East) river, which coming up north, turns then straight to the east. It is narrow here, and in the middle of the bend or elbow lie several large rocks. On either side it is wider, consequently the current is much stronger in the narrow part, and as it is a bend, the water is checked and made to eddy, and then, striking these rocks . . . makes a whirlpool. You must therefore be careful not to approach this whirlpool, especially with small vessels, as you will be in danger of being drawn under. It makes such a whirlpit and whistling that you can hear it for a quarter of an hour's distance, but this is when the tide is ebbing.

15. The story of Thrond and his persecution by King Harald is printed in *Flatey Book*, III, 314-316; see also *Grönlands Historiske Mindesmerker*, II, 608-630.

16. F. Nansen claims that the use of the verb *leita* (ordinarily meaning *to seek*) shows that Vinland at that time was not a known country. He says: "The use of *leita* shows that Wineland was not a known country, it can only

apply to lands about which legends or reports are current" (*In Northern Mists,* II, 29, 30). This is an error because *leita* was also used in making journeys to well-known countries like Iceland. In *Olafs Saga Tryggvasonar* we read that when Queen Aud went to join her brother in Iceland, she *for at leita Island* (*Flateyjarbook,* Ed. 1860, I. 265). *Eirikr Konungr leitadi vestan um haf med her sinn* (King Eirik sailed west with his army), *Fornmanna Sögur,* I. 26.

17. Rafn, *Antiquitates Americanae,* 1837, p. 45; Brögger, Winlandfahrten, Hamburg, 1939, p. 175; Hennig, *Terra Incognitae,* II, Ch. 109. See also Bröndsted's 1948 press release quoted in Chapter XI.

18. Le Clercq, *First Establishment of the Faith,* Shea's translation, N. Y. 1881, p. 1.

19. The investigation of the Beardmore find is fully set forth in J. W. Curran, *Here was Vinland,* Sault Ste. Marie, Ont. 1937, pp. 177-184, 211-234. See also C. T. Currelly, "Viking Weapons Found near Beardmore, Ont." and *Canadian Historical Review,* 1939, pp. 4-7.

20. On the location of Ginnungagap, see Gustav Storm, *Arkiv for Nord. Filologi,* 1889, pp. 340-350.

21. Björn Jonsson of Skardsá (1574-1656) was an Icelander with a very keen interest in history who was requested by Bishop Torlak Skuleson to make copies of as much of the Icelandic literary remains as possible. As the more famous family sagas, like Eyrbyggja, Njal's Saga, Egil's Saga, etc. existed in many copies, Björn passed these by and spent most of his time on strictly historical narratives. Bishop Torlak owned a large collection of these sagas, some of which are known only through Björn's copies.

22. The best identification of these far northern hunting stations has been made by Captain J. K. Tornoe, *Lysstreif over Nogesveldets Historie, Meddelelser,* No. 56, Oslo, 1944.

23. *Meddelelser om Grönland,* 1902, Vol. XXI, p. 322.

23a. *Ibid.* III, 410-415.

24. Rachel L. Carson, *The Sea Around Us,* New York, 1951, pp. 177-180. Dr. Petterson's thesis is set forth in "Climatic Variations in Historic and Prehistoric Times," in *Svenska Hydrog-Biol. Komm. Skrifter,* No. 5, 1912.

25. *Grönlands Historiske Mindesmerker,* II, 90-127. John Fiske has printed the story of Thorgils in the first volume of his *Discovery of America.*

26. *Kongespeilet,* A. W. Brögger's edition, Oslo, 1947, pp. 41-42. This work is supposed to have been written by Einar Gunnarson, Archbishop of Trondheim about 1250. As most of the commerce with Greenland passed through Trondheim, he had the best opportunity of learning from the sea captains of the times about conditions in Greenland.

26a. W. Graah, *Opdagelsereise,* p. 186; cf. 165-168.

27. *Grönlands Historiske Mindesmerker,* III, 259. Also printed in *Purchas his Pilegrimes,* London, 1625, Part III, 518 ff.

28. *Grönlands Historiske Mindesmerker,* II, 459-464; G. Storm, "Om Biskop Gisle Oddsons Annaler" in *Arkiv F. Nordisk Filologi,* 1890, Vol. IV.

29. *Unionsperioden,* I, 313-314. The same interpretation is also given by Gustav Storm, in *Arkiv F. Nordisk Filologi,* VI, 356. Also by Finn Magnuson in *Grönlands Historiske Mindesmerker,* III, 887.

30. Wm. Hovgaard, *Voyages of the Norsemen to America*, New York, 1914, p. 50. Here is also given a photograph of a group of Stefanssons *blond Eskimo*.

31. The lawspeakers were among the most important men in the country, and as a mark of their dignity were permitted to ride with a following of ten men to be entertained at local public expense. P. A. Munch, *Unionsperioden*, I, 433.

32. The original letter of 1354 which belonged to the University Library in Copenhagen was lost in the great fire of 1728. A copy, of which a translation is given above, was made in the 16th century. A photostatic copy is printed in William Thalbitzer's *Two Runic Stones from Greenland and Minnesota*, translated and published by the Smithsonian Institution, *Miscellaneous Collections*, Vol. 116, No. 3.

33. *Historia de gentibus septentrionalibus*, Rome, 1555, Book II, Ch. IX. There is published a Swedish translation entitled *Historia om de Nordiske Folken*, Stockholm, 1909-16. See Vol. II, 92.

34. When Norway in 1319 became loosely connected with Sweden by having a common king, it was with some misgivings. It was therefore provided that the two countries were to have separate kings as soon as the sons of Magnus became of age, fifteen years old. The elder was to have Sweden, the next in age to have Norway. By this arrangement, Haakon, the second son, became King of Norway in 1355. However, several large districts remained in the possession of King Magnus. These were the provinces on both sides of the Oslofjord and also West Gothland in Sweden.

35. Professor Storm writes: "We have a copy of a royal letter from October, 1354, which indicates extraordinary preparations. Paul Knutson of Onarheim, a member of the King's Bodyguard, is appointed leader of the expedition, and he is given special authority to fit it out and choose the members of it. The purpose of the enterprise is stated to be '*to maintain Christianity in Greenland,*' i.e., to fight the Eskimo and to strengthen the colony in general, perhaps also to explore the new lands. In any case we can be sure that the conditions in Greenland and its fate were in those years debated in Bergen from whence the expedition departed and where after a number of years it returned. We know that it had not returned in 1357. It appears most probable that it did not return until 1363 or 1364, because in the last year Ivar Bardson reappears again and not before 1365 is a new bishop to Greenland consecrated." *Studier over Vinlandsreiserne*, 1888, 73-74. The same view is held by P. A. Munch (*Unionsperioden*, I, 314), Helge Gjessing (*Symra*, 1909, p. 124), and even by F. Nansen (*In Northern Mists*, II, 38) who is exceedingly critical of all reports about Norse discoveries in America.

35a. There is some doubt as to what was sent to Breda. He says he received a copy of the inscription made by the manager of the bank, S. A. Siverts; but the latter in a letter to me, dated November 22, 1935, says: "I shipped the stone very carefully packed and by express to Prof. Breda . . . and the stone was returned to me at Kensington in a couple of months." Then it was sent to Professor George Curme at Northwestern University. Before sending the stone away, Mr. Siverts made a very good copy of the inscription which is still on file in the archives of Minnesota Historical Society.

36. The inscription contains two words which need some explanation. One is the word "Goths."

The fact that two nationalities (Goths and Norwegians) are said to have taken part in the expedition has given much offense to the critics. The facts are as follows: In 1319 Norway and Sweden were united under one king, Magnus Erikson who was a member of the great Folkunga family of West Gothland, and he greatly irritated the nobles of other parts of Sweden by his favoritism toward the Goths. It is therefore likely that the sons of prominent families in West Gothland were favored in appointments to the Royal Bodyguard. When the king, in his letter to Sir Paul Knutson (see chapter XIV), instructed him to select some of the men of the Royal Bodyguard to take part in the expedition to find the apostate Greeenlanders, it was likely that these would be Goths. This favoritism finally resulted in open rebellion in Sweden against King Magnus, and West Gothland was the only province that remained loyal to him.

The other word is *daghrise*. In chapter III it has been shown that the Norsemen had a unit of distance called *dagrsigling* (day's sailing). This was based on the average distance covered in a day's sailing or rowing and was equal to about seventy-five English miles or a little more. This unit was also used in recording distances sailed or rowed on rivers and lakes (*Westward From Vinland*, 189-192). When the writer of the inscription says that the island where he left the runic inscription was fourteen *daghrise* from the sea, he means it was fourteen times seventy-five English miles from the sea. This agrees very well with the actual distance from this spot to the mouth of the Nelson River which is almost 1100 miles.

37. This report was published in 1911. Four years later it was re-published with much new material in Minnesota Historical Society *Collections*, Vol. 15.

38. This committee's report was published in *Symra*, Decorah, Iowa, 1909, Vol. 5, pp. 182-189.

39. These three linguistic studies are the following in the order of their appearance: H. R. Holand, *The Kensington Stone*, 1932, pp. 96-133, 225-271; reprinted in *Westward From Vinland*, 1940, pp. 151-189, 289-318. Wm. Thalbitzer, "Kensingtonstenen," *Danske Studier*, Copenhagen, 1947, pp. 10-40. S. N. Hagen, "The Kensington Runic Inscription," *Speculum*, Cambridge, Mass. 1950, Vol. XXV, 321-356.

40. U. S. Department of Agriculture, *Forestry Service Bulletin*, no. 93, p. 17; "Aspens in Central Rocky Mountain Region," U. S. Dept. of Agric. *Bulletin*, 1291, p. 6.

41. Warren Upham, *Glacial Lake Agassiz*, Washington, D. C. Ch. IX.

42. "The tilting of the land which had caused the inclination of the beaches and the submergence of the western part of the shore line of the Nipissing Great Lakes may still be in progress. This was first noticed more than 75 years ago and was afterward studied more carefully, so that we now know something about the rate at which the tilting is going on. To say that a line 100 miles long and trending approximately north-south, is being tilted at such a rate that the southern end of it will be four or five inches below the northern end after the lapse of a century seems to indicate a very slow movement. It may turn out, however, that the tilting is spasmodic, with intervals of movement interrupted by intervals of rest. However this may be, the slow tilting has sufficed to submerge the stumps of trees near Superior, where the trees, of course grew above lake level. The tilting has submerged rapids during the

lifetime of some of the Indians, as indicated at the beginning of this chapter."
Lawrence Martin, *The Physical Geography of Wisconsin*, Bulletin No. 36, p. 464
(1932).

43. *Journal of American History*, 1910, IV, 180.

44. Statement on file in archives of Minnesota Historical Society. For similar
statements by other geologists, see H. R. Holand, *Westward From Vinland*, 1940,
pp. 125-132.

45. The quoted statement is made in a letter from the Geological Survey dated
February 25, 1952. Here, in Ephraim, Wisconsin we have a good and prominent
proof of the correctness of this statement. In 1928 the people of the village
raised a monument in honor of the first settlers. A large flat limestone of good
shape, weighing many tons, was found in the woods. Its face and two sides were
above ground and were deeply weathered, but the under side was white and
fresh in appearance. That stone has now stood upright on its end with a bronze
tablet on it for twenty-seven years, and the under side has been similarly exposed
to the sun, the wind, and the rains for the same period. But that former under
side still remains white and fresh with little noticeable patina.

45a. *Skandiven*, Chicago, May 3, 1899.

46. Report of the Minnesota Historical Society Committee, Minn. Hist. Soc.
Collections, XV, pp. 225, 244. Dr. Hoegh's report is printed in *Symra*, a quarterly, 1909, pp. 182-187; quotation from page 186.

47. Jay Edgerton in *Minneapolis Star*, July 1, 1955.

48. "Norsemen in North America Before Columbus," in *Smithsonian Report
for 1953*, pp. 367-405. Bröndsted's report was printed as a separate item in
January, 1955. The quotation is from p. 400.

49. For further details on this stone, see H. R. Holand, *America, 1355-1364*,
pp. 146-148.

51. For further details, see Holand, *America, 1355-1364*, 1946, pp. 166-177.

55. Bashford Dean, "Evolution of Arms and Armor," *American Museum Journal*, XV, 356-362. See his chart.

56. *Norsk Riksmålsordbok*, Oslo, 1939, p. 1762.

57. *Historia de gentibus septentrionalibus*, 1555, Liber 7, Cap. 21; Liber 9,
Cap. 29.

58. *Aarböger for Nordisk Oldk. og Historie*, 1950, p. 112. Later inquiry has
revealed that there were no Finns in or near Republic, Mich. until after 1870.
As the axe was found in 1878, submerged in the water of a creek, this leaves
a maximum of only eight years for the total decomposition of the wood in
the handle, which, according to Dr. Darrow, would take several hundred years.

59. Benson John Lossing, *Pictorial Fieldbook of the American Revolution*,
1860, Vol. 1, 632-634.

60. "Plowden's New Albion" in *Collections of the New York Historical
Society*, 1869, 213-222.

61. For further details about this "rownde Stone tower" see F. J. Pohl, *The
Lost Discovery*, 1953, pp. 182-186. Mr. Pohl was the first to call public attention
to this item.

62. B. Wick, *Did the Norsemen erect the Newport Tower?* 1911; Camille
Enlart in *Revue de l'art chretien*, LX (1910), p. 139 ff.; F. J. Allen in *The*

Cambridge Antiquarian Society's Communications, XXII (1921), p. 90 ff.; P. A. Means, *Newport Tower,* 1942; H. R. Holand, *America: 1355-1364* (1946), 18-132; *Rhode Island History,* July, 1948; Herbert Pell, *Rhode Island History,* October, 1948; Johannes Bröndsted in *Aarbog f. Nor. Oldk. og Historie,* 1951, pp. 17-63; F. J. Pohl, *The Lost Discovery,* New York, 1952.

63. This needs a word of explanation because there is one round stone tower standing on columns and arches which was (and possibly still is) used for a windmill. This is the Chesterton mill near Leamington in Warwickshire which stands on six columns and arches. However, as Philip Ainsworth Means has so conclusively shown (see his book *Newport Tower,* 1942, pp. 184-187), the Chesterton tower was not built as a mill but as an observatory for Sir Edward Peyto by the architect, Inigo Jones in 1632. There was a water mill on the estate, but about a hundred years later the water supply dried up and the observatory was converted into a windmill.

64. "Problemet om Nordboer i Nordamerika för Columbus" in *Aarbog for Nordisk Oldk. og Historie,* Copenhagen, 1951, pp. 17-63.

65. The complete minutes referring to this matter is printed in *Rhode Island History,* 1948, pp. 71-72.

66. Hugo Frölen, *Nordens Befästa Rundkyrkor,* 1911, Vol. 1, p. 42.

67. "Varnhem," in *Svenska Fornminneplatser,* published by the Kungl, Vitt. Hist. och Antikvitets Akademien, 1947, No. 8, pp. 39-41, Plates XIV, XV.

68. "The Ruined Mill or Round Church of the Northmen in Newport" in *Proceedings of the Cambridge Antiquarian Society* (1931), Vol. 22, 93-94.

69. Professor K. J. Conant objects that these offsets are "functional in the statics of the tower," *Rhode Island History,* January 1948, p. 4. That may well be, but that would not hinder the use of the offsets as bases for the rafters of a putative ambulatory as suggested by architect R. G. Hatfield in *Scribner's Monthly,* 1879, pp. 638-639.

70. These were John Howard Benson, an artist in Newport and descendant of Benedict Arnold, the reputed builder of the Tower; Herbert O. Brigham, Secretary of the Newport Historical Society; and F. J. Pohl, Brooklyn, N. Y.

71. It may be objected that these fractional measurements are only what may be expected when working with rough stone construction. But the outlines of the columns are perfectly straight as may be seen by inspecting figures 18 and 20, and the difficulty of the rough surface is easily overcome. If a straight board is held up against any column, the true diameters of the structure can be obtained by measuring from the edge of the board next to the column to a similar board held against the opposite column. Likewise, the diameter of the columns can be found by using calipers big enough to cover both sides of the column.

There is a geometrical rule for laying out an octagon on an equilateral square. An oblique line is drawn or measured from corner to corner of the square; then one-half the length of this line is used as a radius from each corner to mark the location of the eight points on the sides of the square. If the builders applied this rule on a square of twenty feet on the side, the measurements of their octagon would be about the same as those of the Tower. But as this rule seems to be practically unknown to the builders and contractors of the present time, it is extremely improbable that it would have been known to these explorers of the Middle Ages. Moreover, it would be very difficult to lay out an exact square without the help of a surveyor's transit. Furthermore, while this rule is perfect for determining the exact location of the eight corners of the octagon, the builders of the Tower were far from successful in this particular. It is their principal weakness because the arcades between the columns differ in width as much as three inches. Finally, the builders were obviously influenced by a respect for the sacred number three because all the main measurements are multiples of three. This veneration could not find expression if the octagon was laid out on a square because the dimensions could not then be predetermined.

72. The following are the architect's figures on the (1) height of the bases of the pillars and (2) the height of the bottom of the holes where the beams of the floor above rested:

	Height of bases	Height of bottom of holes for beams
Height of Instrument	100' 0"	100' 0"
Column 1	95' 7"	104' 6"
" 2	95' 7"	104' 4½"
" 3	95' 5"	104' 0"
" 4	95' 5"	103' 9½"
" 5	95' 6"	104' 4"
" 6	95' 0"	104' 6"
" 7	95' 5½"	104' 2"
" 8	95' 6½"	104' 7"

The average height of the beam holes above the bases is 8' 10½". As the height of the top of the floor at the hearth of the fireplace is 12' 5", this makes the floor 3' 7" thick. The reason for this thick floor was explained in the previous chapter.

73. S. G. Arnold, *History of Rhode Island*, 1: 490: see also pp. 125, 139-141, 151, 152.

74. Archbishop Olaus Magnus says he saw the two in St. Halvard's Church in 1505 (see *Historia de gentibus septentrionalibus*, Rome, 1555, Book II, Chap. IX). Claudius Clavus states that he saw two in the Trondheim Cathedral some time before 1429; see A. A. Bjornbo and C. S. Peterson, *Fyenboen Claudius Clavus Swart*, Copenhagen, 1904, p. 179.

75. *Discovery of America to 1525*, 1884, p. 348.

76. There are several versions of Verrazano's report. The passage quoted in this chapter is from J. G. Cogswell's translation published in the New York Historical Society's publication, May, 1841, pp. 37-54. Another version is translated by E. H. Hall and printed in the fifteenth annual report of the American Scenic and Historical Society, 1910, pp. 192-195. Another version is given in Ramusio's *Della Navigatione*, 1556, Vol. III, 420-426. See also J. C. Brevoort, *Notes on the Verrazano map*, 1874.

77. Peter Kalm, *Travels into North America*, translated into English by J. R. Forster, 1771. Kalm was born in 1716 and died in 1779. He was one of the great Linné's most promising students and early became recognized as a leading botanist. In 1748 he was sent to America to study its flora. His book, *Travels into North America*, London, 1773, is translated into many languages.

78. *Ibid.* volume 3, pp. 122-128.

79. On a recent trip into the Mandan country north of Bismarck, North Dakota, I saw many of these pillars. The land is full of many knolls usually surmounted by perpendicular outcroppings of rock.

80. William Thalbitzer, *Two Runic Stones*, Smithsonian Institution, 1951, Fig. 1, pp. 6-13.

81. B. Wick, *Did the Norsemen Erect the Newport Tower?* Cedar Rapids, Iowa, 1911, pp. 23-25.

82. His full inscription reads thus: "Indicatio Groenlandiæ et vicinarum regionum, versus Septentrionem, et Occidentem, ex antiqua quadam mappa, rudi modo delineata, ante aliquot centenos annos ab Islandis, quibus tunc erat ista terra notissima, et nauticus nostri temporis observationibus." Both maps are printed in *Meddelelser om Grönland*, Copenhagen, Vol. IX.

83. This letter is printed in full both in its Latin original and in a Danish translation in *Grönlands Historiske Mindesmerker*, 1845, Vol. III, pp. 165-176.

84. C. Pingel, "Om de vigtigste Rejser . . . for at opsöge det tabte Grönland" in *Grönlands Historiske Mindesmerker*, Copenhagen, 1845, Vol. III, pp. 629-795.

85. It is possible that the old map, which Bishop Resen believed was several centuries old, was made by Ivar Bardsen who gave the first report of the destruction of the Western Settlement. He had been steward of church properties in Greenland for many years and knew the country well. In his description of Greenland he uses the term *höge land* to describe the high mountainous elevation in the southeastern corner of Greenland. This term is also found on the Resen map, but nowhere else. He returned to Norway in 1363 or 1364, apparently in company with the survivors of the royal expedition which was sent out in 1355 and returned about eight years later (see page 286). On the return voyage he would have abundant opportunity to learn about the geographical features of Vinland as shown on the map.

87. A. A. Björnbo, *Cartographia*, 130, 135, Fig. 10.

88. Björnbo, *op. cit.* 117.

89. F. W. Lucas, *The Voyages of the Brothers Zeno*, 1897, p. 101.

90. Volume 40, New York, 1894, p. 418. Hakluyt's report is given in *Principal Navigations*, 1903, Vol. 1, pp. 301-304. See also B. F. De Costa "Arctic Explorations" in *Bulletin of the American Geographical Society*, 1880, pp. 159-192.

90a. A. Bugge, "Handelen Mellem England og Norge," in *Historisk Tidsskrift*, Oslo, 1896.

91. "Philippe de Mezieres" in *Bulletin de la Societe des Antiquares de Picardie*, 1896, XIX, 659-678. N. Jorga, *Philippe de Mezieres, 1327-1405, et la Croisade an XIV Siecle*, Paris, 1896, 244-251.

94. Gustav Storm in *Geografisk Forenings Aarbog*, 1897. A copy of the letter is said to be in the Bodleian Library, Oxford.

95. Larsen, *Discovery of America*, 1-29.

96. Louis Bobe, "Aktstykker til Oplysning om Grönlands besejling," in *Danske Magazin*, 1909. Kiel is in Schleswig-Holstein, which at that time was a part of the Danish domain.

97. *Historia Insulana*, Lisbon, 1717, VI, 2, 12.

98. *Die Entdecker Amerikas*, Leipzig, 1939, 34.

99. F. Nansen, *In Northern Mists*, II, 130.

99a. The letter is printed in *Martin Behaim, His Life and Globe* by E. G. Ravenstein, 1908.

100. In the 12th century Jon and Simon Skolp both married daughters of King Harald Gille. Simon killed King Eystein. P. A. Munch, *Det Norske Folks Historie*, II, 887-889.

101. Larsen, *Discovery of America*, 92.

103. The Pope's letter, with others, is printed in *Norroena*, edited by Julius E. Olson.

104. Samuel E. Morison, *Admiral of the Ocean Sea*, 1942, p. 24. A *braccio*, literally "an arm," was 22.9 inches.

105. J. Fritzner, *Ordbog over det gamle Norske Sprog*, art. *daga;* see also G. Vigfusson, *Icelandic Dictionary*.

106. These are all quoted in Holand, *Westward From Vinland*, 313-314.

107. Axel Kock, *Svensk Ljudhistoria*, 1906, I, 352-354, 430; 299, 400-401.

108. S. N. Hagen, *Speculum*, 1950, 337.

109. Olafur Thorgeirsson, *Almanak*, 1899, 25, 27.

110. Edition of 1862, Vol. 1, p. 310, line 20; p. 61, l. 25; p. 454, l. 3.

111. *Svensk Diplomatarium*, No. 4503.

112. S. N. Hagen has a very good commentary on the use of *of*, see *Speculum*, 1850, 332-333.

113. I have spent thirteen years in traveling through Norwegian settlements in America for the purpose of writing a history of the Norwegian immigration, and my opportunities for observations of this kind have been abundant.

114. Kock, Axel, *Svensk Ljudhistoria*, II, 38-42.

115. *Svenska Språkets Lagar*, IV, 98-101.

116. *Diplomatarium Norwegicum*, Vol. 4, no. 586.

117. Vol. III, p. 457; Vol. I, 554, 557.

118. *Annaler for Nordisk Oldk.*, 1846, p. 36.

119. The ballad was printed by Professor O. E. Hagen in *Samband*, a quarterly published in Minneapolis, 1911, No. 42, pp.363-369, with copious notes. Hagen said he had heard it recited in 1873 by an old Telemarking. This folksong was also communicated by Mr. Tortvei, Moorehead, Minn. to Mr. Thorkel Oftelie, a folklorist in Fergus Falls, Minn. by whom it was printed in *Telesoga*, a small quarterly in 1909, No. 1. Mr. Tortvei was an octogenerian pioneer who, though illiterate, remembered hundreds of old ballads which he had heard in his youth. Oftelie sent this ballad—*Förnesbronen*—to the folklorist Rikard Berge in Telemarken, Norway, who said it was *förstehands*, that is, it was written at about the time of the events described.

120. *St. Paul Dispatch*, December 14, 1909.

121. "The First Prayer in America" in *Columbia* (1933), Vol. V, pp. 10-20.

121a. *Nordisk Familjebok*, Vol. 12, Art. I.

122. *Information*, Nov. 9, 1949.

123. *Aarbog for Nordisk Oldkyndighed og Historie*, 1950, p. 83.

124. *Ibid.* 82.

125. "The Kensington Rune Stone Report to the Minnesota Historical Society by its Museum Committee," 1911, *Minnesota Historical Soc. Collections*, 1915, pp. 225, 244.

126. *Om Runernes Brug til Skrift*, Copenhagen, 1877; *Codex Runicus*, 1877.

127. *Information*, Copenhagen, Nov. 9, 1949.

128. The last rune was used in Greenland to represent *e*. A good explanation of the runic calendar is given by Otto von Friesen in *Runorna i Sverige*, pp. 82-84.

129. *Information*, Copenhagen, Nov. 9, 1949.

130. Hugo Yungner, *Vestergötlands Runinskrifter*, 1940, Vol. V.

131. Moltke, *Information*, Nov. 9, 1949.

132. When Moltke says that "no manuscript, no printed book from before 1500 can show a special sign for consonantal i, that is j," he overlooks a vast amount of use of consonantal j. The expert philologist, Adolf Noreen, in his article on the letter j, written for the great Swedish encyclopedia mentions that Gutenberg in his Gothic-print bible (ca. 1450) uses i as vowel and j as consonant. He also points out that the Provencal-Catalonian literature used j regularly as a consonant as early as the beginning of the 14th century, and it was similarly used in English in the beginning of the 15th century. His claim that the introduction of j as a consonant was first made by Petro Ramus is therefore without basis.

132a. See his article on consonantal J in *Nordisk Familjebok*, Vol. 12, pp. 1123-1124.

133. *Nordisk Kultur*, Vol. VI, p. 8.

134. *Svensk Ljudhistoria*, II, 284.

135. See also excellent facsimiles in Reeves, *The Finding of Wineland the Good*, London, 1890, opp. pp. 144 and 147.

136. *D. N.*, Vol. I, No. 409. A photostat of it is shown in Taranger, *Norges Historia*, III, Part I, p. 144.

137. "En Gammel Gildeskrä fra Trondheim," in *Sproglig Historiske Studier*, 1896, p. 218.

138. A photostatic copy is shown in *D. N.*, I, No. 7.

139. Axel Kock, *Svensk Ljudhistoria*, II, 1-2.

140. Joseph Wright, *Historical German Grammar*, p. 42. Cf. A. Noreen, *Nordisk Familjebok*, art. *ö;* "In Middle High German (1100-1500) the sign ö was used to represent the ö sound."

141. *Scandinavian Studies*, 1953, p. 14.

142. The report is printed in the Minnesota Historical Society *Collections*, Vol. 15, pp. 239-240.

143. *Scandinavian Studies*, 1953, pp. 12-13. This is the third time Moltke has published it.

144. Rygh's transcription with interlinear translation was published in *Morgenbladet* in the spring of 1899. It was reprinted by Breda in *Symra*, Decorah, Iowa, Vol. 6 (1910), p. 73. The first to call attention to Rygh's many mistakes was S. N. Hagen in *Speculum*, 1950, pp. 321-356. See particularly page 324.

146. P. A. Munch, *Unionsperioden*, I, 596-597, 363-364. The same view is expressed by J. Bröndum-Nielsen in *Arkiv* F. Nordisk Filologi, 1918, 103-107; Amund B. Larsen in *Arkiv f. N.F.*, 1897, p. 244, and Falk and Torp in *Dansk-Norskens Syntaks*, 1900, pp. 12-13.

147. *Diplomatarium Norwegicum*, Vol. 6, no. 278.

148. *Dip. Nor.*, Vol. I, No. 409.

149. *Dip. Nor.*, Vol. I, No. 575.

150. *Dip. Nor.*, Vol. IV, No. 501.

151. *Kvartalskrift*, Eau Claire, Wis., Jan. 1919, pp. 24-25.

152. As the printer was unable to reproduce the Gemma Frisius chart, a tracing of *Mare Glaciale* (Hudson Bay) is shown in Figure 32.

Bibliography

Aakjær, Sven. "Maal og vægt," in *Nordisk Kultur,* Vol. 28.

Allen, F. J. "The Ruined Mill or Round Church in Newport," in Cambridge Antiquarian Society *Communications,* 1921, Vol. 22, pp. 90-107.

Almquist, J. L. *Svensk Grammatik,* Stockholm, 1840.

Andersen, Harry. "Amerikas Runesten," in *Danske Studier,* 1949, pp. 37-60.

Anderson, R. B. "Draw your own Conclusions," in *Amerika,* Madison, Wisconsin, May 27, 1910 and *Minneapolis Journal,* June 2, 1910. Refuted by N. H. Winchell in *The Norwegian American,* Northfield, Minnesota, June 6, 1910.

Babcock, W. H. "Early Norse Visits to North America," in *Smithsonian Miscellaneous Collections,* 1913, Vol. 59, No. 19.

"Recent Historical and Present Status of the Vinland Problem," *Geographical Review,* New York, 1921, Vol. II, pp. 265-282.

Bacchiani, A. "Giovanni Verrazzano and his Discoveries in America," English translation by E. H. Hall, printed as appendix in *Fifteenth Annual Report of the American Scenic and Historical Preservation Society,* 1910.

Baker, F. S. "Aspen in Central Rocky Mountain Region," in U. S. Dept. of Agriculture *Bulletin* 1291, 1925.

Bardsson, Ivar. "Report on the Western Settlement in Greenland," *Grönlands Historiske Mindesmerker,* III, 1845.

Beamish, N. L. *The Discovery of America, London,* 1841.

Björnbo, A. A. *Cartographia Groenlandica,* Copenhagen, 1912.

Biggar, H. P. *Voyages of the Cabots and Corti-Reals,* Paris, 1903.

Jonssön, Björn. "Grönlands Annaler," in *Grönlands Historiske Mindesmerker,* III, 1845.

Björnbo, A. A. and Peterson, C. S. *Fyenboen Claudius Clausen Swart,* Copenhagen, 1904.

Breevort, J. C. *Verrazano the Navigator,* New York, 1874.

Brooks, C. T. *Controversy Concerning the Old Stone Mill.* Newport, 1851.

Brögger, A. W. *Vinlandsferdene,* Oslo, 1937. A series of articles against the Kensington Stone in *Dagbladet,* Oslo, Norway, beginning February 12, 1949, followed in each case by reply from H. R. Holand.

Bröndsted, Joh. "Problemet om Nordboer i Nordamerika för Columbus," in *Aarbog for Nordisk Oldkyndighed,* Copenhagen, 1951, pp. 1-122.

Bruun, D. "The Icelandic Colonization of Greenland," in *Meddelelser om Grönland,* 1918, Vol. 57.

Bugge, A. *Olavs- Klostret i Tönsberg,* Oslo, 1932. *Handelen Mellem Norge og England,* 1896.

Bugge, Sophus. "Hönen-Runerne fra Ringerike," in *Norges Indskrifter med de Yngre Runer,* Oslo, 1902.

"Cartographia Groenlandica," in *Meddelelser om Grönland,* Vol. 48.

Catholic Encyclopedia. Article *Altar.* Vol. 1.

Catlin, George. *North American Indians,* New York, 1841.

Cawley, F. S. "The Kensington Stone," in *New England Quarterly,* 1933, pp. 210-217.

Channing, G. G. *Early Recollections of Newport,* 1868.

Chapin, H. M. *Documentary History of Rhode Island,* 1919.

Christensen, T. P. *The Discovery and Rediscovery of America,* 1934. A vigorous support of the Kensington inscription.

Cogswell, J. G. "Verrazano's Report," *N. Y. Historical Society Colls.* Second series, 1: 37-54.

Conant, K. J. "Newport Tower or Mill," in *Rhode Island History,* January, 1948, pp. 2-7. Reply by H. R. Holand in July, 1948 issue.

Curran, J. W. *Here was Vinland,* Sault Ste. Marie, 1939.

Currelly, C. T. "Viking Weapons found near Beardmore, Ontario," in *Canadian Historical Review,* 1919, pp. 4-7.

Curtis, W. E. "Recent Disclosures concerning Pre-Columbian Voyages to America," in *National Geographic Magazine,* 1894, 197-234.

Daa, Ludwig, "Didrik Pining" in *Norsk Kis Tidsskrift,* 1881.

De Costa, B. F. *Pre-Columbian Discovery of America,* Albany, 1889. "Inventio Fortunata, Arctic Explorations, with an account of Nicholas of Lynn," in American Geographical Society *Bulletin,* No. 36, New York, 1880, pp. 159-92.

De Land, Chas. E. "Verendrye's Journey to the Mandans," in South Dakota Historical *Collections,* Vol. 7.

De Roo, P. *History of America before Columbus,* Philadelphia, 1900.

Diplomatarium Norwegicum. Lange and Unger's edition, Oslo, 1847-1901.

Drake, S. G. *The Aborigines of America,* 1860.

Einarsson, Stefan. "The Kensington Stone," in *Speculum,* 1933, pp. 400-408. A favorable philological review.

Ekhoff, E. "Om Kyrkornas forna Egenskap af Forsvarsverk," in *Aarböger for Nordisk Oldkyndighed,* Vol. XIV, 1899.

Espeland, Anton. "Nordmænd i Amerika i Middelalderen," in *Norsk Folkekultur,* Vol. 18, pp. 69-72.

"Hirdmannen Paul Knutsons Reise til Gronland," in *Bergens Aftenblad,* November 18, 1922.

"Runestenen fra Kensington," in *Minneapolis Tidende,* November 8, 1928. All three favorable historical reviews.

Falk, Hjalmar. *Altschwedische Waffenkunde,* Oslo, 1914.

Falk and Torp. *Dansk-Norskens Syntaks,* Oslo, 1900.

Fergusson, J. *History of Architecture,* 1887, Vol. 1.

Fischer, J. *The Discoveries of the Norsemen in America,* 1903.

"Contra facta non valent," cited by R. Hennig in *Vergangenheit und Gegenwart,* 1937. Favorable review of the Kensington inscription.

Fiske, John. *Discovery of America,* Vol. 1, Boston, 1892.

Flatey Book—*Flateyjarbok.* Standard Norse edition, 1860.

Flom, G. T. "The Kensington Stone" in *Transactions* of the Illinois State Historical Society, 1910 (1912), pp. 105-125.

Forssen, A. "Varnhem," in *Kung. Vit. His. och Antik. Akademien,* 1947, No. 8.

Forster, J. R. *Peter Kalm's Journey to America,* London, 1771.

Fossum, A. "A Study of the Language of the Kensington Stone brings Satisfactory Results," in *Norwegian-American,* February 24, 1911.

The Norse Discovery of America, Minneapolis, 1918.

Fraser, A. D. "The Norse Discovery of America," in *Dalhousie Review,* 1937, pp. 175-186. Supports authenticity of Kensington Stone.

Friesen, Otto von, *Runorna,* 1933.

Fritzner, J. *Ordbog over det gamle Norske Sprog,* Oslo, 1886.

Frölen, H. *Nordens Befästa Rundkyrkor,* Stockholm, 1911.

Gathorne-Hardy, G. M. *The Norse Discovery of America,* Oxford, 1921.

"A Recent Journey in Northern Labrador," in *Geographical Journal,* Vol. 59, 1922.

"The Kensington Stone," in *Antiquity,* 1932. Strong defense of the inscription.

"Gisle Oddssons Annaler," in *Grönlands Historiske Mindesmerker,* III, 1845.

Gjerset, K. *History of the Norwegian People,* New York, 1927.

Gjessing, Helge. "Kensington-Stenen," in *Symra,* Decorah, Iowa, 1909. Unfavorable review.

Godfrey, W. S. *The Newport Tower,* report to the Preservation Society of Newport County, 1948.

"The Newport Tower," in *Archaeology,* 1950.

Gray, E. F. *Leif Eiriksson,* New York, 1930.

Grenfell, W. T. *Labrador,* 1909.

Grönlands Historiske Mindesmerker, 3 vols., Copenhagen, 1838-1845.

Gutenberg, Beno. "Changes in Sea Level, Post-glacial Uplift and Mobility of Interior," in *Geological Society of America Bulletin,* 1941, pp. 721-772.

Hagen, O. E. "Conclusions about the Kensington Stone," in *Reform,* Eau Claire, Wisconsin, April 29, 1926. Complete endorsement.

Hagen, S. N. "The Kensington Runic Inscription," in *Speculum,* 1950, pp. 321-356. Expert linguistic vindication.

Hakluyt, R. *The Principal Navigations,* etc., 1903, Vol. I.

"Handbook of American Indians," Smithsonian Institution, Bureau of Ethnology, *Bulletin* 30, 1912.

Harisse, Henry. *The Discovery of North America,* London, 1892.

Hatfield, R. G. "The Old Mill at Newport," in *Scribner's Monthly,* 1879, pp. 632-641. Favors pre-Columbian Norse origin.

Haugen, E. I. *Voyages to Vinland,* 1942.

Hennig, R. *Terrae Incognitae,* I-IV, Leiden, 1936, pp. 268-299.

"Der Runenstein von Kensington," in *Verangenheit und Gegenwart,* 1937, pp. 27-43.

Herrmann, Paul. *Sieben Vorbei und Acht verweht,* Hamburg, 1952. *Conquest of Man,* English translation, London, 1954. Pp. 255-374 deals approvingly with the Kensington Stone.

Hermannsson, H. "The Problem of Vinland," in *The Cornell University Press,* 1944. Rejects Kensington inscription.

Hildebrand, H. "Sveriges Rundkyrkor," in *Svenske Fornminne-forenings Tidsskrift*, 1893.

Holand, H. R. *The Kensington Stone*, Ephraim, Wisconsin, 1932.
Westward From Vinland, New York, 1940.
America, 1355-1364, New York, 1946.

Holm, G. "Some Additions to the Vinland Problem," in *Meddel-elser om Grönland*, 1925.

Holvik, J. A. "Debunking the Rune Stone," in *The Concordian*, Moorhead, Minnesota, November 18, 1949.

Hopkins, R. T. *Old Windmills of England*, New York, 1933.

Horsford, E. N. *The Landfall of Leif Eriksson*, Boston, 1892.

Hovgaard, W. *Voyages of the Northmen to America*, New York, 1914. In this book Professor Hovgaard condemns the Kensington inscription as a fake, but he later became a strong supporter of it. See *Geographical Review*, 1932, Vol. XXII, pp. 507-9 and *The American Scandinavian Review*, XX, pp. 224-30.

Isachsen, G. "Hvor langt mod nord kom de norröne Grönlendere?" in *Norsk Geografisk Tiddskrift*, 1932.

Islandske Annaler. Storm's edition, 1888.

Iverslie, P. P. *Gustav Storms Studier*, 1912.
"The Kensington Stone," in *Norwegian American*, October 17, 1910.
"A Reply to Professor Flom," in *Norwegian American*, March 24 and 31, 1911. Vigorous defense of the Kensington Stone.

Jansson, Sven, B. I. "Kensington Steinen," in *Nordisk Tidsskrift*, Nos. 7 and 8, 1949. Reply by H. R. Holand in following issue.

Jonsson, F. "Opdagelse af og Reiserne til Vinland," in *Aarböger for Nordisk Oldkyndighed*, 1915.
Ivar Bardarsson, 1930.

Journal of American History. A Review of the Kensington Stone, 1932, Vol. 26, pp. 120-145. Favorable.

Kalm, P. *En Resa til Norre Amerika*, Stockholm, 1753.

Koch, L. "The East Greenland Ice," in *Meddelelser om Grönland*, CXXX, 1945.

Kock, A. *Svensk Ljudhistoria*, Lund, Sweden, 1906.

Kohl, J. G. "History of the Discovery of the East Coast of America," in *Maine Historical Society*, Vol. 1, 1869.

Kongespeilet. A. W. Brögger's translation, Oslo, 1947.

Kornerup, B. *Biskop Hans Poulsen Resen*, 1928.

Krause, W. "Runen in Amerika," in *Germanien*, 1937. Unfavorable.

Larson, C. *History of Douglas County, Minnesota,* Minneapolis, 1916.

Larson, L. M. "The Kensington Stone," in *Minnesota History,* 1936, pp. 20-37. Rejects inscription. Reply by H. R. Holand in following issue, pp. 166-188.

Larsen, Sofus. *Discovery of America Twenty Years Before Columbus,* London, 1924.

Lindroth, H. "Statement on the Kensington inscription," quoted by R. Hennig, in *Petermann's Geografische Mitteilungen,* 1938, pp. 89-90. Answers linguistic arguments.

Lossing, B. J. *Pictorial Field Book of the Revolution,* Vol. 1, 1855.

Löve, A. "The Plants of Vinland the Good," Winnipeg, 1951.

Lucas, H. S. "Medieval Economic Relations between Flanders and Greenland," in *Speculum,* 1937, pp. 167-181.

Magnus, Bishop Olaus, see Olaus.

Mallory, A. H. *Lost America,* Washington, 1951.

Martin, L. "The Physical Geography of Wisconsin," in *Geological Bulletin,* 1932, No. 36, pp. 447, 461.

Mason, G. C. "Old Stone Mill at Newport," in *Magazine of American History,* 1879, Vol. 3, pp. 541-549.

Means, P. A. "The Kensington Stone," in *N. Y. Times,* May 26, 1940. A historical defense.
Newport Tower, 1942. The most complete work on this subject. He rejects colonial theory of erection.

Minnesota Historical Society. "Report of Committee on Kensington Rune Stone," in *Minnesota Historical Society Colls.* XV, 221-286.

Mjelde, M. M. "The Eyktarstad Problem," in *Sagabook of the Viking Society for Northern Research,* 1921, Vol. 10, 57-74.

Moltke, E. "Kensington-Stenen," in *Information,* Copenhagen, November 9, 1949. Rejects inscription. The same article is printed in *Antiquity,* 1951, 87-93.
"The Ghost of the Kensington Stone," in *Scandinavian Studies,* 1953, pp. 1-14.

Morison, S. E. *Admiral of the Ocean Sea,* 1942.

Moss, E. L. *Shores of the Polar Sea.*

Munch, P. A. *Det Norske Folks Historie, Unionsperioden,* Vol. 1, 1852.

Naess, Almar. *Hvor Lå Vinland?* Oslo, 1954.

Nansen, F. *In Northern Mists,* New York, 1911.

Nares, George. *Voyage to the Polar Sea,* 1880.

Neckel, Gustav. "Die erste Entdeckung Amerikas," Leipzig, 1934.

Nielsen, K. M. "Kensingtonstenens Runeindskrift," in *Aarbog for Nordisk Oldk.* 1951, pp. 73-88.

Nilsson, M. P. N. *Tideräkningen,* Stockholm, 1934.

Noreen, A. *Altschwedische Grammatik, Halle,* 1904.

Nörlund, P. "Buried Norsemen at Herjulfsness," in *Meddelelser om Grönland,* Vol. 67, 1924.

Nörlund and Roussel. "Norse Ruins at Gardar," in *Meddelelser om Grönland,* Vol. 76, 1930.

Nörlund and Stenberger. "Brattahlid," in *Meddelelser om Grönland,* 1934.

Olaus, Magnus. *Historia de gentibus septentrionalibus,* 1555.

Olsen, Magnus. "Kingigtorsuak-Stenen," in *Norsk Tidsskrift for Sprogvidenskap,* Oslo, 1932.

Pastor, E. "Der Runenstein von Kensington," in *Wacht am Osten,* 1937, pp. 321-328.

Peterson and Björnbo. *Fyenboen Claudius Clavus Swart,* Copenhagen, 1904.

Pierce, C. S. "The Old Stone Mill at Newport," in *Science,* 1884, Vol. 4, pp. 512-514.

Pingel, F. C. "Nye Reiser til Grönland," in *Grönlands Historiske Mindesmerker,* III, 1845.

"Plowdens New Albion," in *Collections* of the New York Historical Society, 1869, pp. 213-222.

Pohl, F. J. *The Lost Discovery,* New York, 1952. "The Newport Tower," in *Archaeology,* 1950, pp. 183-184. "The Ship's Shoring at Follin's Pond," in *Bulletin of the Mass. Archaeological Society,* Vol. 16, pp. 53-60.

Putnam, J. P. *The Open Fireplace in all Ages,* 1882.

Quaife, M. M. "The Myth of the Kensington Stone," in *New England Quarterly,* December, 1934. Reply by H. R. Holand in same publication, 1935.

Rafn, C. C. *Antiquitates Americanae,* 1837.

Ramusio, G. *Delle Navigatione e Vaggi,* Vol. III, 1566.

Rasmussen, K. *Myter og Sagn,* Copenhagen, 1921.

Ravenstein, E. G. *Martin Behaim, his Life and his Globe,* London, 1908.

Reeves, A. M. *The Finding of Wineland the Good,* 1890.

Reman, E. *The Norse Discoveries in America,* Berkeley, 1949.

Reuter, O. S. *Germanische Himmelskunde,* Munich, 1934.

Riant, P. *Expeditions et Pelerinages des Skandinaves,* 1865.

Rosander, K. *Den Kunskaprike Skolmästaren*, 1864.

Roussel, A. "Researches into Norse Culture in Greenland," in *Meddelelser om Grönland*, 1936, Vol. 88.

Rydquist, J. E. *Svenska Språkets Lagar*, Stockholm, 1883.

Sailing Directions for Newfoundland, U. S. Hydrographic Office, 1940.

Schirmer, H. M. "Aare, Rögovn og Peis," in *Annual Report* of Foreningen til Norske Fortidsmindesmerkers Bevaring, Oslo, 1904, 1905.

Shelton, F. H. "More Light on the old Mill at Newport," in *Bulletin of the Newport Historical Society*, No. 21, pp. 3-23, 1917.

Söderwall, A. *Ordbok öfrer Svenska Språket i Medeltiden*, Lund, 1925.

Steensby, H. P. "The Norsemen's Route from Greenland to Vinland," in *Meddelelser om Grönland*, Vol. 56.

Steenstrup, K. J. V. "Om Österbygden," in *Meddelelser om Grönland*, Vol. 9.

Stefansson, V. *Introduction to Frobisher's Three Voyages*, 1938.

Stomberg, A. A. "The Kensington Stone," in *Allsvensk Samling*, August 30, 1932. Favors authenticity.

Storm, G. "Ginnungagap," in *Arkiv for Nordisk Filologi*, 1889, pp. 340-350.

Islanske Annaler, Oslo, 1888.

Styffe, G. C. *Skandinavien under Unionsperioden*, Stockholm, 1911.

Taranger, A. *Norges Historie*, Oslo, 1917.

Thalbitzer, W. "Two Runic Stones from Greenland," in *Smithsonian Miscellaneous Publications*, 1951, Vol. 116, No. 3, pp. 1-71. Favorable philological analysis.

"To Fjærne Runestene," in *Danske Studier*, 1947, pp. 1-40.

Thordarsson, M. "The Vinland Voyages," in *American Geographical Society Research Series*, No. 18, 1930.

Thorsen, P. G. Editor *Codex Runicus*, 1877. *Om Runernes Brug til Skrift*, Copenhagen, 1877.

Tornoe, J. K. "Lysstreif over Norgesveldets Historie," in *Norges-Svalbards Udersökelser*, No. 56, 1944.

Ulldahl, F. "Om Vinduerne i de Jydske Granit-Kirker," in *Aarböger for Nordisk Oldkyndighed*, Vol. IX.

U. S. Coast and Hydrographic Survey: *The Coast Pilot*, Part III, 1912.

Upham, Warren. "The Kensington Stone," in *Records of the Past*, Washington, Vol. 9, 1910.

Van Rennslaer, J. K. *Newport: Our Social Capital*, 1905.

Verendrye, P. "Report on Visit to the Mandans," in *South Dakota Historical Collections*, Vol. 7.

Verrazano, see Bacchiani and Cogswell.

Vigfusson, G. *Icelandic Dictionary*, Oxford, 1874.

Wahlgren, Erik. "The Runes of Kensington," in *University of Kansas Press*, 1952, pp. 57-70. A repetition of old linguistic objections.

Wailes, Rex. "Notes on some Windmills," in *Old Time New England*, 1931, Vol. 21, pp. 99-128.

Wallace, W. S. "Literature relating to Norse Voyages to America," in *Canadian Historical Review*, March, 1939. Supports authenticity of Kensington inscription.

Walsh, J. J. "The First Prayer in America," in *Columbia*, August, 1933. Supports authenticity.

Weigle, W. G. and Frothingham, E. H. "The Aspens: Their Growth and Management," in U. S. Dept. of Agriculture *Forest Service Bulletin*, 1911, No. 93.

Weise, A. J. *The Discovery of America*, 1884.

Wick, B. L. *Did the Norsemen erect the Newport Tower?* 1911, 26 pp.

Will, G. F. and Spinden, H. J. "The Mandans," in *Papers of the Peabody Museum*, III, 1913.

Williams, M. W. "Review of the Kensington Stone," in *Journal of American History*, 1932, pp. 128-129. Favorable.

Social Scandinavia in the Viking Age, New York, 1920.

Winchell, N. H. *The Aborigines of America*, 1911. "Committee Report to Minnesota Historical Society on the Kensington inscription," in *Minnesota Historical Society Colls.*, 1915, pp. 221-268. Unanimous endorsement of authenticity.

"I Believe the Inscription is Genuine," in *Norwegian American*, Northfield, Minnesota, May 13, 1910.

Refutation of R. B. Anderson's allegations about Olaf Ohman and Fogelblad, printed in *Mpls. Journal*, June 2, 1910; in *Norwegian American*, June 6, 1910.

Winsor, Justin, *Narrative and Critical History*, Vol. I, 1889.

Worm, Ole. *Fasti Danici*, Copenhagen, 1643.

Wright, Joseph. *Historical German Grammar*, London, 1907.

Yungner, H. *Vestergötlands Runinskrifter*, Vol. 5, 194.

Index

[375]